Adobe® Acrobat® 5.0

Classroom in a Book®

Adobe

Contents

Lesson 6   **Modifying PDF Files**

Lesson 7   **Using Acrobat in a Document Review Cycle**

Lesson 8   **Creating Forms**

Lesson 9

Creating Adobe PDF from Web Pages

Lesson 10

Designing Online Documents

Lesson 11

Enhancing a Multimedia Project

Lesson 12

Managing Color

Getting Started

Adobe® Acrobat® is the essential tool for universal document exchange. You can use Acrobat to publish virtually any document in Portable Document Format (PDF), preserving the exact look and content of the original, complete with fonts and graphics.

Distribute your PDF documents by e-mail or store them on the World Wide Web, an intranet, a file system, or a CD. Other users can view your work on the Microsoft® Windows®, Mac® OS, and UNIX® platforms. Add interactive elements—from custom hyperlinks and media clips, to form fields and buttons Streamline your document review process with Acrobat comments and digital signatures. Use Acrobat to create a searchable electronic library of files and place security locks on sensitive files.

About Classroom in a Book

Adobe Acrobat 5.0 Classroom in a Book® is part of the official training series for Adobe graphics and publishing software developed by experts at Adobe Systems. The lessons are designed to let you learn at your own pace. If you're new to Adobe Acrobat, you'll learn the fundamental concepts and features you'll need to master the program. If you've been using Acrobat for a while, you'll find Classroom in a Book teaches many advanced features, including tips and techniques for using this latest version.

The lessons in this edition include information on the new Adobe Acrobat user interface, new ways of creating Adobe PDF files, more powerful methods of repurposing the content of Adobe PDF files for use in other applications, and new tools for creating forms and managing color in your PDF files. The design of documents for online viewing is also reviewed.

Although each lesson provides step-by-step instructions for creating a specific project, there's room for exploration and experimentation. You can follow the book from start to finish or do only the lessons that correspond to your interests and needs. Each lesson concludes with a review section summarizing what you've covered.

Prerequisites

Before beginning to use *Adobe Acrobat 5.0 Classroom in a Book*, you should have a working knowledge of your computer and its operating system. Make sure you know how to use the mouse, standard menus and commands, and how to open, save, and close files. If you need to review these techniques, see the printed or online documentation included with your system.

Installing Adobe Acrobat

Before you begin using *Adobe Acrobat 5.0 Classroom in a Book*, make sure that your system is set up correctly and that you've installed the required software and hardware. You must purchase Adobe Acrobat 5.0 software separately. For system requirements and complete instructions on installing the software, see the *HowToInstall.wri* (Windows) or *HowToInstall* (Mac OS) file on the application CD.

You must install the application from the Adobe Acrobat 5.0 CD onto your hard drive; you cannot run the program from the CD. Follow the on-screen installation instructions.

Make sure your serial number is accessible before installing the application. You can find the serial number on the registration card or CD sleeve.

Starting Adobe Acrobat

You start Acrobat just as you would any other software application.

• In Windows, choose Start > Programs > Adobe Acrobat 5.0.

• In Mac OS, open the Adobe Acrobat 5.0 folder, and double-click the Acrobat 5.0 program icon.

The Adobe Acrobat application window appears. You can now open a document or create a new one and start working.

Installing the Classroom in a Book fonts

To ensure that the lesson files appear on your system with the correct fonts, you may need to install the Classroom in a Book font files. The fonts for the lessons are located in the Fonts folder on the *Adobe Acrobat 5.0 Classroom in a Book* CD. If you already have these on your system, you do not need to install them. If you have ATM® (Adobe Type Manager®), see its documentation on how to install fonts. If you do not have ATM, installing it from the Classroom in a Book (CIB) CD will automatically install the necessary fonts.

♀ *You can also install the Classroom in a Book fonts by copying all of the files in the Fonts folder on the Adobe Acrobat 5.0 Classroom in a Book CD to the Program Files/Common Files/Adobe/Fonts (Windows) or System Folder/Application Support/Adobe/Fonts (Mac OS) folder. If you install a Type 1, TrueType, OpenType, or CID font into these local Fonts folders, the font appears in Adobe applications only.*

Copying the Classroom in a Book files

The *Adobe Acrobat 5.0 Classroom in a Book* CD includes folders containing all the electronic files for the lessons. Each lesson has its own folder, and you must copy the folders to your hard drive to do the lessons. To save room on your drive, you can install only the necessary folder for each lesson as you need it, and remove it when you're done.

To install the Classroom in a Book files:

1 Insert the *Adobe Acrobat 5.0 Classroom in a Book* CD into your CD-ROM drive.

2 Create a folder named AA5_CIB on your hard drive.

3 Copy the lessons you want to the hard drive:

• To copy all of the lessons, drag the Lessons folder from the CD into the AA5_CIB folder.

• To copy a single lesson, drag the individual lesson folder from the CD into the AA5_CIB folder.

If you are installing the files in Windows, you need to unlock them before using them. You don't need to unlock the files if you are installing them in Mac OS.

4 In Windows, unlock the files you copied:

• If you copied all of the lessons, double click the unlock.bat file in the AA5_CIB/Lessons folder.

• If you copied a single lesson, drag the unlock.bat file from the Lessons folder on the CD into the AA5_CIB folder. Then double-click the unlock.bat file in the AA5_CIB folder.

Note: If as you work through the lessons, you overwrite the Start files, you can restore the original files by recopying the corresponding Lesson folder from the Classroom in a Book CD to the AA5_CIB folder on your hard drive.

Additional resources

Adobe Acrobat 5.0 Classroom in a Book is not meant to replace documentation provided with the Adobe Acrobat 5.0 program. Only the commands and options used in the lessons are explained in this book. For comprehensive information about program features, refer to these resources:

• The Acrobat 5.0 online Help included with the Adobe Acrobat software, which you can view by choosing Help > Acrobat Help. This guide contains a complete description of all features.

• The Adobe Web site (www.adobe.com/products/acrobat/), which you can view by choosing Help > Adobe Online if you have a connection to the World Wide Web.

Adobe certification

The Adobe Training and Certification Programs are designed to help Adobe customers improve and promote their product proficiency skills. The Adobe Certified Expert (ACE) program is designed to recognize the high-level skills of expert users. Adobe Certified Training Providers (ACTP) use only Adobe Certified Experts to teach Adobe software classes. Available in either ACTP classrooms or on-site, the ACE program is the best way to master Adobe products. For Adobe Certified Training Programs information, visit the Partnering with Adobe Web site at http://partners.adobe.com/.

Lesson 1

1 Introducing Adobe Acrobat

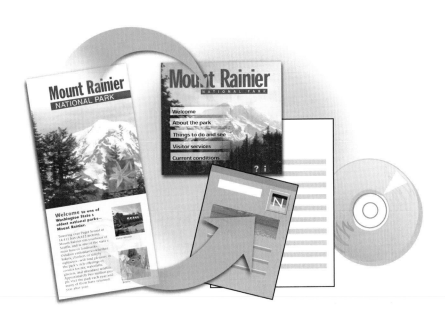

Quality publishing tools are within reach of more people than ever before, and easy access to the Internet and to CD-ROM recorders enables wider distribution of electronic publications. Adobe Acrobat helps you create electronic documents quickly and easily—and Acrobat® Reader® can provide your audience free access to them.

In this lesson, you'll do the following:

• Review the main features of Adobe Acrobat.

• Look at the differences between electronic documents designed for printing and viewing online.

• Identify the types of formatting and design decisions you need to make when creating an electronic publication.

This lesson will take about 20 minutes to complete.

If needed, copy the Lesson01 folder onto your hard drive.

Note: *Windows users need to unlock the lesson files before using them. For information, see "Copying the Classroom in a Book files" on page 3.*

About Adobe PDF

Adobe Portable Document Format (PDF) is a universal file format that preserves all of the fonts, formatting, colors, and graphics of any source document, regardless of the application and platform used to create it. Adobe PDF files are compact and can be shared, viewed, navigated, and printed exactly as intended by anyone with the free Adobe Acrobat Reader or Acrobat® eBook Reader™. You can convert any document to Adobe PDF using Adobe Acrobat software.

• Adobe PDF preserves the exact layout, fonts, and text formatting of electronic documents, regardless of the computer system or platform used to view these documents.

• PDF documents can contain multiple languages, such as Japanese and English, on the same page.

• PDF documents print predictably with proper margins and page breaks.

• PDF files can be secured with passwords to lock against undesired changes or printing, or to limit access to confidential documents.

• The view magnification of a PDF page can be changed using controls in Adobe Acrobat or Acrobat Reader. This feature can be especially useful for zooming in on graphics or diagrams containing intricate details.

About Adobe Acrobat

Adobe Acrobat lets you create, work with, read, and print Portable Document Format (PDF) documents.

Creating Adobe PDF

Your workflow and the types of documents you use determine how you create an Adobe PDF file.

• Use Acrobat® Distiller® to convert almost any file to Adobe PDF, including those created with drawing, page-layout, or image-editing programs.

• Use Adobe PDFMaker to create Adobe PDF files from within Microsoft Office for Windows applications. Simply click the Convert to Adobe PDF button on the Microsoft Office for Windows toolbar.

• Use the Open as Adobe PDF command to quickly convert a variety of file formats to Adobe PDF and open them in Acrobat.

• Use an application's Print command to create Adobe PDF directly from within common authoring applications.

• Scan paper documents and convert them to Adobe PDF.

• Use the Open Web Page command to download Web pages and convert them to Adobe PDF.

Lesson 3, "Creating Adobe PDF Files" and Lesson 9, "Creating Adobe PDF from Web Pages," give step-by-step instructions for creating Adobe PDF using these methods.

Working with PDF files

Working with PDF files has never been easier.

• Add hyperlinks, electronic bookmarks, media clips, and page actions to create a rich multimedia experience. (Lesson 5, "Putting Documents Online"; Lesson 10, "Designing Online Documents"; Lesson 11, "Enhancing a Multimedia Project"; and Lesson 13, "Distributing Document Collections.")

• Use the powerful new content repurposing tools to re-use content in other applications by saving text in Rich Text Format, extracting images in image formats, and converting PDF pages to image formats. (Lesson 6, "Modifying PDF Files.")

• Use built-in or third-party security handlers to add sophisticated protection to your confidential PDF documents, preventing users from copying text and graphics, printing a document, or even opening a file. (Lesson 3, "Creating Adobe PDF Files.")

• Add digital signatures to approve the content and format of a document. Compare signed documents to identify differences between different versions. Digitally sign documents in your Web browser. (Lesson 7, "Using Acrobat in a Document Review Cycle.")

• Add comments and files, and markup text in a totally electronic document review cycle. Work groups can share comments on a Web browser. (Lesson 7, "Using Acrobat in a Document Review Cycle.")

• Create interactive electronic forms or add form fields to existing documents. (Lesson 8, "Creating Forms.")

• Use the same color management system as is used in Adobe® Photoshop® and Adobe® Illustrator® for a reliable and consistent color experience. (Lesson 12, "Managing Color.")

• Use Acrobat® Catalog to organize and index document collections for distribution on CD-ROMs. (Lesson 13, "Distributing Document Collections" and Lesson 14, "Building a Searchable PDF Library and Catalog.")

Reading PDF files

You can read PDF documents using Acrobat, Acrobat Reader, or Acrobat eBook Reader. You can publish your PDF documents on network and Web servers, CDs, and disks.

• Acrobat Reader can be downloaded free of charge for all platforms from the Adobe Web site at www.adobe.com. If you need to read a PDF document and have not purchased Adobe Acrobat, you would use Acrobat Reader to do so.

• Acrobat eBook Reader is designed to give you an optimum reading experience with high-fidelity eBooks on your laptop or desktop computer. Acrobat eBook Reader can be downloaded free of charge for all platforms from the Adobe Web site at www.adobe.com.

Adobe PDF on the World Wide Web

The World Wide Web has greatly expanded the possibilities of delivering electronic documents to a wide and varied audience. Because Web browsers can be configured to run other applications inside the browser window, you can post PDF files as part of a Web site. Your users can then download or view these files inside the browser window using Acrobat Reader.

When including a PDF file as part of your Web page, you should direct your users to the Adobe Web site so that the first time they look at a PDF document, they can download Reader free of charge.

PDF documents can be viewed one page at a time and printed from the Web. With page-at-a-time downloading, the Web server sends only the requested page to the user, decreasing downloading time. In addition, the user can easily print selected pages or all pages from the document. PDF is a suitable format for publishing long electronic documents on the Web. PDF documents print predictably, with proper margins and page breaks.

You can use a Web search engine to index PDF documents for rapid searching on the Web.

Looking at some examples

Publishing your document electronically is a flexible way to distribute information. Using Adobe PDF, you can create documents for printing, for multimedia presentations, or for distribution on a CD or over a network. In this lesson, you'll take a look at some electronic documents designed for printing on paper and at some designed for online reading.

1 Start Acrobat.

2 Choose File > Open. Select Introduc.pdf in the Lessons/Lesson01 folder, and click Open. If necessary, use the scroll bars to bring the bottom part of the page into view.

The previews in this document are links to the corresponding electronic documents. The top three previews link to documents designed to be both distributed and viewed electronically; the bottom three previews link to documents intended to be distributed online, but printed out for reading.

3 Click the Schedule preview in the bottom row to open the corresponding PDF file.

This document is a work schedule that has been converted to Adobe PDF for easy electronic distribution.

4 Look at the status bar at the bottom of the document window. Notice that the page size is a standard 8-1/2-by-11 inches, a suitable size for printing on a desktop printer.

You might glance at the schedule online, but you'd also want to print out a hard-copy version for handy reference.

2. Pub. with Adobe Acrobat	n/a	
Acrobat family sidebar	X	X
Pub. with Acrobat: an overview	X	X
3. Identifying Your Audience	X	X
Online view. vs. printed view.	X	X
Determ. dist. & view. media	X	X

5 Click the Go to Previous View button (◀) in the toolbar to return to the previews in the Introduc.pdf document.

Another example of a publication designed for printing is the Documentation file. This text-intensive document is much easier to read in printed format than online.

6 Click the Documentation preview in the bottom row to look at the file, and then click the Go to Previous View button to return to the previews.

7 Click the Slide Show preview in the top row to open that document.

This document is a marketing presentation designed to be shown and viewed exclusively on-screen. Notice that the presentation opens in Full Screen mode to occupy all available space on the monitor.

8 Press Enter or Return several times to page through the presentation. The colorful graphics, large type size, and horizontal page layout have been designed for optimal display on a monitor.

The Full Screen preference settings let you control how pages display in this mode. For example, you can have a full-screen document with each page displayed automatically after a certain number of seconds.

9 Press the Escape key to exit Full Screen mode.

10 Click the Go to Previous View button until you return to the previews in the Introduc.pdf document.

An online help publication or an electronic catalog are further examples of documents for which on-screen viewing is suitable and even preferred. Electronic publishing offers intuitive navigational features, such as hypertext links, which are well-suited for publications meant to be browsed or used as quick reference guides.

Designing documents for online viewing

Once you have identified the final format for your publication, you can begin to make the design and production decisions that will help make the publication attractive and easy to use. If you're simply converting an existing paper document to electronic format, you'll inevitably weigh the benefits of reworking the design against the time and cost required to do so. If your publication will be viewed on-screen and on paper, you'll need to make the design accommodate the different requirements of both.

First you'll take a look at a document designed to be browsed online but printed out for closer viewing.

1 In the Introduc.pdf file, click the Brochure preview at the bottom of the page to open the corresponding document.

This document is a printed brochure that was converted exactly as it was to electronic format. Converting the document to Adobe PDF is a good way to distribute it cheaply and easily. It also enables you to use features such as hypertext links to make navigation of the online brochure both easy and intuitive.

2 If necessary, click the Fit in Window button ( ) to view the entire page. Click the Next Page button ( ) in the toolbar a few times to page through the brochure.

Notice, however, that while the online brochure is useful for quick browsing and printing selected pages, it is not designed to be read on-screen. The long and narrow pages are inconveniently shaped for the screen, and the small image and type sizes make reading a strain for the user.

Now you'll look at the same brochure redesigned and optimized for online reading. The topics in the brochure have been reorganized as a series of nested, linked topic screens that lead the reader through the document.

3 Click the Go to Previous View button ( ) until you return to the Introduc.pdf file, and click the Park Kiosk preview at the top of the page to open that document.

4 If necessary, click the Fit in Window button to view the entire page.

Notice that the horizontal page orientation is well-suited for display on a monitor.

5 Click About the Park to activate that link.

The About the Park topic screen appears, with its own list of subtopics. Notice how the larger image and type sizes make this document easier to view than the online brochure.

Notice also the use of sans serif fonts in the publication. Sans serif fonts have simpler and cleaner shapes than serif fonts, making them easier to read on-screen.

M ount Rainier was established on March 2, 1899 as the country's fifth national park. The park encompasses 378 square miles (980 square kilometers). Elevation ranges from 880 feet (282 meters) at the Carbon River rainforest to 14,411 feet (4,612 meters) at the summit of the glacier-covered peak. Approximately two million people visit the park each year.

6 Click Flora & Fauna to jump to that topic screen. Then click Lowland Forest to view a specific information screen about the Olympic Elk in this region.

Notice that the pages of the original brochure have been redesigned to accommodate a navigational structure based on self-contained, screen-sized units.

The formatting considerations of on-screen publications—fonts, page size, layout, color, and resolution—are the same as those of other kinds of publications; however, each element must be reevaluated in the context of on-screen viewing. Decisions about issues such as color and resolution, which in traditional publishing may require a trade-off between quality and cost, may require a parallel trade-off between quality and file size in electronic publishing. Once you have determined the page elements that are important to you, you need to choose the publishing tools and format that will best maintain the desired elements.

7 Click the Go to Previous View button until you return to the Introduc.pdf file.

8 Click the Online Booklet preview to see another example of a PDF document designed for online viewing.

9 Choose Window > Close All to close all the open PDF files.

In this lesson, you have examined a variety of electronic documents designed in different file formats for different purposes. Later on in this book, you'll get some hands-on practice in creating and tailoring your own electronic documents.

Review questions

1 Describe some of the features of Adobe Acrobat 5.0.

2 How do electronic documents designed for printing differ from documents optimized for online use?

3 What hardware and software do you need to view PDF documents?

4 What kinds of media can you use to distribute PDF documents?

5 What kinds of fonts or typefaces and type sizes are best suited for on-screen display?

Review answers

1 Adobe Acrobat 5.0 is used for creating, modifying, printing, and viewing PDF documents. Among the things you can do with Acrobat are add hyperlinks, electronic bookmarks, media clips, and page actions to PDF documents; organize and index document collections for distribution on CD-ROMs; add password protection to prevent users from copying text and graphics, printing a document, or even opening a file; digitally sign documents; add comments and files, and markup text; create electronic forms or add form fields to existing documents; color proof documents before sending them to a printer.

2 Electronic documents designed for paper output tend to be longer, text-intensive documents. Optimized online documents have been redesigned for optimal display on a monitor and may contain more graphics and screen-based navigational features.

3 You can view PDF documents on Windows, Mac OS, or UNIX computer systems. In addition to a computer, you need Acrobat Reader, Acrobat eBook Reader, or Adobe Acrobat to view PDF documents.

4 You can distribute PDF documents via floppy disk, CD, electronic mail, corporate intranet, or the World Wide Web. You can also print PDF documents and distribute them as printed documents.

5 Large fonts or typefaces with simple, clean shapes display most clearly on the screen. Sans serif fonts are more suitable than serif fonts, which contain embellishments more suitable for the printed page.

Lesson 2

2 Getting to Know the Work Area

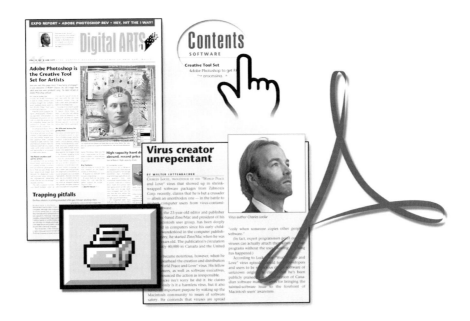

In this lesson, you'll familiarize yourself with the Acrobat toolbars and palettes. You'll learn how to navigate through a PDF document, paging through an online magazine using controls built into Adobe Acrobat. You'll use the Acrobat 5.0 online Help and get some tips on printing PDF files.

In this lesson, you'll learn how to do the following:

• Work with Acrobat tools and palettes.

• Page through a PDF document using Acrobat's built-in navigational controls.

• Change how a PDF document scrolls and displays in the document window.

• Change the magnification of a view.

• Retrace your viewing path through a document.

• Use the Acrobat 5.0 online Help.

This lesson will take about 60 minutes to complete.

If needed, remove the previous lesson folder from your hard drive and copy the Lesson02 folder onto it.

Note: *Windows users need to unlock the lesson files before using them. For information, see "Copying the Classroom in a Book files" on page 3.*

Opening the work file

You'll practice navigating through a fictional online magazine called *Digital Arts. Digital Arts* is a glossy, tabloid-style magazine that contains news from the computer world. In addition to buying the printed magazine from newsstands, readers can view and download the electronic version.

Digital Arts was created using Adobe® PageMaker® and then converted to PDF.

1 Start Acrobat.

2 Choose File > Open. Select Digarts.pdf in the Lessons/Lesson02 folder, and click Open. Then choose File > Save As, rename the file **Digarts1.pdf**, and save it in the Lesson02 folder.

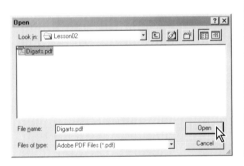 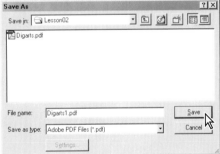

Using the work area

The Acrobat work area includes a window with a document pane for viewing PDF documents and a navigation pane showing bookmarks, thumbnails, comments, and other navigation elements related to the document. A menu bar, status bar, and several toolbars around the outside of the window provide other controls you need to work with documents.

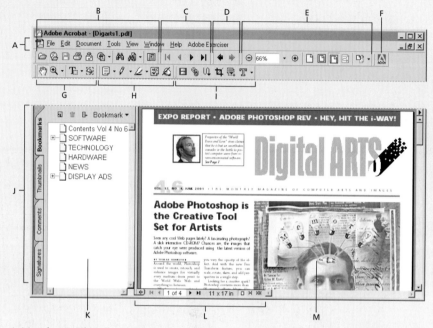

A. Menu bar B. File toolbar C. Navigation toolbar D. View History toolbar E. Viewing toolbar
F. Adobe Online button G. Basic Tools toolbar H. Commenting toolbar I. Editing toolbar   J. Tab palettes
K. Navigation pane L. Status bar M. Document pane

The buttons and menus in the status bar and the Viewing toolbar provide quick ways to change your on-screen display and to navigate through documents.

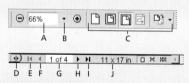

A. Magnification level
B. Magnification pop-up menu
C. Page Layout buttons
D. Navigation Pane button
E. First Page button
F. Previous Page button
G. Current page
H. Next Page button
I. Last Page button
J. Page size

Using the Acrobat tools

The Acrobat toolbars contain tools for scrolling, zooming, changing the appearance of text, cropping pages, adding comments, and making other changes to the current PDF document. This section introduces the toolbars and shows you how to select tools, including hidden tools. As you work through the lessons, you'll learn more about each tool's specific function.

To see the name of a toolbar, position the pointer over the toolbar's separator bar. A separator bar is located at the beginning of each toolbar.

Separator bar

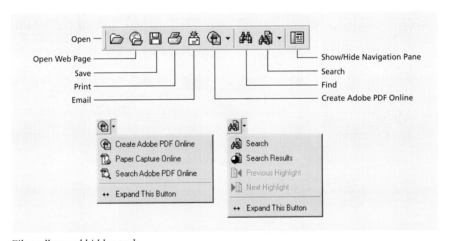

File toolbar and hidden tools

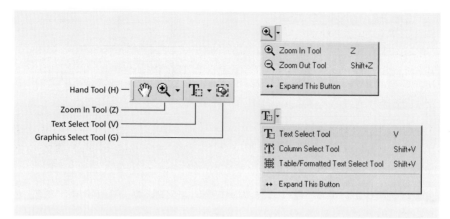

Basic Tools toolbar and hidden tools

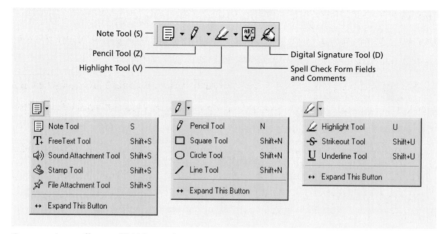

Commenting toolbar and hidden tools

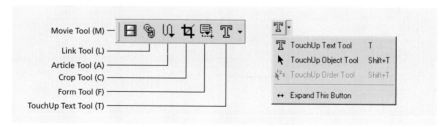

Editing toolbar and hidden tools

Navigation toolbar   View History toolbar

1 To select a tool, you can either click the tool in the toolbar or press the tool's keyboard shortcut. For example, you can press Z to select the zoom-in tool from the keyboard. Selected tools remain active until you select a different tool.

If you don't know the keyboard shortcut for a tool, position the mouse over the tool until its name and shortcut are displayed in a tooltip.

2 Some of the tools in the toolbars have a small triangle to their right, indicating the presence of additional hidden tools.

• Hold down the mouse button on either the tool or the triangle next to the tool until the additional tools appear, and then drag to the tool you want.

• Hold down Shift and press the tool's keyboard shortcut repeatedly to cycle through the group of tools. For example, press Shift+Z to select the zoom-in tool ($\oplus$). Press Shift+Z again to select the zoom-out tool ($\ominus$).

• To place hidden tools in the toolbar alongside the visible tools, hold down the mouse button on either the tool or the triangle next to the tool until the additional tools appear, and then drag to select the Expand This Button option. To collapse the hidden tools, click the triangle to the right of the tools.

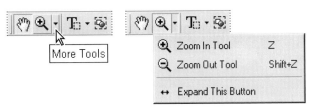

Show hidden tools.   Drag to select desired tool.

Customizing the toolbars

Toolbars can be hidden, expanded, moved into the document or navigation pane, separated, and docked. You can customize your toolbars to put the ones you use most frequently together in the most convenient location.

1 To hide a toolbar, with the hand tool (🖑) selected, choose Window > Toolbars, and choose a name of a toolbar (such as Basic Tools) from the pop-up menu. A checkmark appears next to the name of any toolbar that is currently visible. Try hiding and showing different toolbar combinations.

You can also show or hide a toolbar by right-clicking (Windows) or Control-clicking (Mac OS) in the toolbar area, and then selecting the toolbar name from the pop-up menu.

2 To move a toolbar, drag it by the separator bar. Release the mouse button when the toolbar is located in its new position. Try dragging a toolbar to another location in the toolbar area or into the document pane. For example, drag a toolbar from the upper row to the lower row. Then drag the bar back to its original location and reattach it. (If you drag a toolbar into the document pane or navigation pane and position it vertically, the separator bar is positioned at the top of the toolbar.)

3 Drag a toolbar (by the separator bar) to the navigation pane or document pane. Now drag a second toolbar on top of the floating toolbar to combine them in a single floating window.

4 Change the orientation of floating toolbars by right-clicking (Windows) or Control-clicking (Mac OS) within the toolbar area. Choose Horizontal, One Column, or Two Column.

Experiment with expanding and collapsing toolbars, reordering them, and creating floating palettes.

Using Acrobat palettes

Acrobat provides palettes to help you organize and keep track of a document's bookmarks, thumbnails, comments, signatures, articles, and destinations. Palettes can be docked inside the navigation pane or floated in windows over the work area. They can also be grouped with other palettes. This section introduces the navigation pane and shows you how to display palettes. As you work through the lessons, you'll learn more about each palette's specific function.

Displaying palettes

You can display palettes in a variety of ways. Experiment with several techniques:

• To show or hide the navigation pane as you work, click the Show/Hide Navigation Pane button (▤) in the toolbar, the Navigation Pane button (◀▶) in the status bar at the bottom of the Acrobat window, or click the left border of the document pane.

• To show or hide a palette, choose the palette's name from the Window menu. The palette that is currently active is checked. Palettes appear in the navigation pane or in a floating window.

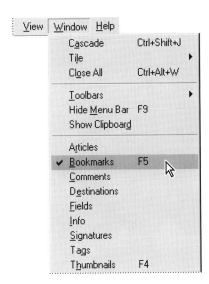

Changing the palette display

You can change the palette display in a variety of ways. Experiment with several techniques:

- To change the width of the navigation pane while it's visible, drag its right border.

- To bring a palette to the front of its group, click the palette's tab.

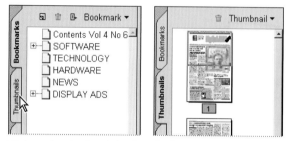

Click a palette's tab to bring it to the front.

- To move a palette to its own floating window, drag the palette's tab to the document pane. To return the palette to the navigation pane, drag the palette's tab back into the navigation pane.

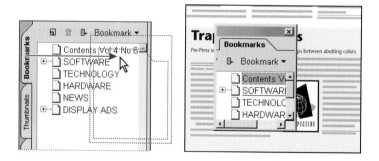

- To move a palette to another group, drag the palette's tab to the other group.

• To display a palette menu, hold down the mouse button on the palette name and triangle in the upper right corner of the palette. Drag to select a command. To hide a palette menu without making a selection, click in the blank space in the navigation pane.

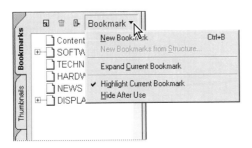

Using context menus

In addition to menus at the top of your screen, context menus display commands relevant to the active tool, selection, or palette.

To display a context menu, position the pointer over an item (such as a bookmark or thumbnail in a palette, for example), and right-click (Windows) or Control-click (Mac OS).

Position the pointer over the *Software* bookmark in the Bookmarks palette and right-click (Windows) or Control-click (Mac OS). After you have looked at the commands available in the context menu, click in a blank area anywhere outside the context menu to close it without choosing a command.

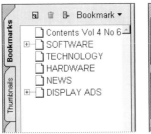
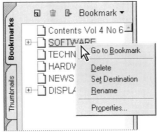

About the on-screen display

Take a look at the status bar located at the bottom of the document window and the Viewing toolbar located at the top of the document window. Notice that the magazine is tabloid size (11-by-17 inches) and currently appears at 100% magnification on-screen.

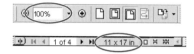

The magnification shown in the status bar does not refer to the printed size of the page, but rather to how the page is displayed on-screen. Acrobat determines the on-screen display of a page by treating the page as a 72 ppi (pixels-per-inch) image. For example, if your page has a print size of 2-by-2 inches, Acrobat treats the page as if it were 144 pixels wide and 144 pixels high (72 x 2 = 144). At 100% view, each pixel in the page is represented by 1 screen pixel on your monitor.

How large the page actually appears on-screen depends on your monitor size and your monitor resolution setting. For example, when you increase the resolution of your monitor, you increase the number of screen pixels within the same monitor area. This results in smaller screen pixels and a smaller displayed page, since the number of pixels in the page itself stays constant. The following illustration shows the variation among 100% displays of the same page on different monitors.

Pixel dimensions and monitor resolution

Regardless of the print size specified for an image, the size of an image on-screen is determined by the pixel dimensions of the image and the monitor size and setting. A large monitor set to 640-by-480 pixels uses larger pixels than a small monitor with the same setting. In most cases, default PC monitor settings display 96 pixels per inch, and default Macintosh monitor settings display approximately 72 pixels per inch.

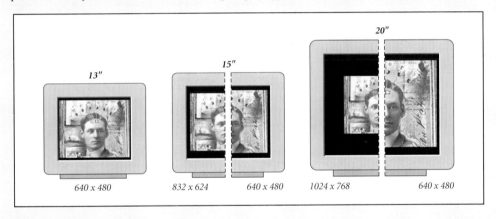

Navigating the document

Acrobat provides a variety of ways for you to move through and adjust the magnification of a PDF document. For example, you can scroll through the magazine using the scroll bar at the right side of the window, or you can turn pages as in a traditional book using the browse buttons in the Navigation toolbar or the status bar. You can also jump to a specific page using the status bar at the bottom of the window or the thumbnails in the Thumbnails palette.

Browsing the document

1 If needed, click the Show/Hide Navigation Pane button (▤) to hide the navigation pane. In addition, if you have a palette displayed in a floating window, select the palette's name in the Window menu to hide the palette.

2 Click the Actual Size button (▯).

3 Select the hand tool (✋) in the toolbar, position your pointer over the document. Hold down the mouse button. Notice that the hand pointer changes to a closed hand when you hold down the mouse button.

4 Drag the closed hand in the window to move the page around on the screen. This is similar to moving a piece of paper around on a desktop.

Drag with hand tool to move page.   *Result*

5 Press Enter or Return to display the next part of the page. You can press Enter or Return repeatedly to view the document from start to finish in screen-sized sections.

6 Click the Fit in Window button (▣) to display the entire page in the window. If needed, click the First Page button (◀) to go to page 1.

7 Position the pointer over the down arrow in the scroll bar, and click once.

The document scrolls automatically to display all of page 2. In the next step, you'll control how PDF pages scroll and display.

8 Click the Continuous button (▤) in the status bar, and then use the scroll bar to scroll to page 3.

The Continuous option displays pages end to end like frames in a filmstrip.

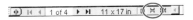

9 Now click the Continuous - Facing button (▦) in the status bar to display page spreads, with left- and right-hand pages facing each other, as on a layout board.

10 Click the Fit Width button (▣) to maximize your viewing area.

Continuous option   *Continuous - Facing option*

11 Click the First Page button to go to page 1.

In keeping with the conventions of printed books, a PDF document always begins with a right-hand page.

12 Click the Single Page button (▢) to return to the original page layout.

You can use the page box in the status bar to switch directly to a specific page.

13 Move the pointer over the page box until it changes to an I-beam, and click to highlight the current page number.

14 Type **4** to replace the current page number, and press Enter or Return.

You should now be viewing page 4 of *Digital Arts*.

The scroll bar also lets you navigate to a specific page.

15 Begin dragging the scroll box upward in the scroll bar. As you drag, a page status box appears. When page 1 appears in the status box, release the mouse.

A. *Scroll box* **B.** *Page status box*

You should now be back at the beginning of *Digital Arts*.

Browsing with thumbnails

Thumbnails are miniature previews of your document pages that are displayed in the Thumbnails palette, which is docked in the navigation pane to the left of the document pane.

In this part of the lesson, you'll use thumbnails to navigate and change the view of pages. In Lesson 6, "Modifying PDF Files," you'll learn how to use thumbnails to reorder pages in a document.

1 Click the Actual Size button (🗋) to view the page at 100% magnification. You should be looking at page 1.

2 Click the Show/Hide Navigation Pane button (🗐) to display the navigation pane. Click the Thumbnails tab to bring the Thumbnails palette to the front.

With Acrobat 5.0, thumbnails for every page in the document are displayed automatically in the navigation pane. The thumbnails represent both the content and page orientation of the pages in the document. Page-number boxes appear beneath each thumbnail.

If your document is a long one, you may need to use the scroll bar to view all the thumbnails.

3 Double-click the page 3 thumbnail to go to page 3.

The page number for the thumbnail is highlighted, and a 100% view of page 3 appears in the document window, centered on the point that you clicked.

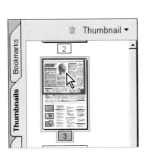

Take a look at the page 3 thumbnail. The rectangle inside the thumbnail, called the page-view box, represents the area displayed in the current page view. You can use the page-view box to adjust the area and magnification being viewed.

4 Position the pointer over the lower right corner of the page-view box. Notice that the pointer turns into a double-headed arrow.

Drag lower right corner of   *Result*
page-view box upward.

5 Drag to shrink the page-view box, and release the mouse button. Take a look at the status bar and notice that the magnification level has increased to accommodate the smaller area being viewed.

6 Now position the pointer over the bottom border of the page-view box. Notice that the pointer changes to a hand.

7 Drag the page-view box within the thumbnail, and watch the view change in the document window.

8 Drag the page-view box down to focus your view on the contents at the bottom of the page.

Thumbnails provide a convenient way to monitor and adjust your page view in a document.

9 Click the Show/Hide Navigation Pane button to hide the navigation pane.

Changing the page view magnification

You can change the magnification of the page view using controls in the toolbar and status bar, or by clicking or dragging in the page with the zoom-in or zoom-out tool.

1 Click the Fit Width button ( ). This control adjusts the magnification to spread the page across the whole width of your screen. A new magnification appears in the Viewing toolbar.

2 Click the Previous Page button (◀) to move to page 2. Notice that the magnification remains the same.

3 Click the Actual Size button ( ) to return the page to a 100% view.

4 Click the arrow to the right of the magnification pop-up menu in the Viewing toolbar to display the preset magnification options. Drag to choose 200% for the magnification.

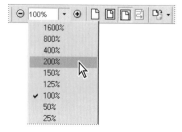

You can also enter a specific value for the magnification.

5 Move the pointer over the magnification box in the Viewing toolbar until it changes to an I-beam, and click to highlight the current magnification.

6 Type **75** to replace the current magnification, and press Enter or Return.

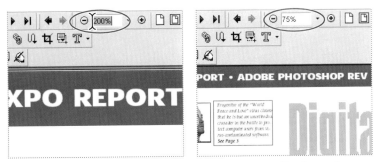

Click to highlight magnification.   *Type in new magnification, and press Enter or Return.*

7 Now click the Fit in Window button ( ) to display the entire page in the window.

Next you'll use the zoom-in tool to magnify a specific portion of a page.

8 Type **3** in the page box, and press Enter or Return to go to page 3. Then select the zoom-in tool ( ) in the toolbar.

9 Click in the top right section of the page to increase the magnification. Notice that the view centers around the point you clicked. Click in the top right section of the page once more to increase the magnification again.

10 Hold down Ctrl (Windows) or Option (Mac OS). Notice that the zoom pointer now appears with a minus sign, indicating that the zoom-out tool is active.

11 With Ctrl or Option held down, click in the document to decrease the magnification. Ctrl-click or Option-click once more to decrease the magnification again, and then release Ctrl or Option.

The entire page should fit on your screen again.

Now you'll drag the zoom-in tool to magnify the Contents area.

12 Position the pointer near the top left of the Contents, and drag over the text as shown in the following illustration.

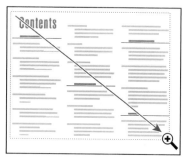

Marquee-zooming

The view zooms in on the area you enclosed. This is called *marquee-zooming*.

Following links

In a PDF document, you don't always have to view pages in sequence. You can jump immediately from one section of a document to another using custom navigational aids such as links.

One benefit of placing *Digital Arts* online is that you can convert traditional cross-references into links, which users can use to jump directly to the referenced section or file. For example, you can make each item under the contents list of *Digital Arts* into a link that jumps to its corresponding section. You can also use links to add interactivity to traditional book elements such as glossaries and indexes. In this lesson you'll follow links; in later lessons, you'll create links.

Now you'll try out an existing link. You should be viewing the Contents at the bottom of page 3.

1 Select the hand tool (🖑). Move the pointer over the Trapping Pitfalls listing in the Contents. The hand tool changes to a pointing finger, indicating the presence of a link. Click to follow the link.

This item links to the Trapping Pitfalls section at the bottom of the first page.

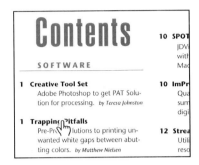 

2 Click the Go to Previous View button (◀) to return to your previous view of the Contents.

You can click the Go to Previous View button at any time to retrace your viewing path through a document. The Go to Next View button (▶) lets you reverse the action of your last Go to Previous View.

In this section, you have learned how to page through a PDF document, change the magnification and page layout mode, and follow links. In later lessons, you'll learn how to create links and create and use other navigational features, such as bookmarks, thumbnails, and articles.

Printing PDF files

When you print Adobe PDF files, you'll find that many of the options in the Acrobat Print dialog box are the same as those found in the Print dialog boxes of other popular applications. For example, the Acrobat Print dialog box, as with the Print dialog boxes of many applications, lets you print an entire file or a range of pages within a PDF file.

Here's how you can print non-contiguous pages or portions of pages in Acrobat.

1 In the *Digital Arts* document, do one of the following:

• To select pages to print, open the Thumbnails palette and click the thumbnails corresponding to the pages you want to print. You can Ctrl-click (Windows) or Command-click (Mac OS) thumbnails to select non-contiguous pages, or Shift-click to select contiguous pages.

- To print an area on a page (rather than the entire page), select the graphics select tool ( ), and drag on the page to draw the area you want to print.

2 If you have a printer attached to your system and turned on, choose File > Print. Make sure the name of the printer attached to your system is displayed. Note that the Selected Pages (Windows) or Selected Thumbnails (Mac OS) option or the Selected Graphic option is automatically selected in the Print dialog box.

In Mac OS, choose Acrobat 5.0 from the pop-up menu to display the correct Print dialog box.

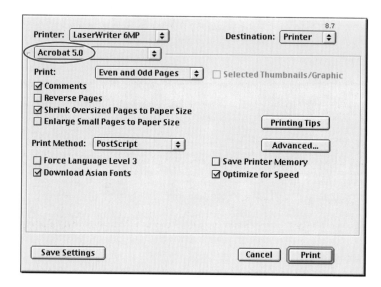

3 Click OK or Print to print your selected pages. Click Cancel to abort the printing operation.

If you have an Internet connection and a Web browser installed on your system, you can click Printing Tips in the Print dialog box to go to the Adobe Web site for the latest troubleshooting help on printing.

For information on printing comments, see "Printing comments" on page 184.

4 Choose File > Close.

⬛ For information on the Advanced Print dialog box, which offers features such as the ability to tile oversize page for printing on 8-1/2 x 11 pages for fast review and proofing and the ability to emit halftones, transfer functions, and undercolor removal and black generation, see "Printing PDF documents" and "Managing color on a printer" in the Acrobat 5.0 online Help.

Using the Acrobat 5.0 online Help

For complete information on all the Acrobat tools, commands, and features for both Windows and Mac OS systems, you can use the Acrobat 5.0 online Help. The Acrobat 5.0 online Help is easy to use because you can look for topics in several ways:

- Scanning the table of contents.
- Using the bookmarks.
- Searching for keywords.
- Using an index.
- Jumping from topic to topic using related topics links.

Opening the Acrobat 5.0 online Help

Choose Help > Acrobat Help from the Help menu or press F1 to open the Acrobat 5.0 online Help.

Acrobat Help opens in a new document window with the bookmark pane open. If the bookmark pane is not open, choose Window > Bookmarks, or press F5.

Note: The accessible PDF format of the online Help is designed to provide easy navigation online, as well as easy reading using third-party screen readers compatible with Windows. The file can also be printed out to provide a handy desktop reference.

Using bookmarks

Since the Acrobat 5.0 online Help opens with the Bookmarks palette visible, try looking for a topic using the bookmarks. Look for information on how to use bookmarks to navigate the Acrobat 5.0 online Help.

In the Bookmarks palette, click the plus sign (Windows) or triangle (Mac OS) next to the Using Help bookmark to expand the bookmark. Click the Using Bookmarks bookmark. The document pane shows the section of online Help describing how to use bookmarks.

Experiment with expanding and collapsing the bookmarks. Note that some bookmarks have multiple nested levels.

Using the index

If you can't find the topic you need in the Bookmarks palette, try using the index. You can get to the index in several ways:

• Click the Index bookmark in the Bookmarks palette to go to the first page of the index. You can also expand the Index bookmark and click on the individual letters to go directly to that portion of the index.

• Click the Index link at the top or bottom of any page in the Acrobat 5.0 online Help to go to the first page of the index. You can then click on any of the letter links at the top of each index page to go to that portion of the index.

When you find the index entry you're looking for, click the page number next to the entry to go to that topic. If the index entry has more than one page number, after you have checked the information on the first page number cited, click the Go to Previous View button (◀) to return to your place in the index and then click the next page number. You can also use the Back link at the top or bottom of each page to retrace your path.

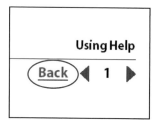

Using Adobe Online

Another way to get information on Adobe Acrobat or on related Adobe products is to use Adobe Online. If you have an Internet connection and a Web browser installed on your system, you can access the U.S. Adobe Systems Web site (at www.adobe.com) for information on services, products, and tips pertaining to Acrobat.

Adobe Online provides access to up-to-the-minute information about services, products, and tips for using Adobe products.

1 In Acrobat, choose Help > Adobe Online.

2 Select Preferences, and specify automatic update options.

3 Select how often you would like to check for updates from the Check for Updates pop-up menu, and select whether you want to see the progress of the download and have the installer launch automatically. You should plan on checking for updates on a regular basis.

4 Click OK to accept the settings and return to the Adobe Online dialog box.

5 In the Adobe Online dialog box, click Updates to see the Adobe Product Updates dialog box, which lists new updates and summarizes all available updates.

6 Click Choose to specify where to install the updates.

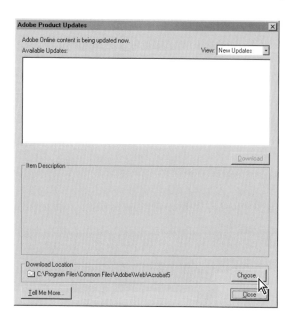

7 Select the required updates in the Available Updates text box, and click Download. (Click Close to close the dialog box without performing a download.)

The updates are downloaded, and depending on the options you selected in the Adobe Online Preferences dialog box, installed. You must close and restart Acrobat for the updates to take effect.

8 If necessary, click Close to close the Adobe Update Products dialog box.

The Go Online button takes you to the Acrobat home page on the Adobe Web site.

9 Close all the Adobe Online dialog boxes. Close and restart Adobe Acrobat if needed.

10 Choose File > Close to close the online Help.

Now that you're familiar with the Acrobat 5.0 work area, you can move through the lessons in this book and learn how to create and work with Adobe PDF files.

Review questions

1 How do you select a hidden tool?

2 Name several ways in which you can move to a different page.

3 Name several ways in which you can change the view magnification.

4 How would you find a topic in the Acrobat 5.0 online Help?

5 How would you print a graphic or a selected portion of text rather than the entire page?

Review answers

1 You can select a hidden tool by holding down the mouse button on either the related tool or the triangle next to the related tool until the additional tools appear, and then dragging to the tool you want. You can hold down Shift and press the letter key shown in the tool tip to cycle through the group of tools, or you can expand the toolbar by holding down the mouse button on the related tool or the triangle next to it until the additional tools appear, and then selecting the Expand This Button option.

2 You can switch pages by clicking the Previous Page or Next Page button in the toolbar; dragging the scroll box in the scroll bar; highlighting the page box in the status bar and entering a page number; or clicking a bookmark, thumbnail, or link that jumps to a different page.

3 You can change the view magnification by clicking the Actual Size, Fit in Window, or Fit Width button in the toolbar; marquee-zooming with the zoom-in or zoom-out tool; choosing a preset magnification from the magnification menu in the Viewing toolbar; or highlighting the magnification box and entering a specific percentage.

4 You can look for a topic using the Acrobat 5.0 online Help bookmarks. You can look for topics on the Contents page of the Acrobat 5.0 online Help. You can look in the index for keywords. You can search for words in the Acrobat 5.0 online Help using the Find command or Search command.

5 You can print a graphic from a mixed text and graphics page by selecting the graphic using the graphics select tool. When you open the Print dialog box, Selected Graphic is selected for the Print Range, and when you click Print, only the graphic will print. You can use this same technique to print a portion of text.

Lesson 3

3 Creating Adobe PDF Files

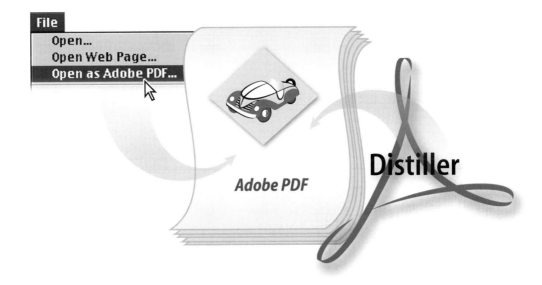

Acrobat provides a variety of ways for you to create Adobe PDF files quickly and easily from existing electronic files or documents. You can use the Print command from within your authoring application, you can open files using the Open as Adobe PDF command, and you can convert scanned documents using Acrobat® Capture® or the Adobe Paper Capture Online service.

In this lesson, you'll learn how to do the following:

• Use an authoring application's Print command to convert a file to Adobe PDF.

• Open a text file in Acrobat, automatically converting it to Adobe PDF.

• Create an Adobe PDF file by exporting a file from Adobe PageMaker.

• Specify security settings for a file.

• View security information for a document.

• Correct PDF files created by converting paper documents to Adobe PDF using a scanner and the Web-based Paper Capture Online service.

This lesson will take about 50 minutes to complete.

If needed, remove the previous lesson folder from your hard drive, and copy the Lesson03 folder onto it.

Note: Windows users need to unlock the lesson files before using them. For information, see "Copying the Classroom in a Book files" on page 3.

Using fonts with this lesson

In this lesson, you'll work with several source files that contain specific fonts. If you receive a message indicating that the necessary fonts are not installed, see "Getting Started" at the beginning of this book, and install the fonts from the Classroom in a Book CD.

About PDF documents

Adobe Acrobat is not a program that enables you to create content. The content of any PDF document must be created in a program other than Acrobat. You can use any word-processing, page-layout, graphic, or business program to create content and then convert that content to Adobe PDF at the time you would normally print to paper. You can think of Adobe PDF files as the electronic equivalents of your printed documents.

You can also create PDF documents by "capturing" scanned images of paper documents (see "Converting paper documents to Adobe PDF" on page 69) and converting Web pages (see Lesson 9, "Creating Adobe PDF from Web Pages").

About Acrobat Distiller

Acrobat mostly uses Acrobat Distiller to create Adobe PDF files. All the necessary components are installed and configured automatically when you perform a typical installation of Acrobat so that you're ready to create Adobe PDF files right away.

Adobe PDF files created with Acrobat Distiller maintain all the formatting, graphics, and photographic images of the original document. Although Distiller has very powerful options that let you control many aspects of your Adobe PDF file, including the amount of compression applied to images, whether or not fonts are embedded, and how color is managed, most users will probably use only the four sets of predefined Distiller job options:

- eBook

- Screen

- Print

- Press

In this lesson, you'll use these predefined Distiller job options to create Adobe PDF files. For information on customizing Distiller job options, see Lesson 4, "Customizing Adobe PDF Output Quality" and "Setting job options" on page 45 in the Acrobat 5.0 online Help.

Using an application's Print command

When you install Acrobat on your system, you automatically install an Acrobat Distiller "printer" (Windows) and a Create Adobe PDF "printer" (Mac OS) that appear in the Print dialog box of many authoring applications. These printers let you create an Adobe PDF file directly from your authoring application.

In this part of the lesson, you'll create an Adobe PDF version of a contract between Adeline and Associates, a fictitious company that repairs and restores antique automobiles, and their agency.

1 Start your word processor.

2 Choose File > Open. Select Contract.doc in the Lessons/Lesson03 folder, and click Open.

Note: If your word processing program won't open the Contract.doc file, open the Contract.pdf file in the Lesson03/Supply folder and skip to "Viewing the PDF contract" on page 55.

Take a minute to look at the contract document. Notice that the document contains a simple graphic logo at the top of the page. (On some platforms and with some word processing programs, you may not see the graphic. The graphic should still print when you create the PDF file, however.)

Creating the Adobe PDF file

Creating an Adobe PDF file is as easy as printing. However, because printing is different on Windows and Mac OS, this section has been organized by platform. Follow the steps in the Windows or Mac OS section.

In Windows:

1 From within your word processing program, choose File > Print.

2 Choose Acrobat Distiller from the Name pop-up menu in the Printer section of the Print dialog box. In some applications, you may need to click Setup in the Print dialog box to access the Name menu.

In this lesson, you'll use the default Distiller parameters (eBook) to create the Adobe PDF file. First though, take a minute to see how you would change the Distiller parameters (job options), if you needed to. (The options available in the Print dialog box may vary depending on your word processing application.)

3 Click the Properties button to open the Acrobat Distiller printer properties dialog box.

4 Click the Adobe PDF Settings tab. You can choose a predefined set of job options from the Conversion Settings pop-up menu, or you can click Edit Conversion Settings to customize the job options. (Any set of job options that you have previously defined and saved in Acrobat Distiller will appear in this pop-up menu.) For information on Adobe PDF Settings, see "Setting job options" in the Acrobat 5.0 online Help.

5 Click Cancel or OK without changing any of the default settings until you return to the Print dialog box.

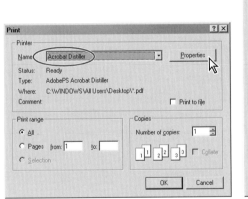
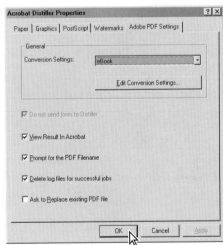

6 Click OK or Print.

7 In the Save PDF File As dialog box, name the PDF document **Contract1.pdf**, and save it in the Lesson03 folder.

8 Exit your word processor.

For alternative ways of converting Microsoft Office application files to Adobe PDF, see "Converting Microsoft Office application files (Windows)" on page 74 and "Converting Microsoft Office application files (Windows)" in the Acrobat 5.0 online Help.

In Mac OS:

1 From within your word processing program, choose File > Print.

💡 *After you install Acrobat, open the Chooser and select any PostScript® printer. A Create Adobe PDF printer will be defined automatically. In your word processing program, choose File > Page Setup, and select Create Adobe PDF as the printer. If you do not have a PostScript printer defined in the Chooser, visit the Adobe Web site for instructions on installing and using the AdobePS™ printer driver.*

2 In the word processing program's Print dialog box, make sure that Create Adobe PDF is selected as the printer, that File is selected for Destination, and that PDF Settings is selected from the pop-up menu. (The options available in the Print dialog box may vary depending on your word processing application.)

Now you'll choose the Distiller job options to be used in creating the Adobe PDF file.

3 Open the Job Options pop-up menu to view the job options available. In addition to the standard job options (eBook, Screen, Print, and Press), any set of job options that you have previously defined and saved in Acrobat Distiller will appear in this pop-up menu. Select eBook, the default Distiller job options.

In Mac OS, you can customize the Distiller job options settings only from Distiller, as described in "Setting job options" in the Acrobat 5.0 online Help.

4 For After PDF Creation, choose Launch Nothing.

The Launch Adobe Acrobat option automatically opens Acrobat and displays your newly created PDF document.

5 Click Save. Name the PDF document **Contract1.pdf**, and save it in the Lesson03 folder.

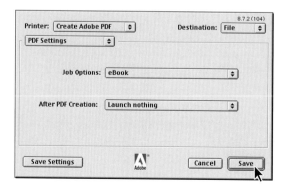

6 Exit or Quit your word processor. You don't need to save any changes.

Creating PostScript files

Not all authoring applications offer a mechanism for creating Adobe PDF files directly. In these cases, you must first create a PostScript file and then convert this PostScript file to Adobe PDF. Advanced users may also want to use this two-step method so they can insert Distiller parameters into the PostScript file to more closely control the creation of the PDF file. (See "Setting the Distiller Advanced job options" in the Acrobat 5.0 online Help.) You may also prefer to create PostScript files if you routinely convert multiple PostScript files to Adobe PDF in a watched folder or need to combine multiple PostScript files into a single Adobe PDF file. (See "Setting up watched folders" and "Combining PostScript files" in the Acrobat 5.0 online Help.)

You create PostScript files using the AdobePS driver and an Acrobat Distiller PPD with the source application. The AdobePS driver and an Acrobat Distiller PPD are installed automatically in the default Acrobat installation. (The PScript driver is installed on Windows 2000 systems.)

—From the Acrobat 5.0 online Help.

Viewing the PDF contract

1 Start Acrobat.

2 Choose File > Open. Select Contract1.pdf in the Lesson03 folder, and click Open.

Note: *If you need to use the supplied PDF document, locate and open the Supply folder inside the Lesson03 folder. Select Contract.pdf from the list of files, and click Open. Choose File > Save As, name the file Contract1.pdf and save it in the Lesson03 folder.*

Take a moment to look at the document. Distiller has re-created the original document, maintaining the format, fonts, and layout.

Just as easily as you would print a paper copy of your file, you have created an Adobe PDF version of your file that you can share with users on any platform, e-mail, or post on the Web.

Creating Adobe PDF from a text file

With the Open as Adobe PDF command in Acrobat, you can convert a variety of file formats—BMP, Compuserve GIF, HTML, JPEG, PCX, PICT (Mac OS only), PNG, Text, or TIFF files—to Adobe PDF by simply opening the files in Acrobat.

Before the agency would sign the contract with Adeline and Associates, they asked for a cancellation clause to be added. Rather than redoing the contract, Adeline and Associates prepared a simple text document containing a cancellation clause. You'll convert this text document to Adobe PDF by opening it in Acrobat using the Open as Adobe PDF command, and then you'll append it to the Sales Agency Agreement document.

1 With the Contract1.pdf file still open, choose File > Open as Adobe PDF. For File of Type (Windows) or Show (Mac OS), select Text (*.txt, *.text). Select Cancel.txt in the Lesson03 folder, and click Open.

2 In the alert, select Create New Document. Click OK.

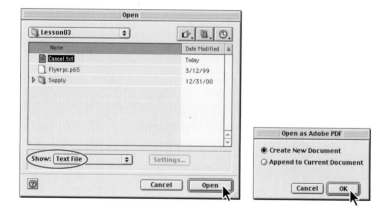

Your text file is automatically converted to an Adobe PDF file.

3 Choose File > Save As. Name the file **Cancel.pdf** and save it in the Lesson03 folder.

4 Choose Window > Tile > Vertically to show the two documents, Contract1.pdf and Cancel.pdf, side-by-side.

Now you'll add the converted file to end of the contract by dragging its thumbnail into the navigation pane of the Contract1.pdf document.

5 Click in one of the document panes to activate it, and then click the Show/Hide Navigation Pane button (▣) to show the navigation pane. Repeat this process for the second document pane.

6 In each navigation pane in turn, click the Thumbnails tab to bring the Thumbnails palette to the front.

7 Select the Cancel.pdf thumbnail in the Thumbnails palette.

8 Drag the selected thumbnail into the Thumbnails palette of Contract1.pdf. When the insertion bar appears below (or to the right of) the Contract1.pdf thumbnail, release the mouse button.

9 Click in the Cancel.pdf document to activate it, and choose File > Close to close the file.

10 Resize the Contract.pdf window.

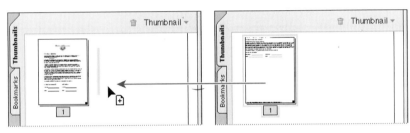

Drag thumbnail between documents.

Page through the document to check that the page was inserted correctly.

11 Choose File > Save to save your work.

Editing text in a PDF file

In the previous section, you converted a simple text file to Adobe PDF and inserted the converted page at the end of the contract file. As you look at the inserted page, you see a header that is not required. Also, the font used in the addendum is very different from that used in the body of the contract. You can edit text in a PDF file using the touchup text tool. However, you can edit only one line at a time so you should do major editing in the authoring application before you create the PDF version. In this file, you'll just remove the unwanted header and format the first heading.

First, you'll check the font and font size used in the headings on page 1 of the contract file so that you can use the same font and font size on the page that you added.

1 Go to page 1 of the contract. Select the touchup text tool (⊤), and click in the heading Sales Agency Agreement. A box appears around the text. Drag to highlight the text within the box.

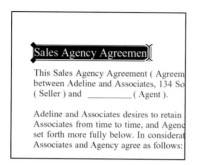

2 Choose Tools > Touchup Text > Text Attributes.

The Text Attributes box displays the name of the font used and the font size. You'll use this information to modify the headings on the addendum.

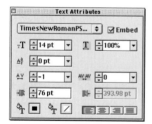

3 Close the Text Attributes dialog box, and go to page 2 of the contract.

Now you'll delete the unwanted header.

4 With the touchup text tool still selected, click in the unwanted header. In the selection box, drag the cursor to select the entire line of text. Press Delete. (If needed, click the Actual Size button ( ) to show the document at 100%.)

Text can be deleted and edited only if the security settings of the PDF file are set to allow such actions. This addendum was created with no security settings applied.

Now you'll change the font and font size of the heading on page 2.

5 Click in the heading Addendum to Sales Agency Agreement, and drag the cursor to select the line of text.

6 Choose Tools > Touchup Text > Text Attributes.

7 In the Text Attributes dialog box, choose the font and point size you identified in Step 2. (If necessary, close any font alert boxes.)

8 Close the Text Attributes dialog box, and click in a blank area of the page to see the newly formatted text.

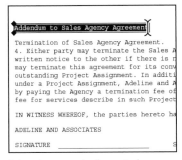

Select the text to be formatted.

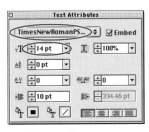

Define new formatting.

Result

The heading text is now in the same font and type size as the headings on page 1. Because the touchup text tool edits only one line at a time, it is not useful for major editing tasks. However, it is a very useful for making minor last-minute corrections such as changing a font or adding color.

9 Select the hand tool (🖑).

10 Choose File > Close. Click Yes (Windows) or Save (Mac OS) to save the file in the Lesson03 folder.

Changing the Distiller job options

At the beginning of this lesson, you created an Adobe PDF file (Contact1.pdf) using Acrobat Distiller in Windows or Create Adobe PDF in Mac OS. In both cases, Distiller used the default Distiller eBook job options to create your Adobe PDF file. (The ebook job options create a PDF file that provides the best balance between file size and image quality for most uses.) In this section, you'll use the Press job options, a predefined set of job options tailored for high-quality printed output.

Distiller provides four job options settings that control the quality of the resulting PDF document for different output needs:

• eBook job options create Adobe PDF files appropriate for reading primarily on screen—on desktop or laptop computers or devices for reading eBooks, for example. This set of options balances file size against image resolution to produce a relatively small self-contained file. PDF files created using the eBook job options are compatible with Acrobat 4.0 (and later).

• The Screen job options create Adobe PDF files appropriate for display on the World Wide Web or an intranet, or for distribution through an e-mail system. This option set produces the smallest PDF file size. It also optimizes files for byte serving.

• The Print job options create Adobe PDF files that are intended for printers, digital copiers, publishing on a CD-ROM, or distribution as a publishing proof. This option set compresses the PDF file size while striving to preserve the color, image quality, and font attributes of the original document.

• The Press job options create Adobe PDF files that are intended for high-quality printed output. This option set produces the largest file size, but preserves the maximum amount of information about the original document.

To see the difference in image quality produced using different Distiller job options, see Lesson 13, "Distributing Document Collections."

In this part of the lesson, you'll convert an Adeline and Associates flyer document to Adobe PDF using the Press Distiller job options.

About Fast Web View

The Distiller 5.0 job options automatically create Adobe PDF files that are optimized for Fast Web View. However, if you are working with older files or with files that were not created using Acrobat 5.0, you should check whether the files have been optimized for Fast Web View.

Optimizing or creating Fast Web View files

You should convert your PDF files to Fast Web View PDF files—that is, optimize them—before distributing them. This minimizes file size and facilitates page-at-a-time downloading. In most cases, converting your PDF files to Fast Web View PDF files by optimizing them reduces their file size significantly.

Fast Web View also restructures a PDF document to prepare for page-at-a-time downloading (byte-serving) from Web servers. With page-at-a-time downloading, the Web server sends only the requested page of information to the user, rather than the entire PDF document. This is especially important with large documents, which can take a long time to download from a server.

To find out if a PDF document has been converted to Fast Web View:

Choose File > Document Properties > Summary, and look at the Fast Web View option.

To create a Fast Web View document:

1. *Choose Edit > Preferences > General. Select Options in the left panel of the General Preferences dialog box. Select Save As Optimizes for Fast Web View (This option is set by default.) Click OK.*

2. *Use the File > Save As command to save your file.*

—From the Acrobat 5.0 online Help.

Opening the flyer document

Saved in Adobe PageMaker format, the flyer document contains general information about Adeline and Associates and their repair and restoration of antique automobiles.

Note: If you do not have Adobe PageMaker, proceed to "Adding security to PDF files" on page 65 and open the Flyer.pdf file that has been supplied in the Lesson03/Supply folder.

1 Start PageMaker.

2 Choose File > Open. Select Flyerpc.p65 (Windows) or Flyermc.p65 (Mac OS) in the Lesson03 folder, and click Open (Windows) or OK (Mac OS). (Clear any alerts regarding missing printers. They are not important in this lesson.)

3 Choose File > Save As, rename the file **Flyer1.p65** and save it in the Lesson03 folder.

Take a minute to look at the flyer document. Notice that the flyer contains a number of photographic and graphic elements.

If you get an alert indicating that fonts are missing, see "Getting Started" at the beginning of this book, and install the fonts from the Classroom in a Book CD. If you don't want to install the fonts, you can accept substitute fonts, but the appearance of the document may not be true to the original.

Choosing a Distiller job options setting

The informational flyer is going to be printed by a commercial printer so it can be handed out at automotive shows. For this reason, the source file for the commercial printer needs to contain text graphics of the highest quality—file size is not a problem. To create this Adobe PDF file, you'll use the Distiller Press job options.

1 In Acrobat, choose Tools > Distiller to start Acrobat Distiller.

2 In the Acrobat Distiller dialog box, for Job Options, choose Press.

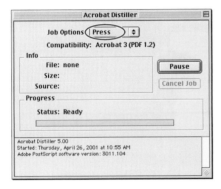

3 Exit or quit Distiller.

In general, the predefined Distiller job options produce good results. However, you may want to set custom options to control the appearance of converted pages and to fine-tune the quality and compression of images. For information on using these advanced Distiller features, see Lesson 4, "Customizing Adobe PDF Output Quality." For even more control over the PDF creation process, you may want to convert your document first to a PostScript language file, and then convert the PostScript file to Adobe PDF using Distiller. For information on creating PostScript files, see "Creating PostScript files" in the Acrobat 5.0 online Help.

Creating the Adobe PDF file

Now that you've specified a Distiller job options setting, you can convert the flyer directly to Adobe PDF from PageMaker. You'll use a special PageMaker feature that exports an Adobe PDF file using Distiller.

1 Return to the PageMaker flyer document in PageMaker.

2 Choose File > Export > Adobe PDF.

3 Deselect Override Distiller's Options. Accept the remaining settings, and click Export.

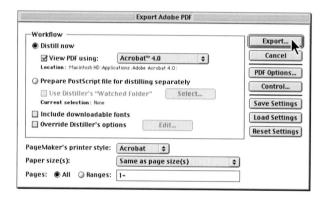

4 Save the PDF file as **Flyer1.pdf** in the Lesson03 folder. Distiller will open, and you can see the progress of the conversion.

5 Exit or quit Distiller when the conversion is finished.

6 Exit or quit PageMaker. You don't need to save any changes to the PageMaker flyer document.

7 If necessary, choose File > Open and open Flyer1.pdf in the Lesson03 folder.

Your PageMaker document has been converted to Adobe PDF—fonts, text and graphics look just as they did in the original PageMaker document (unless you allowed font substitution).

Adding security to PDF files

When you share confidential documents by e-mail or on the Web, it is critical that the information doesn't end up in the wrong hands. Acrobat allows you to apply different levels of security so that only designated people can open files or only certain people can open and edit files. Even if your files are being distributed widely, you can protect them against being copied or changed. For example, now that you have a finished PDF file for the flyer, you'll want to protect the file from accidental changes before you send it to the printer.

Setting file security

You should have the Flyer1.pdf file open.

If you did not create a Flyer1.pdf file in the last section, in Acrobat, open the Flyer.pdf file in the Lesson03/Supply folder. Save the file as Flyer1.pdf in the Lesson03 folder.

1 Choose File > Document Security, and choose Acrobat Standard Security from the Security Options menu.

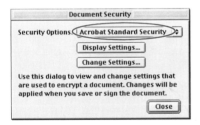

A dialog box appears. You can specify two passwords—one for opening the file and one for changing permissions and passwords to the file. These passwords are case-sensitive. In most situations, you won't want to set a password for opening a document, only for changing the document. You'll set both passwords here for practice.

2 Check Password Required to Open Document, and enter **Cars** for User Password.

3 Check Password Required to Change Permissions and Passwords, and enter **Classic** for Master Password.

Consider leaving the encryption level at the default value (40-bit), which is backwards compatible with Acrobat 4.0 and 3.0. While the 128-bit encryption level offers more sophisticated security, files secured with this encryption level cannot be opened with versions of Acrobat prior to 5.0.

4 For Permissions, select No Changing the Document and No Adding or Changing Comments and Form Fields. Click OK.

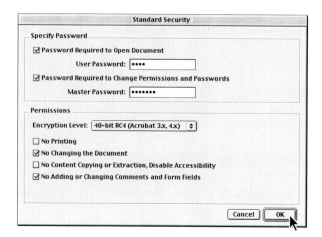

A dialog box appears asking you to confirm your Open password.

5 Enter **Cars,** and click OK. Remember that passwords are case-sensitive.

A second dialog box appears asking you to confirm your Master password.

6 Enter **Classic,** and click OK.

7 Click Display Settings to check the security settings you have applied to the file. Click OK, and then click Close to exit the Document Security dialog box.

8 Choose File > Close, and click Yes (Windows) or Save (Mac OS) to save your changes. You have to save and close the file for changes to take effect.

If you want to make sure that only certain people can open and edit a particular document, you should set the security using Acrobat Self-Sign Security (in the Document Security dialog box) or an equivalent security handler.

Testing file security

Now you'll test the security that you just applied to the file.

1 Choose File > Open. Select Flyer1.pdf, located in the Lesson03 folder, and click Open.

A dialog box appears asking you for the Open password.

2 Enter **Cars,** and click OK.

Notice that even though a password was required to open the document, many commands under the Edit and Document menus are dimmed, indicating that you cannot invoke them. Notice also that many of the tools in the toolbar are dimmed.

3 Try to select the note tool (🗒). The note tool is dimmed, indicating that you can't even add notes to this document.

4 Choose File > Document Security.

5 In the Document Security dialog box, click Change Settings.

A dialog box appears asking you for the Master password.

6 Enter **Classic,** and click OK.

7 Deselect the Password Required to Open Document option.

8 For Permissions, deselect No Adding or Changing Comments and Form Fields, and click OK. Then click Close.

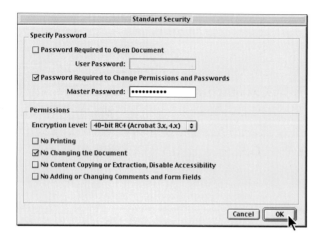

9 Choose File > Close, and click Yes (Windows) or Save (Mac OS) to save changes.

You have to close and save the file for changes to take effect.

10 Choose File > Open, and re-open the Flyer1.pdf file.

You no longer need a password to open the document.

11 Select the note tool (⊟) and click in the document to add a note. The tool is no longer disabled.

12 Select the hand tool.

13 Close the Flyer1.pdf file. You do not need to save your changes.

Now that you have investigated the security settings in Acrobat, you can protect all your sensitive PDF files from unauthorized changes.

Converting paper documents to Adobe PDF

Earlier in this lesson you used several different methods to create Adobe PDF files from electronic files. You can also use the Import Scan command of Acrobat in conjunction with a scanner to convert paper documents to Adobe PDF files. The resulting PDF file is PDF Image Only format in which elements on the page can be edited only as bitmap images; text characters cannot be searched or edited. If your converted document contains text, you may want to convert the document to PDF Normal format so that the text can be edited and searched in Acrobat. You use Acrobat Capture (not included with Acrobat 5.0) or the Paper Capture Online Web-based service provided by Adobe to convert documents to PDF Normal format.

Scanning text you plan to capture

• *For normal text, set up the scanner to create black-and-white (or 1-bit) images.*

• *Black-and-white images and text must be scanned at 200 to 600 dpi. Color images and text must be scanned at 200 to 400 dpi.*

Note: Pages scanned in 24-bit color, 300 dpi, at 8.5-by-11 inches result in very large files (24 MB); your system must have at least twice that amount of virtual memory available to be able to scan. If you're scanning in color, check that you have at least 50 MB of space available on your hard drive before beginning the scanning process.

• *For color or grayscale pages with large type, consider scanning at 200 dpi for faster processing.*

• *For most pages, scanning at 300 dpi produces the best captures. However, if a page has many unrecognized words or very small text (9 points or below), try scanning at a higher resolution (up to 600 dpi). Scan in black and white whenever possible.*

• *Do not use dithering or halftone scanner settings. These settings can improve the appearance of photographic images, but they make it difficult to recognize text.*

• *For text printed on colored paper, try increasing the brightness and contrast by about 10%. If your scanner has color-filtering capability, consider using a filter or lamp that drops out the background color.*

• *If your scanner has a manual brightness control, adjust it so that characters are clean and well formed. If characters are touching because they are too thick, use a higher (brighter) setting. If characters are separated because the characters are too thin, use a lower (darker) setting.*

Characters that are too thin, well-formed characters, and characters that are too thick

Your office just received a fax announcing a meeting to discuss team strategy. Rather than take the time to retype the information in an e-mail, you'll convert a TIFF image of the fax to Adobe PDF. You can send the resulting Adobe PDF file to your colleagues as an e-mail attachment. We've provided a fax document, scanned as a TIFF file, for you to experiment with.

1 Choose File > Open as Adobe PDF. For File of Type (Windows) or Show (Mac OS), choose TIFF. Select Fax.tif in the Lesson03 folder, and click Open.

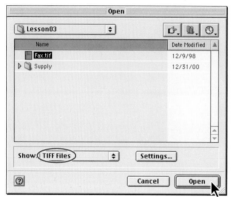 

Acrobat automatically converts the TIFF file to Adobe PDF.

2 Choose File > Save As, rename the file **Fax1.pdf**, and save it in the Lesson03 folder. (Be sure to select PDF as the format for the saved file.)

3 Select the touchup text tool ($\mathbb{T}$), and click in the fax text.

Notice that you cannot edit the text in the document. The file is a PDF Image Only file; that is, all elements in the document, including the text, behave as bitmap pictures.

You convert the file to PDF Normal format using Acrobat Capture or the Web-based Paper Capture Online service (Tools > Paper Capture Online) offered by Adobe. A PDF Normal document contains editable text that can be altered, scaled, and reformatted.

In case you don't have a connection to the Internet, we have "captured" the fax for you.

4 Choose File > Close, and close the converted fax without saving changes.

5 Choose File > Open. Select Capture.pdf in the Lesson03/Supply folder, and click Open.

6 Choose File > Save As, rename the file **Capture1.pdf**, and save it in the Lesson03 folder.

7 With the touchup text tool selected, click in the document. Notice that you can now edit all horizontal text. The vertically oriented text along the side of the page is still treated as a bitmap image.

The quality of the original fax was poor, as is often the case. As a result, a number of words couldn't be recognized with any degree of accuracy. In the next section, you'll correct these suspect words.

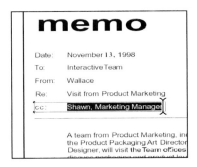

Finding suspect words

Acrobat Capture converts a bitmap text image into its equivalent text characters. If Acrobat suspects that it has not recognized a word correctly, it displays the bitmap image for the word in the document and hides its best guess for the word behind the bitmap. You can view these *suspect* words in the captured document.

Choose Tools > TouchUp Text > Show Capture Suspects.

The suspect words are identified in the document. You'll examine each suspect and correct or accept Acrobat's best guess for the word.

Correcting suspect words

1 Choose Tools > TouchUp Text > Find First Suspect.

The original bitmap word appears enlarged in the Capture Suspect window, and Acrobat's best guess for the word appears highlighted in the document. You can correct a suspect word by typing in the desired characters, or you can accept Acrobat's best guess for the word.

2 If needed, click Accept (Windows) or Accept & Next (Mac OS) until you arrive at the suspect word "launch."

 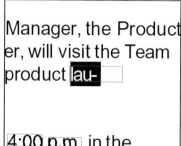

Since Acrobat's guess is obviously wrong, you'll type in the correct word.

3 Type **launch** on the keyboard. Notice that the word is updated in the document as you type. Then click Accept (Windows) or Accept & Next (Mac OS) to convert the image text to the word you just typed.

Notice that the word you corrected is incorrectly spaced. You'll adjust the word spacing using the touchup text tool in a moment. First, you'll finish correcting the capture suspects.

4 Click Accept (Windows) or Accept & Next (Mac OS) as necessary to finish the correction process.

Now you can go back and correct the spacing of the word "launch."

5 Select the touchup text tool (T), and click in the line containing the word "launch."

6 Drag to highlight the crowded letters.

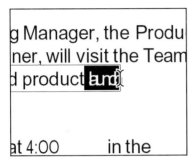

7 Choose Tools > Touchup Text > Text Attributes.

8 In the Text Attributes dialog box, change the letter spacing to 2.

9 If there are any extra characters or letter spaces, drag to highlight the characters or letter spaces, and press Delete. Click outside the selection to view the result of the text touchup.

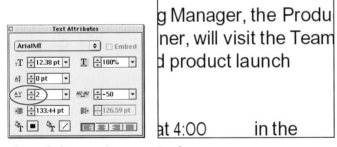

Change the letter spacing.   *Result*

10 Close the Text Attributes dialog box when you are satisfied with your correction.

11 Select the hand tool.

12 Choose File > Save, and save your work.

13 Choose File > Close to close the file.

Converting Microsoft Office application files (Windows)

If you are using Microsoft Office applications in Windows, you have an additional route for creating Adobe PDF files. The default Acrobat installation in Windows includes Adobe PDFMaker 5.0 which allows you to create Adobe PDF files quickly and easily from within Microsoft Office applications. PDFMaker works with Microsoft Word 97, Word 2000, Excel 97, Excel 2000, PowerPoint 97, and PowerPoint 2000, automatically generating tagged Adobe PDF and preserving hyperlinks, styles, and bookmarks present in the source document.

PDFMaker uses the Distiller job options (settings) last defined unless you change them.

Experiment by opening the Contract.doc file you used earlier in this lesson, and choose Acrobat > Convert to Adobe PDF from the Word menu bar. PDFMaker will use your current Distiller job options to create the Adobe PDF file.

To change the settings used in the conversion of the file, choose Acrobat > Change Conversion Settings. Click Help in the PDFMaker dialog box to access the online Help for changing these settings, many of which are the same as for Distiller.

Review questions

1 How can you create a PDF file from within an authoring program, such as Adobe® FrameMaker®?

2 What file formats can you use with the Open as Adobe PDF command?

3 What are the default Distiller job options, and what are they recommended for?

4 What types of passwords can you assign to a document?

5 What are the properties of a PDF Image Only file? A PDF Normal file?

6 How do you make a scanned page searchable and editable in Acrobat?

7 What is a "suspect" word?

Review answers

1 Use the Print command in the authoring program, choose Acrobat Distiller (Windows) or Create Adobe PDF (Mac OS) as the printer, and then print to a file.

2 The Open as Adobe PDF command works on text files, HTML files, and a variety of image files. The types of files supported are listed in the Open dialog box in the Files of Type (Windows) or Show (Mac OS) pop-up menu.

3 The eBook job options are the default Distiller job options. They are used to create Adobe PDF files that balance size with image and text quality to give a relatively small PDF file that is designed primarily to be read on screen—on desktop or laptop computers or on devices for reading eBooks.

4 You can assign a password that lets users open the document and one that lets users change the security options for the document.

5 In a PDF Image Only file, all the pictures and text are treated as images. You cannot edit the text using the touchup text tool or search the text using the Find or Search command. A PDF Normal file contains searchable and editable text.

6 To convert a scanned PDF Image file to a searchable, editable PDF Normal file, use Acrobat Capture or the Paper Capture Online service offered by Adobe. Both use optical character recognition to convert bitmap text to searchable, editable text.

7 A suspect word is a word that has probably been recognized incorrectly during the capture process. Acrobat provides its best guess for the characters in the suspect word and lets you correct its mistakes.

Lesson 4

4 | Customizing Adobe PDF Output Quality

You control the output quality of your files by specifying appropriate job options used by Acrobat Distiller to convert the files to Adobe PDF. In addition to default job options designed to produce satisfactory results for common output needs, Distiller lets you customize job options for your specific needs.

In this lesson, you'll learn how to do the following:

• Choose Acrobat Distiller compression and resampling job options.

• Compare the output of Adobe PDF files converted with different default Distiller job options.

• Explore the color management settings in the default Distiller job options.

• Set up watched folders for batch-processing of PDF files.

• Convert PostScript files to Adobe PDF using the drag-and-drop method.

This lesson will take approximately 35 minutes to complete.

If needed, remove the previous lesson folder from your hard drive, and copy the Lesson04 folder onto it.

Note: Windows users need to unlock the lesson files before using them. For information, see "Copying the Classroom in a Book files" on page 3.

Controlling Adobe PDF output quality

Acrobat Distiller produces Adobe PDF files that accurately preserve the look and content of the original document. When creating Adobe PDF files, Distiller uses various methods to compress text, line art, and bitmap images so that they use less file space. In this lesson, you'll learn how to choose and customize compression options to create the Adobe PDF quality and file size appropriate to your output needs.

In Lesson 3, "Creating Adobe PDF Files," you learned how to convert a source document directly to Adobe PDF using Distiller. Behind the scenes of this conversion process, Distiller creates an intermediate file in PostScript format before producing the final Adobe PDF file. For greater control over the creation of Adobe PDF files, you may want to create your own PostScript file from the source document and then process the PostScript file manually using Distiller. Creating PostScript files manually gives you greater control over page descriptions and compression options, and allows you to automate the creation of Adobe PDF files using watched folders. Although you'll not do so in this lesson, you can easily create PostScript files from many source applications.

[?] For information on setting up your system to create PostScript files, see "Creating PostScript files" in the Acrobat 5.0 online Help.

About compression and resampling

Distiller lets you choose from a variety of file compression methods designed to reduce the file space used by color, grayscale, and monochrome images in your document. Which method you choose depends on the kind of images you are compressing.

In addition to choosing a compression method, you can *resample* bitmap images in your file to reduce the file size. A bitmap image consists of digital units called *pixels,* whose total number determines the file size. When you resample a bitmap image using Distiller, the information represented by several pixels in the image is combined to make a single larger pixel. This process is also called *downsampling* because it reduces the number of pixels in the image.

Managing color with Distiller

Distiller 5.0 gathers color management controls in a single Color Settings dialog box.

When you use Distiller to convert a PostScript file to Adobe PDF, you can choose to use the color management information contained in the PostScript file or you can choose to change aspects of that color management information. If you choose to modify any color management information in the PostScript file, you do so through the Color tab in the Distiller job options dialog box.

Note: In Acrobat, color is managed through the Color Management preferences (in the General Preferences dialog box).

Specifying how color is managed

To specify whether Distiller uses color management information contained in the PostScript file or CSFs defined in the Color tab of the Distiller job options dialog box, do one of the following:

• To use information contained in the PostScript file to manage color, choose None in the Settings File pop-up menu. Set the color management policy and working spaces to determine how Distiller converts or tags unmanaged color spaces in the PostScript file. The options other than the Setting File options vary with the compatibility option selected in the General tab. (The default Settings File value for the eBook, Press, Print, and Screen job options is None; settings for the related color management policies, working spaces, and device-dependent data are defined for each of the default job options settings.)

• To use a Distiller color settings file to manage color, choose the required CSF from the Settings File pop-up menu. The Color Management Policies and Working Spaces options are grayed out because they are pre-defined for each CSF. Set the device-dependent data options as required.

--From the Acrobat 5.0 online Help.

Using default compression settings

In this section, you'll compare the image quality and file size of four different PDF files prepared by converting a sample PostScript file to Adobe PDF four times, using a different predefined set of job options each time.

1 Start Acrobat.

2 Choose File > Open, and select the four Adobe PDF files—Color1.pdf, Color2.pdf, Color3.pdf, and Color4.pdf—in the Lessons/Lesson04 folder. (You can shift-click to select contiguous files.) Click Open.

Color1.pdf was created using the Distiller eBook job options, Color2.pdf was created using the Distiller Press job options, Color3.pdf was created using the Distiller Print job options, and Color4.pdf was created using the Distiller Screen job options.

3 Choose Window > Tile > Vertically to display all the files in the document pane. If needed, use the scroll bars to display the same area in each of the files.

At the default magnification, all four images look very similar.

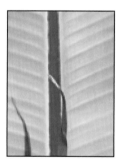

Color1.pdf   *Color2.pdf*   *Color3.pdf*   *Color4.pdf*

4 Click several times with the zoom-in tool (⊕) or use the magnification pop-up menu to display each image at 400% magnification. Scroll as needed so that you can see the same area in each of the files.

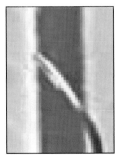   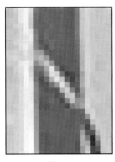

Color1.pdf   *Color2.pdf*   *Color3.pdf*   *Color4.pdf*

In comparison with the other images, Color4.pdf (the screen-optimized file) has a more jagged display quality. Since Color4.pdf is intended for low-resolution, on-screen use, and especially for Web use where download time is important, it does not require as detailed a display quality. Screen-optimized files display more quickly than files with higher resolution images.

5 Select the hand tool (✋).

6 With the Color4.pdf window active, choose File > Close, and close the Color4.pdf file without saving any changes.

7 Choose Window > Tile > Vertically to resize the remaining three images.

8 Select the zoom-in tool and click twice in each document pane to display Color1.pdf, Color2.pdf, and Color3.pdf at 800% magnification. Scroll as needed to display the same area in the three files.

Color1.pdf (the eBook-optimized file) has the coarsest display quality. The eBook job options are chosen to balance image quality with a reasonable file size. The display quality of Color3.pdf (the print-optimized file) is very close to that of Color2.pdf (the press-optimized file). Color2.pdf is intended for high-resolution printing—it contains the most detailed image quality and has the largest file size.

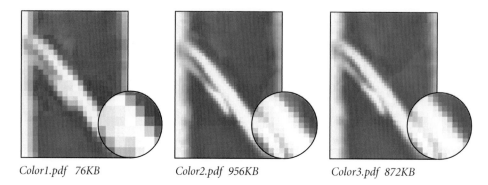

Color1.pdf 76KB   *Color2.pdf 956KB*   *Color3.pdf 872KB*

9 Choose Window > Close All to close all three files without saving them.

Now you'll compare the file sizes of the four Adobe PDF files. (File size may vary depending on your platform.)

10 In Windows, use Windows Explorer to open the Lesson04 folder, and note the sizes of the four files. In Mac OS, open the Lesson04 folder, shift-click the Color1.pdf, Color2.pdf, Color3.pdf, and Color4.pdf to select all four files, and then choose File > Get Info > General Information.

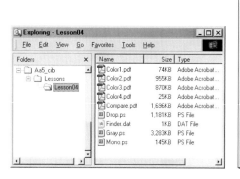

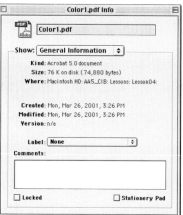

Color4.pdf has the lowest image quality and the smallest file size, while Color2.pdf has the highest image quality and the largest file size. Note that the significantly smaller Color1.pdf file does indeed balance image quality with small file size.

Note: *File sizes may vary slightly depending on whether you are using a Windows or Mac OS system.*

11 Close all open windows.

PDF creation often involves a trade-off between image quality and file compression. More compression means smaller file sizes but also coarser image quality, while finer image quality is achieved at the expense of larger file sizes. For information on the default job options, see "Changing the Distiller job options" in Lesson 3.

Using custom compression settings

The default Distiller job options are designed to produce optimum results in most cases. However, you can set job options manually if you want to fine-tune the compression methods used by Distiller. In this part of the lesson, you'll practice applying custom compression and resampling settings to the color PostScript file.

Note: *Compression and resampling do not affect the quality of either text or line art.*

Changing the Distiller job options

By combining the appropriate compression and downsampling job options, you can greatly reduce the file size of a PDF document without losing noticeable detail in an image. You'll apply your custom settings to the original high-resolution PostScript file Color.ps.

1 In Acrobat, choose Tools > Distiller.

2 In the Acrobat Distiller dialog box, choose Screen from the Job Options pop-up menu.

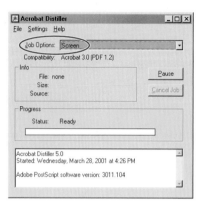

3 Choose Settings > Job Options, and click the Compression tab.

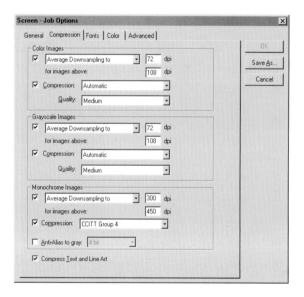

The default compression values associated with the Screen settings are displayed. You'll now adjust several options to produce your own custom setting (using the Screen settings as your base) for optimizing on-screen PDF display.

4 In the Color Images area, choose Average Downsampling To from the pop-up menu.

Average downsampling averages the pixels in a sample area and replaces the entire area with the average pixel color at the specified resolution. A slower but more precise approach is to use bicubic downsampling, which uses a weighted average to determine pixel color. Bicubic downsampling yields the smoothest tonal gradations. Subsampling, which chooses a pixel in the center of the sample area and replaces the entire area with that pixel at the specified resolution, significantly reduces the conversion time but results in images that are less smooth and continuous.

5 Enter **108** dpi for the resampling value and for the Images Above option.

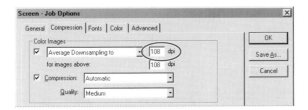

This will downsample the original PostScript color image file (assuming the image resolution is above 108 dpi) to a resolution of 108 dpi. Options you enter in the Color Images section of the dialog box affect only color images. Any changes you make to the grayscale or monochrome options have no effect on color images. Distiller recognizes the type of PostScript image file, and applies the appropriate color, grayscale, or monochrome compression settings.

Note: The minimum resolution of images that will be downsampled is determined by the resampling value you choose.

6 Leave the Compression set to Automatic to allow Acrobat to determine the best compression method, and leave the Quality set to Medium.

With the Automatic option, Acrobat determines the best compression method and quality for your color or grayscale images: JPEG is applied to 8-bit grayscale images and to 8-bit, 16-bit, and 24-bit color images when the images have continuous, smooth tones; ZIP is applied to 2-bit, 4-bit, and 8-bit grayscale images, to 4-bit color images and indexed 8-bit color images, and to 16-bit and 24-bit color images when the images have sharp color changes.

7 Since the Color.ps file you'll be converting contains no grayscale or monochrome images, you'll leave the default values in these sections.

If the Optimize for Fast Web View option is selected in the General tab, text and line art are compressed regardless of whether you select the Compress Text and Line Art option in the Compression tab.

Now you'll save the custom setting that you have specified so that you can use it again in the future.

8 Click Save As. Save the custom setting using the default name **Screen(1).joboptions**. You cannot overwrite the default Distiller job options.

Your custom setting will now be available from the Distiller Job Options menu, along with the default settings.

9 Click OK to exit the job options. Leave the Distiller window open.

About methods of compression

Distiller applies ZIP compression to text and line art; ZIP or JPEG compression to color and grayscale bitmap images; and ZIP, CCITT Group 3 or 4, or Run Length compression to monochrome images.

• ZIP is a compression method that works well on images with large areas of single colors or repeating patterns, such as screen shots and simple images created with paint programs, and for black-and-white images that contain repeating patterns. Acrobat provides 4-bit and 8-bit ZIP compression options. If you use 4-bit ZIP compression with 4-bit images, or 8-bit ZIP with 4-bit or 8-bit images, the ZIP method is lossless, which means it does not remove data to reduce file size and so does not affect an image's quality. However, using 4-bit ZIP compression with 8-bit data can affect the quality, since data is lost.

Note: *Adobe's implementation of the ZIP filter is derived from the zlib package of Jeanloup Gailly and Mark Adler, whose generous assistance we gratefully acknowledge.*

• The JPEG (Joint Photographic Experts Group) compression method is suitable for grayscale or color images, such as continuous-tone photographs that contain more detail than can be reproduced on-screen or in print. JPEG is lossy, which means that it removes image data and may reduce image quality, but it attempts to reduce file size with the minimum loss of information. Because JPEG eliminates data, it can achieve much smaller file sizes than ZIP compression.

Acrobat provides five JPEG options, ranging from Maximum quality (the least compression and the smallest loss of data) to Minimum quality (the most compression and the greatest loss of data). The loss of detail that results from the Maximum and High quality settings are so slight that most people cannot tell an image has been compressed; at Minimum and Low, however, the image may become blocky and acquire a mosaic look. The Medium quality setting usually strikes the best balance in creating a compact file while still maintaining enough information to produce high-quality images.

• The CCITT (International Coordinating Committee for Telephony and Telegraphy) compression method is appropriate for black-and-white images made by paint programs and any images scanned with an image depth of 1 bit. CCITT is a lossless method.

Acrobat provides the CCITT Group 3 and Group 4 compression options. CCITT Group 4 is a general-purpose method that produces good compression for most types of monochrome images. CCITT Group 3, used by most fax machines, compresses monochrome bitmaps one row at a time.

• Run Length is a lossless compression option that produces the best results for images that contain large areas of solid white or black.

--From the Acrobat 5.0 online Help.

Processing the color file with custom settings

Now you're ready to try out your new job options setting.

1 In Distiller, choose File > Open. Select Color.ps in the Lesson04 folder, and click Open.

2 Name the Adobe PDF file **Color5.pdf**, and click Save to save it in the Lesson04 folder. (The default is to save the file on the desktop.)

The conversion of the PostScript file is shown in the Distiller window.

3 In Acrobat, choose File > Open. Select Color5.pdf and Color4.pdf (the other screen-optimized PDF file) in the Lesson04 folder, and click Open.

4 Choose Window > Tile > Vertically to display the files side-by-side, and view both files at 200% magnification. If needed, use the scroll bars to display the same area in each of the files.

Color5.pdf is smoother than Color4.pdf. Because Color5.pdf has a higher resolution (108 dpi rather than 72 dpi), it contains more pixel detail and finer image quality.

 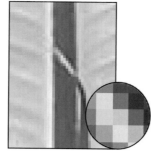

Color5.pdf 42KB　　　*Color4.pdf 25KB*

5 Choose Window > Close All to close the files without saving them.

6 Compare the file size of the two images. In Windows use Windows Explorer; in Mac OS, choose Get Info > General Information from the File menu. Color5.pdf is significantly larger than Color4.pdf.

Processing grayscale and monochrome images

You can experiment with applying default compression and resampling settings to a grayscale and a monochrome PostScript image file. This part of the lesson is optional.

You'll convert the sample PostScript files Gray.ps and Mono.ps, located in the Lesson04 folder to Adobe PDF using the eBook job options. (We converted the two PostScript files using the Press, Print, and Screen job options for you; however, you can experiment with creating the files yourself using these job options if you have time. You can also customize the job options settings as you did in the previous section.)

1 In the Distiller window, choose eBook from the Job Options menu.

The eBook setting creates output appropriate for on-screen display, such as desktop computers, laptops, and eBook reading devices.

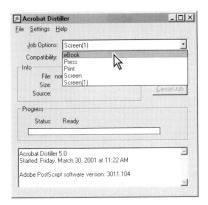

2 Choose File > Open. Select Gray.ps in the Lesson04 folder on your hard drive, and click Open.

3 Name the resulting Adobe PDF file **Gray1.pdf**, and save it in the Lesson04 folder. Distiller shows the status of the conversion process to Adobe PDF.

4 Repeat steps 1 through 3 for the Mono.ps file, naming the resulting Adobe PDF file Mono1.pdf.

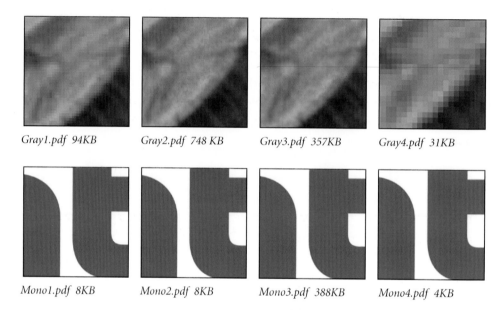

Gray1.pdf 94KB   Gray2.pdf 748 KB   Gray3.pdf 357KB   Gray4.pdf 31KB

Mono1.pdf 8KB   Mono2.pdf 8KB   Mono3.pdf 388KB   Mono4.pdf 4KB

5 In Acrobat, open the "Gray" series of files and the "Mono" series of files, and compare the image quality and file size as you did for the Color1.pdf, Color2.pdf, Color3.pdf, and Color4.pdf files in "Using default compression settings" on page 82.

You'll notice that images with larger file sizes do not necessarily yield better display quality. Downsampling a monochrome file may not significantly reduce its size. When converting your images to Adobe PDF, choose compression and resampling options that will give you adequate quality at the smallest file size possible.

6 When you've finished comparing image quality and file size, choose Window > Close All to close all the files without saving them.

Managing color in Distiller

Any image in a file created by an ICC-compliant application such as Photoshop or Illustrator may have an ICC profile—a description of a device's color space—attached. Distiller can interpret embedded ICC profiles to automatically manage color, and it can assign ICC profiles to unmanaged color spaces.

When you use Distiller to convert a PostScript file to Adobe PDF, you can choose to use the color management information contained in the PostScript file, or you can modify any embedded color management information using the color settings in the job options file.

Take a few minutes to explore the color management settings in the default Distiller job options.

Note: In Acrobat, color is managed through the Color Management preferences (in the General Preferences dialog box).

1 In Distiller, select eBook from the Job Options pop-up menu, and then choose Settings > Job Options. Click the Color tab.

For each of the default Distiller Job Options, eBook, Press, Print, and Screen, the Settings File is set to None—that is, Distiller uses color management information contained in the PostScript file. If the PostScript file contains unmanaged color spaces, however, Distiller converts or tags those spaces based on the color management policy and working spaces settings set in this dialog box.

2 Open the Settings File pop-up menu.

If you are working in a well-defined color workflow, you can select a color settings file (CSF) from the Settings File pop-up menu. Notice that these color settings files mirror those used in Photoshop and Illustrator. These files cannot be edited.

3 Choose U.S. Prepress Defaults.

Notice that the Color Management Policies and Working Spaces options cannot be edited for these predefined color settings files.

4 Click Cancel to close the Job Options dialog box without making any changes.

For more information on these color settings, see "Setting the Distiller Color job options" in the Acrobat 5.0 online Help.

Distiller job options	Acrobat compatibility level	Color management policy
eBook	4.0	Convert all colors to sRGB.
Press	4.0	Leave color unchanged.
Print	4.0	Tag everything for color management.
Screen	3.0	Convert everything to CalRGB.

Using watched folders

To automate the process of creating Adobe PDF files, you can set up a watched folder on your system or network server. When Distiller watches a folder, it periodically checks the folder for PostScript files. When a PostScript file is saved or copied into a watched folder, Distiller automatically converts the file to Adobe PDF and moves it to an Out folder.

In this part of the lesson, you'll set up a watched folder on your system and use it to convert a PostScript file to Adobe PDF.

Setting up a watched folder

You'll configure Distiller to check a folder periodically for PostScript files and to process these files for on-screen Adobe PDF output.

1 Create a folder on your desktop, and name it **Watch**.

2 In Distiller, choose eBook from the Job Options menu.

3 Choose Settings > Watched Folders.

The Watched Folders dialog box lets you specify how frequently Distiller checks a watched folder and how to handle files after they are processed.

4 Click Add.

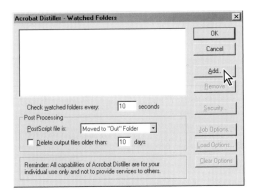

5 Select the Watch folder on your desktop, and click OK (Windows) or click Choose (Mac OS).

The Watch folder appears in the Watched Folder list.

 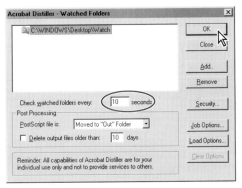

6 Select Watch in the Watched Folder list. For Check Watched Folders Every, enter **10** to process PostScript files every 10 seconds. Under Post-Processing, choose Moved to "Out" Folder.

7 Click Job Options. You can set different options for each watched folder.

8 Click the Compression tab to display the compression and resampling options. Under Color Images and Grayscale Images, choose High for the compression quality. Then click OK.

9 Click OK again to close the Watched Folders dialog box.

Converting a file using a watched folder

Your new Watch folder has an In folder and an Out folder in it, as well as a job options file. You'll place a sample PostScript file in the In folder. When Distiller is finished processing the file, you'll retrieve the resulting Adobe PDF file from the Out folder.

1 In Windows Explorer (Windows) or the Finder (Mac OS), open the Watch folder.

2 Open the Lesson04 folder. Drag Drop.ps from the Lesson04 folder to the In folder within the Watch folder.

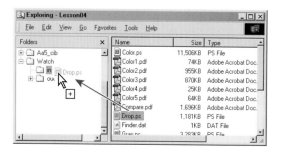

If the Distiller window is still visible, you should be able to see information about the processing in the Distiller window.

Note: *Distiller will not process Read-Only files in watched folders.*

3 Open the Out folder within the Watch folder. You should now have a Drop.pdf file and a Drop.ps file in this folder.

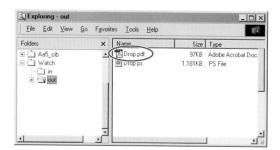

4 Double-click Drop.pdf to view it in Acrobat.

5 When you are finished viewing the file, close it and drag it to the Lesson04 folder.

Removing watched folders

If you no longer need Distiller to watch a particular folder, you should remove it from the list of watched folders. If you do not remove it from the list, Distiller will waste resources checking that folder and ultimately slow down the processing of other tasks.

If you haven't done so already, you should drag Drop.pdf to the Lesson04 folder.

1 In Distiller, choose Settings > Watched Folders.

2 Select Watch from the list.

3 Click Remove, and then click OK.

4 Exit or quit Distiller and Acrobat.

In this lesson, you learned several methods to convert PostScript files to Adobe PDF, and how to manage output quality. The conversion method you use depends on your system resources and working habits. You may not always use the same Distiller settings. You should experiment to find the best solution for your needs.

Exploring on your own

Dragging one or more PostScript files onto the Acrobat Distiller window will launch Distiller and begin the conversion to Adobe PDF. You can also drag the file onto the Distiller icon.

By default, Distiller does not display the Save As dialog box when you use the drag-and-drop method. Instead, it places PDF files into the same folder as the source PostScript files and adds the extension .pdf or .PDF to the original filename. It also uses the current job options defined in Distiller.

1 In Windows Explorer (Windows) or the Finder (Mac OS), open the folder containing the PostScript file you want to process.

2 Drag the PostScript file from the source folder into the Distiller window or onto the Distiller icon.

3 When Distiller is finished processing, double-click the resulting Adobe PDF file located in the source folder to view it in Acrobat. (By default, Distiller saves the PDF file in the same folder as the PostScript file.)

Review questions

1 How do you specify different compression and resampling methods in Distiller?

2 What is resampling? What is downsampling?

3 How often does Distiller check a watched folder for a PostScript file?

4 When you drag and drop a PostScript file onto the Distiller window, where is the resulting Adobe PDF file saved?

Review answers

1 You can specify default compression and resampling methods by choosing one of the predefined sets of job options (eBook, Press, Print, Screen) from the Job Options menu. You can specify custom settings by choosing Settings > Job Options, and customizing the settings on the Compression tab.

2 Resampling refers to reducing the number of pixels in an image to minimize the file size. Multiple pixels in the original image are combined to make a single, larger pixel that represents approximately the same image area. Downsampling is the same as resampling.

3 Distiller checks watched folders as frequently as you specify. Choose Settings > Watched Folders, and enter a value for the Check Watched Folders Every option.

4 When you drag and drop a PostScript file onto the Distiller window, the resulting Adobe PDF file is saved by default in the source folder containing the PostScript file.

Lesson 5

5 Putting Documents Online

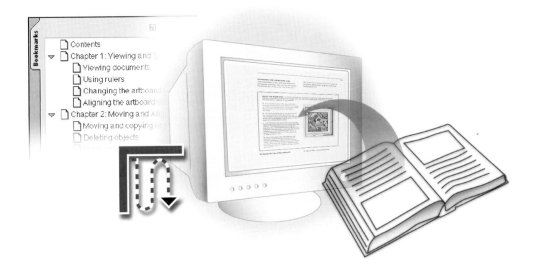

This lesson guides you through the process of putting printed documents online. You'll start with a PDF file of a book, set an opening view for the online version, and work with hyperlink features, such as bookmark and articles, to enhance your electronic publication.

In this lesson, you'll review and learn how to do the following:

- Set an opening view for an online document.
- Create custom bookmarks that link to specific views in the document.
- Create, follow, and edit an article thread.
- Replace a page of a PDF file with a page from a different PDF file.
- Examine the design differences between online and print publications.

This lesson will take about 50 minutes to complete.

If needed, remove the previous lesson folder from your hard drive, and copy the Lesson05 folder onto it.

Note: Windows users need to unlock the lesson files before using them. For information, see "Copying the Classroom in a Book files" on page 3.

About this lesson

In this lesson, you'll work with a reference manual about Adobe Illustrator. You'll create an electronic print-on-demand version of it without altering the content or design of the original book. Then you'll compare your print-on-demand document with another electronic version that has been redesigned for online viewing. In a later lesson, you'll learn how to design a document specifically for online viewing.

Viewing the work file

You'll start by opening a PDF version of the Adobe Illustrator manual.

This version was created from the original Adobe FrameMaker file by first making a PostScript file and then using Acrobat Distiller to convert it to Adobe PDF.

For information on using this technique to create a PDF file, see "Creating PostScript files" in the Acrobat 5.0 online Help.

1 Start Acrobat.

2 Choose File > Open. Select Ai.pdf in the Lessons/Lesson05 folder, and click Open. Then choose File > Save As, rename the file **Ai1.pdf**, and save it in the Lesson05 folder.

Note: On Windows, you may need to resize your document pane when you open a new PDF file after using the Windows > Tile command.

To maximize the screen area used for display, the Adobe Illustrator book has been set to open with the navigation pane closed. You use the Show/Hide Navigation Pane button in the toolbar to display the navigation pane.

3 Click the Show/Hide Navigation Pane button (▥) to show the Bookmarks palette. If needed, click the Bookmarks tab to bring the Bookmarks palette to the front.

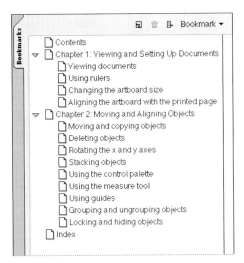

The PDF file contains two chapters, a table of contents, and an index, just as in the original FrameMaker file. The table of contents entries, cross-references, index entries, and text flows in the FrameMaker file have been converted to bookmarks, links, and articles in the PDF file.

You can automatically generate PDF links from files that have been properly formatted in an application that supports this capability, such as Adobe FrameMaker or Adobe PageMaker.

Setting an opening view

You can set the opening view of a PDF document for your user, including the opening page number and magnification level, and whether bookmarks, thumbnails, the toolbar, and the menu bar are displayed. You can change any of these settings to control how the document displays when it is opened.

In this section, you'll set the opening view to display the bookmarks automatically so the user is sure to find them, and you'll set the view to Fit in Window.

1 Choose File > Document Properties > Open Options.

2 Under Initial View, choose Bookmarks and Page to open the navigation pane with the bookmarks in front. The document pane is also opened.

3 From the Magnification pop-up menu, choose Fit in Window to size the page so that it fits entirely in the window.

4 From the Page Layout menu, choose Single Page to display one page of the document at a time.

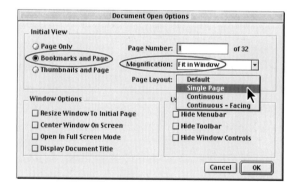

5 Click OK to accept the settings.

6 Choose File > Close, and click Yes (Windows) or Save (Mac OS) in the alert box to save the changes before closing the file.

Changes do not take effect until you save and close the file.

7 Choose File > Open, and open the Ai1.pdf file.

The file now opens with the bookmarks displayed and the entire first page displayed in the document window.

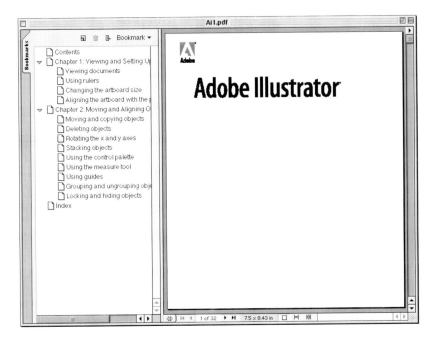

For more information on setting the opening view for a collection of documents, see Lesson 13, "Distributing Document Collections."

Looking at bookmarks and links

A bookmark is a link represented by text in the Bookmarks palette. Bookmarks that are created automatically by an authoring program such as Adobe FrameMaker or Adobe PageMaker are generally linked to headings in the text or to figure captions.

You can also use bookmarks to create a brief custom outline of a document or to open other documents. For information on linking to other documents, see "Adding links to a Welcome document" on page 348 in Lesson 13.

Additionally, you can use electronic bookmarks as you would paper bookmarks—to mark a place in a document that you want to recall or return to later. Later in this lesson, for example, you'll create custom bookmarks that are linked to an area on a page in the document.

1 If needed, drag the right border of the Bookmarks palette (a double-headed arrow appears) to resize the Bookmarks palette so that you can see more of the bookmark text.

2 Select the hand tool (✋), and click the Contents bookmark to view the table of contents.

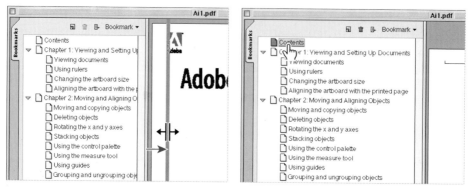

Drag to resize palette.　　　　　　　　　Click to view the table of contents.

Notice that the icon for the Contents bookmarks is highlighted, indicating that the bookmark is linked to the current page of the document. If desired, you can hide this icon highlighting. To do so, click on the triangle in the upper right corner of the Bookmarks palette to display the Bookmark palette menu, and choose Highlight Current Bookmark. (A check mark appears next to the command name when this feature is enabled.) Click outside the palette menu to close it without making a selection.

3 Move the pointer over the contents list in the document pane and notice that the pointing finger appears over each linked entry.

Acrobat automatically linked the table of contents, which was generated using Adobe FrameMaker, to the headings in the document.

4 Click the Index entry at the bottom of the table of contents to view the index listings. In the index, each page number listing links to the appropriate reference in the text. Depending on your monitor, you may need to select the zoom-in tool (🔍) and click in the document pane to increase the magnification. Reselect the hand tool when the magnification is sufficient.

5 Position your pointer over the number next to the "artboard" entry so that the pointing finger appears. Click to jump to the section about the Illustrator artboard.

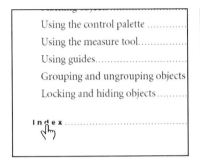
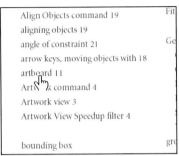

The index for this user guide was originally created in Adobe FrameMaker and then converted automatically to a linked PDF index during the Distiller conversion process. The following chart outlines the procedure for generating a PDF index from a FrameMaker file.

Index creation from a FrameMaker book file

You can convert an index generated in FrameMaker to an interactive PDF index whose entries link to the referenced document pages.

1. Add index markers to FrameMaker documents.

2. Name documents exactly as you want PDF filenames to appear. For example, rename "Exchange.fm" to "Exchange." Then create the book file for these documents.

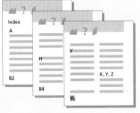

3. Generate index.

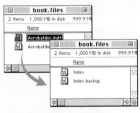

4. In Windows Explorer or the Finder, rename generated index to final PDF name.

5. In book file, redirect index path to renamed index.

6. Print book file to PostScript. Enter * (asterisk) as book filename to preserve original document filenames and create links.

Adding bookmarks

Although the basic bookmarks and links for the Adobe Illustrator book have already been generated, you can add your own custom bookmarks and links using the tools in Acrobat. In this part of the lesson, you'll use different methods to add some new bookmarks that link to the charts, or sidebars (for example, the About the Work Area sidebar you're looking at), in the book.

Creating bookmarks

You'll create three new bookmarks—one placeholder labeled *Sidebars* and two subsidiary bookmarks linked to specific sidebars in the Adobe Illustrator book. (A sidebar is a text insert, with or without graphics, that is formatted differently from the rest of a document.) The placeholder bookmark will not be linked to the document; it will serve only as a hierarchical placeholder.

First you'll create the placeholder bookmark.

1 From the Magnification pop-up menu, choose 100%. A bookmark always displays a page at the magnification set when the bookmark was created.

2 Click on the triangle in the upper right corner of the Bookmarks palette to display the Bookmark palette menu, and choose New Bookmark. Or click the Create New Bookmark button (⌘) at the top of the Bookmarks palette (Mac OS). A new bookmark appears at the bottom of the Bookmarks palette, and the text is selected.

3 Type **Sidebars** to name the bookmark. Click outside the bookmark to deselect it.

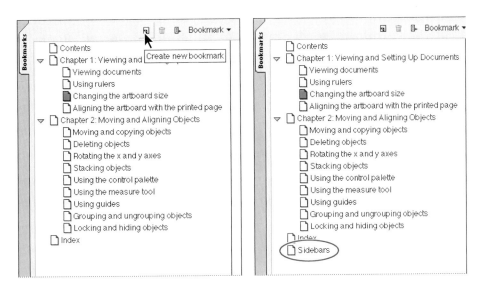

Now you'll create the remaining two bookmarks. You'll create the first bookmark using the keyboard shortcut for the New Bookmarks command. (Many Acrobat commands can be executed using keyboard shortcuts, which appear next to the command names in the menus.) You'll create and name the second bookmark by selecting text in the book itself.

4 To create a new bookmark using a keyboard shortcut, press Ctrl+B (Windows) or Command+B (Mac OS), and name the bookmark **Work area**. Click outside the bookmark to deselect it.

5 Click the Next Page button (▶).

Click each of the new bookmarks in turn. Notice that the Sidebars bookmark links to whatever page was open when you set the link. The Work area bookmark also links to the that same page unless you changed the page view between creating links. You'll change the destination of these links in the next section.

Now you'll create the third bookmark using a different method—one that automatically sets the correct link.

6 Choose Document > Go to Page, enter 25, and click OK. You should be looking at the sidebar titled "Using the Control Palette."

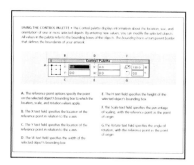

7 If needed, scroll down to bring the sidebar into view.

8 Select the text select tool (T) in the toolbar.

9 Move the I-beam into the page, and drag to highlight the text "Control palette" on the first line. (Don't select the title of the sidebar unless you want your bookmark text to be in capital letters.)

If you have trouble highlighting the text, hold down Ctrl (Windows) or Option (Mac OS) and drag a marquee around the text.

Be sure to leave the magnification at 100%. Whatever magnification is used will be inherited by the bookmark.

10 Choose New Bookmark from the Bookmark palette menu. A new Control palette bookmark appears at the bottom of the bookmarks list—the highlighted text from the document pane has been used as the bookmark name. By default, the new bookmark links to the current page view displayed on your screen.

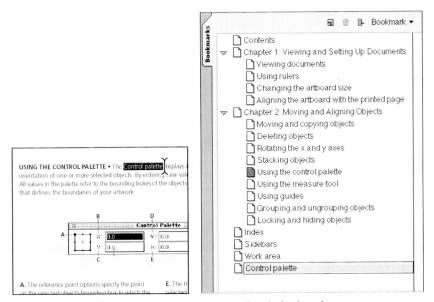

Text selected in the document pane . . .   . . . is used as the bookmark name.

If no bookmarks are selected when you create a new bookmark, the new bookmark appears at the bottom of the list.

11 Click in the blank space beneath the bookmark list to deselect the bookmark text.

12 Test the new bookmark by clicking the First Page button (◄) to go to the beginning of the book. Select the hand tool (✍), and click the Control palette bookmark to jump to the corresponding sidebar.

13 Choose File > Save to save your work.

Moving bookmarks

After creating a bookmark, you can easily move it to its proper place in the Bookmarks palette by dragging.

Before you set links for the two bookmarks you created earlier, you'll nest the Work area and Control palette bookmarks under the Sidebars bookmark.

1 Hold down Shift and click the Work area and Control palette bookmarks to select them both, and then release Shift.

2 Position the pointer on one of the selected bookmarks, hold down the mouse button and drag the bookmarks up and slightly to the right. When the black bar appears under the "S" in the Sidebars bookmark, release the mouse. Click OK at the prompt.

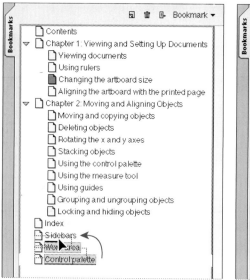
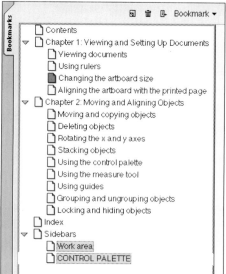

Drag bookmarks up and to the right . . .   *. . . to nest them.*

3 Click in the blank area of the Bookmarks palette to deselect the bookmarks.

4 Choose File > Save to save your work.

Resetting bookmark destinations

Whenever you create a bookmark, the bookmark destination is set automatically to the current document view that your screen displays. Sometimes it is easier to create a series of bookmarks and set the destinations later (as with the first two bookmarks you created); sometimes it is easier to set the destination as you create the bookmark (as with the third bookmark you created).

Now you'll assign a correct destination and action to the Sidebars and Work area bookmarks.

1 Click the Work area bookmark to select it.

2 If needed, go to page 11 in the document pane by dragging the scroll bar or by choosing Document > Go to Page, entering **11**, and clicking OK.

3 Select the zoom-in tool (🔍), and marquee-drag to magnify the sidebar.

4 Choose Set Bookmark Destination from the Bookmark palette menu. At the prompt, click Yes.

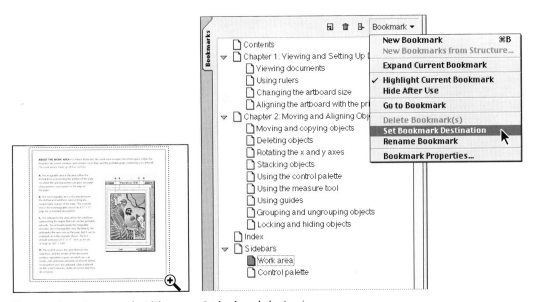

Use zoom-in tool to magnify sidebar.　　Set bookmark destination.

Next, you'll turn the Sidebars bookmark into a placeholder heading for its nested bookmarks.

5 Select the hand tool (☝).

6 Click the minus sign or triangle to the left of the Sidebars bookmark to hide its nested bookmarks.

7 Click the Sidebars bookmark or its page icon to select the bookmark.

8 Choose Edit > Properties. From the Type pop-up menu in the Bookmark Properties dialog box, choose None as the action type, and click Set Action.

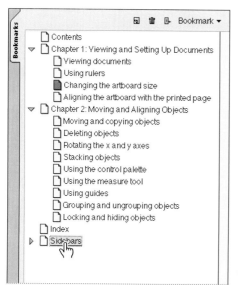

Select bookmark.

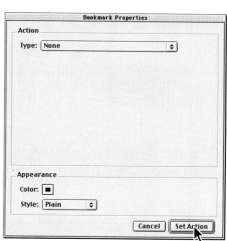

Choose None, and click Set Action.

9 In the Bookmarks palette, click in the blank area to deselect all bookmarks. Click the plus sign or triangle next to the Sidebars bookmark to display its nested bookmarks.

10 Use the hand tool to test your new bookmarks. Notice that nothing happens when you click the Sidebars bookmark. This bookmark now functions not as a link but as a hierarchical placeholder.

11 Choose File > Save to save your work.

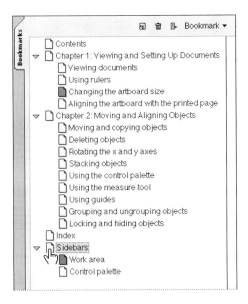

For information on using bookmarks to trigger actions, such as playing a sound file, see Lesson 11, "Enhancing a Multimedia Project."

Looking at articles

Although the Adobe Illustrator book has been converted to an online format, it still uses a layout associated with printed documents. The restrictions of the screen can make the reading of some documents quite difficult. For example, documents created in a column format can be particularly difficult to follow using the traditional page-up or page-down tools.

Acrobat's article feature lets you guide users through material organized in columns or across a series of nonconsecutive pages. You use the article tool to create a series of linked rectangles that connect the separate sections of the material and follow the flow of text. You can also generate article threads automatically from a page layout file when you convert the file to Adobe PDF using Acrobat Distiller.

In this part of the lesson, you'll examine an article that was created automatically. Later in this lesson, you'll learn how to create a customized article thread.

1 Click the Viewing Documents bookmark to jump to its corresponding section of information. Then move your pointer over the column of text and notice the downward pointing arrow inside the hand pointer that indicates an article thread.

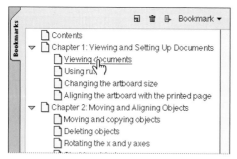

Click the bookmark to go to the text.

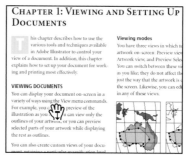

A downward arrow indicates an article thread.

2 Click to enter the article. Click again to follow the article. Press Enter or Return several times to continue to follow the article thread.

When you read an article, Acrobat zooms in or out so the current part of the article fills the screen.

Because this article thread was created automatically, it treats the image area on each page as one article box. Now you'll redefine the article to more conveniently follow the column layout. You'll also edit the thread.

Deleting an article

First you'll delete the existing article.

1 If the Articles palette is not visible, choose Window > Articles to display the palette. Drag the Articles tab to the navigation pane to dock the palette. Click the Articles tab to bring the palette to the front. If needed, close the Destinations palette to give yourself a clear view of the document pane.

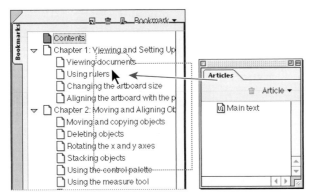

Dock the Articles palette in the navigation pane.

Click the Articles tab to bring the palette to the front.

2 Double-click Main text in the Articles palette to go to the beginning of the article.

3 Select the article tool (⟲) from the toolbar.

The first article box, labeled 1-1, is displayed. (You may have to scroll up to see the top of the article box.)

4 With the Main text article selected in the Articles palette, click on the palette name and triangle in the upper right corner of the Articles palette to display the palette menu.

5 Choose Delete (Windows) or Clear (Mac OS). Click OK in the alert box to delete the article.

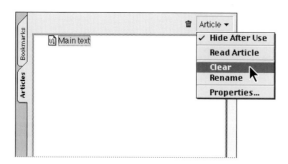

Defining an article

You have deleted the article box that was defined automatically. Now you'll replace it with your own article thread to connect the text columns.

1 Click the Fit in Window button (▣) to view the entire page.

2 Choose View > Grid if you want to use the grid lines as guides when you create the article box. Choose View > Snap to Grid to toggle the snap-to-grid feature on or off. (We didn't use the grid when we created out article boxes.)

3 With the article tool (↻) still selected, drag a marquee around the left column of text. (When you first use the article tool, it appears as a cross-hair pointer in the document window.) An article box appears around the enclosed text, and the pointer changes to the article pointer (↻).

The 1-1 label at the top of the article box indicates that this is the first box of the first article in the file. Now you'll add another article box to continue the thread.

4 Go to the top of the right text column, and drag a marquee around the column of text. An article box, labeled 1-2, appears around the enclosed text.

5 Go to the next page by clicking the Next Page button (▶) or by choosing Document > Go to Page.

Important: *Don't use the status bar to advance to another page; if you do, you'll break the article thread.*

6 Repeat steps 3 through 5 twice more. We created article boxes on three pages. (Do not create an article box for the tip on page 5.)

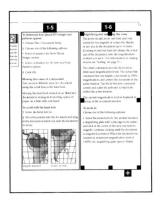

7 Press Enter or Return to end the article thread, or click End Article in the status bar.

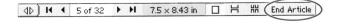

The Article Properties dialog box appears.

Note: *You can also display the Article Properties dialog box by selecting an article with the article tool and choosing Edit > Properties.*

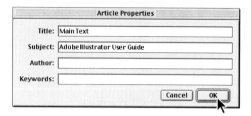

8 Do the following:

• For Title, enter **Main text**, and press Tab. (This is the text that appears in the Articles palette.)

• For Subject, enter **Adobe Illustrator User Guide**.

• Leave the Author and Keywords fields blank, and click OK.

9 Choose File > Save to save your work.

Note: *If you make a mistake when creating the article boxes, select the incorrect box in the thread, press Delete, and at the prompt, click Box. Then select the prior box, click on the plus sign at the bottom of the article box (be careful to click on the plus sign only once), and then drag to create a new article box.*

Reading an article

In this section, you'll look at the various ways you can move through an article.

1 Select the hand tool (🖐).

2 Double-click Main text in the Articles palette.

The contents of the first article box you created appear on-screen.

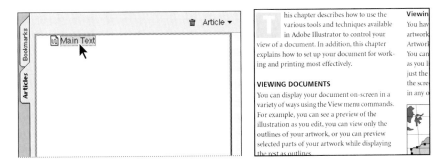

You control the magnification of article boxes by adjusting the Max "Fit Visible" Zoom Magnification preference, which you set in the Display Preferences dialog box.

3 Choose Edit > Preferences > General. Click Display in the left pane to display the Display Preferences dialog box.

4 For Max "Fit Visible" Zoom Magnification, choose 150, and click OK.

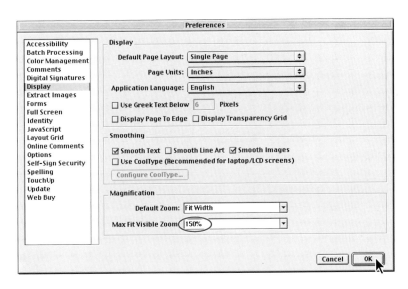

5 Move the hand pointer over the top left corner of the page, and click to enter the article. Look at the status bar and notice that the article box now appears at 150% magnification.

If desired, experiment with different Max "Fit Visible" Magnification settings and notice how they affect your article view.

6 Move through the article using any of these techniques:

• To advance through the article, press Enter or Return.

• To move backward through the article, hold down Shift and press Enter or Return.

• To move to the beginning of the article, hold down Ctrl (Windows) or Option (Mac OS) and click inside the article.

7 To exit the article before reaching the end, press Shift-Ctrl (Windows) or Shift-Option (Mac OS) and click in the document pane.

Inserting an article box

You can edit an existing article thread using the article tool at any time. In this part of the lesson, you'll add an article box, inserting a tip into the article thread you just created.

1 Navigate to page 5, and click the Fit in Window (▣) button.

2 Select the article tool (◊). Click inside the left text column (box 1-5) to select the article box. Handles appear at the corners and along the sides of an article box when it is selected.

You'll insert a new article box after box 1-5.

3 Position your pointer over the plus sign at the bottom of box 1-5 so that the article pointer appears, and click. (Be careful to click on the plus sign only once.)

From now on, the pointer appears as the article pointer (◊). In addition, "End Article" appears in the status bar, indicating that you are editing the article thread.

4 Use the article pointer to drag a box around the tip in the left margin. Notice that this new article box is labeled 1-6 and that the article box around the right text column is now labeled 1-7.

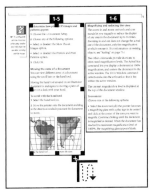

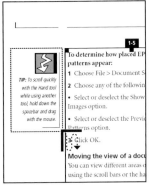

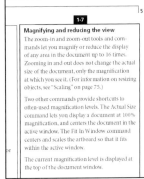

Click on the plus sign at the bottom of box 1-5.

Drag to create an article box around the tip.

Subsequent article boxes are renumbered.

5 Click End Article in the status bar.

6 Select the hand tool (☝). In the Articles palette, double-click Main text to examine your edited article thread.

7 Press Enter or Return to progress to the new article box you inserted.

8 Click the Show/Hide Navigation Pane button (▦) to close the navigation pane when you have finished viewing the article.

9 Choose File > Save to save your work.

Replacing a page

Sometimes you may want to replace an entire page in a PDF file with another PDF page. For example, if you want to change the design or layout of a PDF page, you can revise the source page in your original design application, convert the modified page to PDF, and use it to replace the old PDF page. When you replace a page, only the text and graphics on the original page are replaced. The replacement does not affect any interactive elements associated with the original page, such as bookmarks or links.

The plain title page that currently opens the PDF document is the first page of the printed version of the user guide. To make your PDF user guide look more like an actual book, you'll replace this title page with the full-color illustration that was used to create the front cover of the printed guide.

1 Click the First Page button (◄) to display the current title page, and click the Fit in Window button.

2 Choose Document > Replace Pages.

3 Select Cover.pdf in the Lesson05 folder, and click Select.

4 In the Replace Pages dialog box, make sure that you are replacing page 1 with 1, and click OK and then Yes. The new cover illustration appears as page 1 of the document.

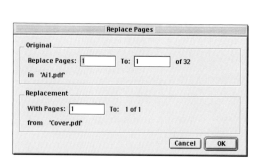 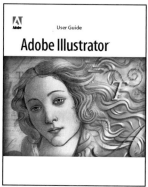

5 Choose File > Save to save the Ai1.pdf file. Leave the file open.

Looking at online document design

Other than replacing the title page, the content and layout of the user guide were not changed before the Ai1.pdf document was created. This print-on-demand document represents the quickest and least expensive option for converting a printed book to online.

In this section of the lesson, you'll open another PDF version of the user guide that has been redesigned for online use.

1 Choose File > Open, select Online.pdf in the Lesson05 folder, and click Open. Then choose File > Save As, rename the file **Online1.pdf**, and save it in the Lesson05 folder.

2 Choose Window > Tile > Vertically to view the two open documents side-by-side.

3 If needed, adjust the magnification to fit the Online1.pdf document on-screen. The tall, narrow page size has been designed for side-by-side viewing next to the Adobe Illustrator application window. This view lets users conveniently look up reference information without closing their illustration window.

Notice also that Online1.pdf contains a hypertext list of elements in the document. A few book elements have been created especially for the optimized online guide.

4 In the online guide artwork, click How to Use This Guide to jump to the section which explains basic navigational techniques to the user. Click the Go to Previous View button (◀) in the toolbar when you have finished viewing the instructions.

Jump to How to Use This Guide . . .   *. . . to learn how to navigate through the guide.*

5 Click List of Topics to view the text contents of the document.

Notice that you jump to a screen listing the main topic titles.

6 Click Viewing and Setting up Documents to display the subtopics under this topic.

7 Now click in the Ai1.pdf document window to make it active, and go to page 2, the Contents page. Click the Actual Size button (⬚) to display this page at 100%.

Compare the table of contents in Ai1.pdf (the print-on-demand guide) with the topic screens in Online1.pdf (the online guide). Online1.pdf arranges its content listings in nested, hierarchical screens, while Ai1.pdf lists the main topics and their subtopics linearly on one page. Although the linear arrangement follows the conventional organization of a printed book, the hierarchical structure is better suited for an online environment where the most intuitive action involves clicking a link to follow a trail of information.

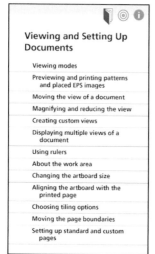

Contents of online guide   Contents of printed guide

8 Click Using Rulers under the Chapter 1 heading to jump to that page of text. If needed, use the scroll bars to move the right column of the page into view.

9 Now return to Online1.pdf, and click Using Rulers in the list of subtopics. If needed, click the Fit in Window button ( ) to view the entire page.

Notice that pages in the online guide have been redesigned so that each topic has its own page. Related topic titles appear as red, linked text.

10 Now click the target icon at the top of the page to return to the parent list of subtopics, and then click About the Work Area, about midway in the list.

This link jumps you to an overview text section that contains its own links to subtopics and art. Click the Jump to Art icon to view a diagram of the work area with all of its components labeled and linked.

11 Return to Ai1.pdf, and navigate to page 11 to view the linear equivalent of the About the Work Area section. If needed, adjust the magnification and use the scroll bar to view the entire section. Compare the text-intensive pages of Ai1.pdf with the more balanced text blocks in Online1.pdf.

By breaking longer topics into their subtopic components and placing these sections on separate pages, you minimize the amount of text shown on each page. As a result, you can display text in a larger, clearer typeface that users can read more easily. In addition, the smaller, self-contained pages reduce the need for scrolling and readjusting the page view. Ideally, a user of Online1.pdf should be able to navigate to any part of the document solely by clicking linked text and icons in the page.

12 Return to Online1.pdf, and click the book icon at the top of the page to return to the opening contents screen. Then click Index.

Like the index for the print-on-demand guide, the page-number listings in the online index link to their referenced section. However, the online index also includes an alphabet tab along the left of the page, which lets you jump to specific parts of the index quickly. Also, the larger font and single-column format make the index easier to read.

13 Choose Window> Close All to close all open files.

For more information on how to design your own online book, see Lesson 10, "Designing Online Documents."

Exploring on your own

Here's an idea you can try on your own to identify content changes in two PDF documents. The Compare Pages command in Acrobat compares every page in two documents, looking at PDF information that describes the pages precisely to find even the most subtle differences between pages. You can use Compare Pages to identify both content changes between documents and changes that may not be visible.

💡 *The Compare Pages command is especially useful for comparing PDF documents that are nearly identical.*

The Compare Pages command looks at the two most recently active PDF documents and produces a third document, a comparison file that shows every page that differs between the documents and highlights the differences on the pages.

1 Choose File > Open, select Ai.pdf in the Lesson05 folder, and click Open.

2 Choose File > Open, select Ai1.pdf in the Lesson05 folder, and click Open.

3 Make active the original Ai.pdf document; this document will be on the right in the comparison file. Then make active the Ai1.pdf document; this document will be on the left.

4 Choose Tools > Compare > Two Documents.

5 In the Compare Documents dialog box, check that the file names of your two documents are in the Compare and the To text boxes.

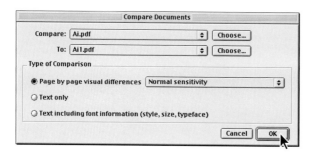

6 Under Type of Comparison, select Page by Page Visual Differences, and choose Normal Sensitivity from the pop-up menu.

7 Click OK.

The two documents appear side-by-side in a read-only comparison file.

The comparison file begins with a summary page that gives the document filenames and describes how many pages were altered, added, moved, or deleted. The rest of the file shows the pages that differ between the documents. In the document on the left, the pages are listed in ascending order and are paired with pages from the document on the right.

Note: *The pages on the right may not be in ascending order if any content or pages have been rearranged in the documents.*

The differences are highlighted in magenta on the pages.

The highlighted differences are stored as pencil comments in the comparison file. You can use the Comments palette to see a list of all the differences, and you can double-click a difference in the palette to go to that place on a page. To display the Comments palette, click the Comments tab.

Note: *The side-by-side display of pages in comparison files is designed for two-up printing. If you are printing only one page, select Fit to Page in the Print dialog box to be sure you include all highlights and the page numbering in the printed copy.*

Choose Window > Close All to close all open files.

Review questions

1 How do you generate a PDF index automatically when converting a FrameMaker file?

2 How do you manually create bookmarks in a document?

3 How can you control how a bookmark behaves?

4 How do you create an article thread?

5 How do you end an article thread?

6 How can the table of contents for a printed publication differ from the table of contents for a strictly online publication?

Review answers

1 Acrobat Distiller generates a linked PDF index automatically from the index markers inserted in a FrameMaker file.

2 To create a bookmark, you choose New Bookmark from the Bookmark palette menu and navigate to the page containing the information you want to bookmark. Then you choose Set Bookmark Destination from the Bookmark palette menu and verify the destination.

3 To control a bookmark's behavior, you select a bookmark, choose Edit > Properties, and specify the bookmark's action using the Type pop-up menu.

4 To create an article thread, you use the article tool and drag an article box. Then you go to the next desired page in the article using the scroll bar or the Document > Go To Page command, and drag another article box. You repeat this process for as many article boxes as desired. To end the article, you press Enter or Return.

5 To end an article thread, you press Enter or Return or you click End Article in the status bar.

6 The table of contents for a printed publication lists the main topics and their subtopics linearly on the page, whereas an online publication arranges its content listings in nested, hierarchical screens. Although the linear arrangement follows the conventional organization of a printed book, the hierarchical structure is better suited for an online environment where the most intuitive action involves clicking a link to follow a trail of information.

Lesson 6

6 Modifying PDF Files

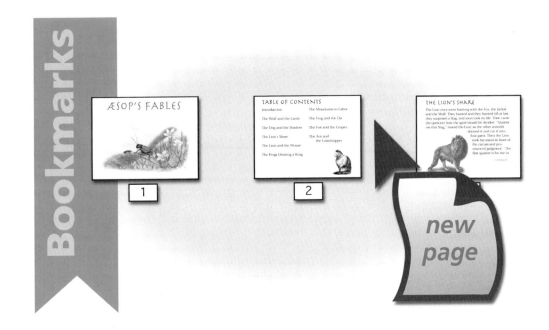

Once you have converted your document to PDF, you can use Acrobat to make final edits and modifications. In addition to adding links and bookmarks, you can edit text and images, and insert, reorder, and extract pages. Powerful new tools let you repurpose Adobe PDF content. You can save text in rich text format, you can save images in a variety of image formats, and you can save entire pages in JPEG, PNG, or TIFF format.

In this lesson, you'll learn how to do the following:

- Convert a TIFF image file to Adobe PDF.

- Rotate and crop pages.

- Use thumbnails to rearrange pages in a document and navigate through a document.

- Insert and extract pages from a document.

- Copy all the text from a document in rich text format.

- Copy all the art from a document.

- Renumber pages.

- Edit the placement and contents of images in a document.

- Create links and bookmarks that play actions.

- Create an image file from a PDF file.

This lesson will take about 50 minutes to complete.

If needed, remove the previous lesson folder from your hard drive, and copy the Lesson06 folder onto it.

Note: Windows users need to unlock the lesson files before using them. For information, see "Copying the Classroom in a Book files" on page 3.

Opening and examining the work file

You'll work with an edition of *Aesop's Fables* that has been designed for online viewing and converted to PDF. Because this online book has passed through multiple designers and review cycles, it contains a number of mistakes. In this lesson you'll use Acrobat to correct the problems in this PDF document and optimize *Aesop's Fables* for the next generation of youngsters.

Later in the lesson, you'll copy all the text out of the file in rich text format (RTF) so that you can use it in the development of a Web page, and then you'll copy all the art into individual TIFF files ready for reuse in your authoring applications.

1 Start Acrobat.

2 Choose File > Open. Select Afables.pdf, located in the Lessons/Lesson06 folder, and click Open. Then choose File > Save As, rename the file **Afables1.pdf**, and save it in the Lesson06 folder.

Notice that bookmarks for the individual fables in this document have already been created.

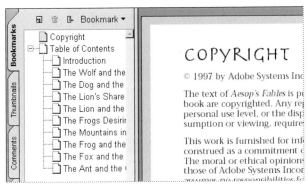

Bookmarks for Aesop's Fables

3 Select the hand tool (☝), and click the Table of Contents bookmark to go to the table of contents.

4 Move the pointer into the document pane. Notice that the titles in the list have already been linked.

Move pointer into document.

This example of *Aesop's Fables* was originally designed using Adobe PageMaker. When the PageMaker file was converted to Adobe PDF, the entries in the formatted table of contents were converted to PDF bookmarks and links automatically.

Certain page-layout and book-publishing programs, such as Adobe PageMaker and Adobe FrameMaker, work in conjunction with Acrobat to automate the creation of links and bookmarks during the conversion to Adobe PDF. In Windows also, you can preserve links created in Microsoft Office applications including Microsoft Word 97, Word 2000, PowerPoint 97, PowerPoint 2000, Excel 97, or Excel 2000.

5 Click The Fox and the Grapes to follow its link.

6 Click the Go to Previous View button (◆) to return to the table of contents. You'll continue exploring this edition of *Aesop's Fables*.

Editing pages

Take a few moments to page through *Aesop's Fables*. Go to the first page of the document and notice that the book has no title page. We've created a separate title page for you by scanning a printed image into a computer and saving the image as a TIFF file.

Importing an image

To add a title page to the document, you'll import and convert the TIFF image we created and crop the page to fit the rest of the book.

1 Choose File > Open as Adobe PDF.

2 For Files of Type (Windows) or Show (Mac OS), choose TIFF Files.

3 Select Cover.tif in the Lesson06 folder.

Notice that the Settings button is no longer grayed out. Click Settings and explore the conversion options available when you import TIFF files. For this file, you'll use the default value—JPEG(Quality:Medium). Click OK to return to the Open dialog box.

4 Click Open.

The Open as Adobe PDF dialog box appears.

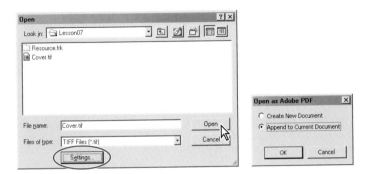

5 Select Append to Current Document, and click OK.

The cover image is appended to the end of the document. The imported page is converted to PDF Image Only mode, meaning that only the image objects (not the text) in the page can be edited in Acrobat.

6 Click the Last Page button (▶|) to go to page 17, the newly created and imported page.

Converting image, HTML, and text files

You can convert BMP, Compuserve GIF, HTML, JPEG, PCX, PICT (Mac OS only), PNG, Text, or TIFF files to Adobe PDF by opening the files in Acrobat using the Open as Adobe PDF command or by dragging the file onto the Acrobat icon or window.

Files are converted to the PDF Image Only format—images and text are bitmaps, and therefore text cannot be edited. If your converted image has text, you may want to "capture" the image to change the bitmap text to regular PDF text that can be edited and searched in Acrobat.

For information on capturing PDF Image Only files, see Lesson 3, "Creating Adobe PDF Files"

An imported image can be saved in a new PDF file or appended to an existing file.

Rotating a page

Now that you have imported the new title page, you'll rotate it to the correct orientation.

1 Click the Fit in Window button (![icon]) to view the whole page you imported. Notice that the page orientation is incorrect—a problem that occurs often when scanning an image.

2 Choose Document > Rotate Pages.

The Rotate Pages dialog box lets you rotate one or more pages by 90° in a specified direction.

3 For Direction, select Counterclockwise 90 degrees. For Pages, make sure that you are rotating only page 17 of the document (From 17 to 17 of 17).

4 Click OK. Click Yes in the alert box to rotate the page.

 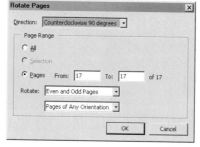 

Imported image . . .   *. . . is rotated . . .*   *. . . to correct orientation*

5 Select the Thumbnails tab in the navigation pane, and if needed, scroll down in the Thumbnails palette to view the thumbnail for the page you just rotated.

You can see that this page is larger than the other pages in the book. You'll crop the imported page to make it exactly the same size as the other pages.

Cropping a page

You'll use the Crop Pages dialog box to enter dimensions for the imported page that match the other pages in the document.

1 Choose Document > Crop Pages.

The Crop Pages dialog box appears, which lets you specify the margins.

2 For Left, enter **2.13**. A line representing the crop location appears both in the preview in the dialog box and in the document.

You may need to drag the Crop Pages dialog box out of the way to view the crop line in the document.

3 If needed, use the up and down arrows for Left in the Crop Pages dialog box to fine-tune the location of the crop line so that it aligns with the left edge of the title border.

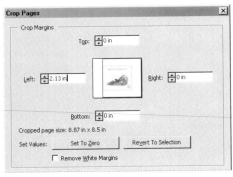

Setting location of left crop mark   *Result*

4 For Top, enter **1.55**. If needed, use the up and down arrows to align the crop line with the top edge of the title border.

5 Enter the following values for the remaining crop text boxes: **2.13** for Right and **1.58** for Bottom. Then use the up and down arrows to fine-tune the crop lines.

If the incremental movement of the crop lines is not fine enough for you, you can experiment with changing the page units in the Display Preferences. (To see the Display Preferences dialog box, choose Edit > Preferences > General, and select Display in the left pane.) Page units of millimeters or points give you finer control over the crop lines.

Note: *You can also use the crop tool (⊐) to crop the page.*

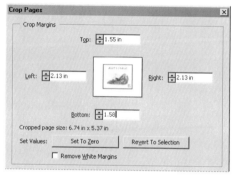 

Adding crop marks to remaining image edges   Result

6 For Page Range, make sure that you are cropping only page 17 of the document, and click OK.

7 Choose File > Save to save the Afables1.pdf file.

Moving a page

Now that you have corrected the size and page orientation of the cover, you'll move it to the front of the book. You rearrange pages in a PDF document by using thumbnails.

1 Hold down the mouse button on the triangle in the upper right corner of the Thumbnails palette to display the Thumbnail palette menu, and choose Small Thumbnails. This command displays the thumbnails in the document in columns.

Thumbnails offer convenient previews of your pages. You can use them for navigation—they are especially useful if you are looking for a page that has a distinctive appearance, and you can drag them to alter the pagination.

2 If needed, scroll to view the page 17 thumbnail, and click to select it. A solid border outlines the thumbnail, indicating that you can move it.

3 Drag the selected thumbnail upward in the Thumbnails palette (the palette scrolls automatically). Drag upward until the insertion bar appears to the left of the page 1 thumbnail, and release the mouse button.

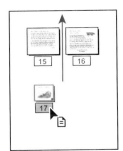
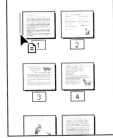

Drag thumbnail to reposition page.   *Insertion bar indicates new location.*

The cover page is repositioned in the document as page 1, and the remaining page numbers change accordingly.

Note: The size of small thumbnails may sometimes vary. The page size is correct, regardless of the size of the thumbnail.

Moving multiple pages

Next you'll move two pages of a fable that were placed in the wrong section of the book.

1 Click the page 3 thumbnail to go to the table of contents.

2 Click the Fit Width button ( ) to display all of the contents.

3 Using the hand tool ( ), click "The Ant and the Grasshopper" to jump to that fable. Although listed last in the contents, it is not the last fable in the book.

4 Click the page 13 thumbnail to select it. Hold down Shift and click the page 14 thumbnail to select it as well. Release Shift.

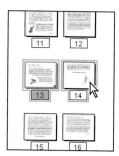

The technique of holding down Shift as you click thumbnails lets you select multiple thumbnails.

5 Drag the page 13 thumbnail down until the insertion bar appears to the right of the page 17 thumbnail. Because the page 14 thumbnail is part of the selection, you're also moving that thumbnail.

6 Release the mouse button to insert the thumbnails into their new position.

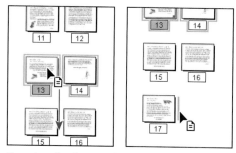

Drag thumbnail to new location.

"The Ant and the Grasshopper" fable is now last in the book.

Inserting a single page

Next you'll insert a page from a different file to complete a fable in this book. You use thumbnails to insert a single page into a document.

1 Select Large Thumbnails in the Thumbnail palette menu to view the thumbnails in a single column.

2 Click the thumbnail for page 14. Then click the Fit in Window button (⬛).

You are viewing "The Frog and the Ox." Notice that this fable is supposed to be continued on another page.

3 Click the Next Page button (▶).

Unfortunately, you can't read the end of the fable because it isn't there. You'll open the PDF document that contains the missing page and insert the page into this file.

4 Choose File > Open. Select Frog_ox.pdf in the Lesson06 folder, and click Open.

5 Choose Window > Tile > Vertically to arrange the two document windows side-by-side.

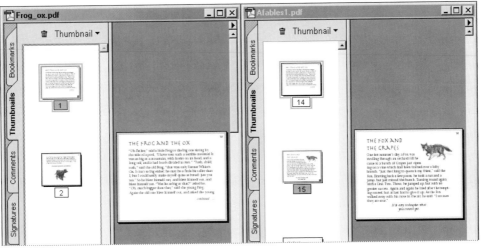

Displaying two document windows side-by-side with Window > Tile > Vertically

You can insert pages by dragging thumbnails between document windows.

6 Select the page 2 Frog_ox.pdf thumbnail.

7 Drag the selected thumbnail into the Thumbnails palette for Afables1.pdf. When the insertion bar appears between the page 14 and page 15 thumbnails, release the mouse button.

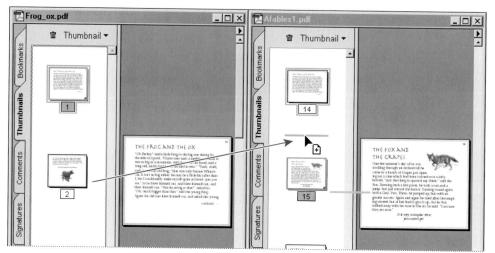

Dragging thumbnail between documents

The second page of the Frog_ox.pdf file becomes page 15 in the book.

8 Close Frog_ox.pdf, and resize the Afables1.pdf window to fill your desktop.

9 Double-click the page 15 thumbnail to view your newly inserted page.

10 Choose File > Save to save your work.

Inserting an entire file

In Acrobat, you can insert a page, a specified range of pages, or all pages from one PDF document into another. In the previous section, you used thumbnails to insert a page from one PDF document into another. Now you'll add a fable to the Afables1.pdf file by inserting all the pages of another file. You can insert an entire file easily by using the Insert Pages command.

1 Click the Bookmarks tab in the navigation pane to display the bookmarks. If needed, resize the navigation pane to view the entire bookmark text.

Although The Lion's Share bookmark appears in the list, the corresponding fable is missing from the book. You'll insert the missing fable from another document.

2 Drag the scroll box in the scroll bar to go to page 9 (9 of 18).

3 Choose Document > Insert Pages. Select Lions.pdf in the Lesson06 folder, and click Select.

The Insert Pages dialog box appears.

4 For Location, choose Before.

5 Select Page, enter **9** in the page text box, and then click OK.

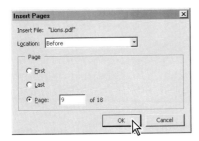

The fable entitled "The Lion's Share" is inserted where it belongs.

6 Page through the document to verify that the fable has been inserted in the correct location. "The Lion's Share" should appear after "The Dog and the Shadow" and before "The Lion and the Mouse."

7 Choose File > Save to save your work.

Updating a bookmark destination

Now that you have inserted the "Lion's Share" fable in the book, you'll update its bookmark link.

1 Go to page 9 of the document.

2 In the navigation pane, click The Lion's Share bookmark to select it. Then choose Set Bookmark Destination from the Bookmark palette menu, and click Yes to the confirmation message to update the bookmark destination.

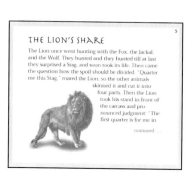

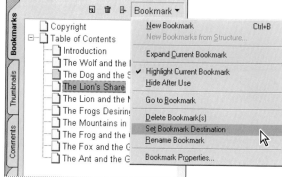

Go to page 9.

Choose Set Bookmark Destination from Bookmark palette menu.

3 Choose File > Save to save the Afables1.pdf file.

Extracting a page

Now you'll remove an unnecessary page from the document and save it as a separate PDF file.

1 Go to page 6, which functions as a second title page.

Although a second title page might be appropriate for a printed book, it seems repetitive and unnecessary in an online document, in which readers will probably not flip through the pages in order.

2 Choose Document > Extract Pages.

3 Make sure that you are extracting from page 6 to 6 of the document, and select Delete Pages after Extracting. Click OK. When the confirmation message appears, click Yes.

Go to page 6.   *Extract Pages dialog box*

The title page is deleted from the Afables1.pdf file and opened as a new one-page document.

4 Choose File > Save As. Name the document **Title.pdf**, and save it in the Lesson06 folder.

5 Close the Title.pdf file.

You can page through the document to verify that the extra title page has been deleted from the fables book.

Renumbering pages

You may have noticed that the page numbers on the document pages do not always match the page numbers that appear below the thumbnails and in the status bar. An Acrobat viewer automatically numbers pages with arabic numerals, starting with page 1 for the first page in the document, and so on.

1 Click the Thumbnails tab in the navigation pane to display the thumbnails. If necessary, resize the navigation pane so that the thumbnails are arranged in a single column.

2 Click the page 3 thumbnail to go to the table of contents.

The first three pages of the document contain front matter such as the cover, copyright page, and table of contents. You'll renumber these pages using lowercase roman numerals.

3 Choose Document > Number Pages.

4 For Pages, select From and enter pages from **1** to **3**. For Numbering, select Begin New Section, choose "i, ii, iii" from the Style pop-up menu, and enter **1** in the Start text box. Click OK.

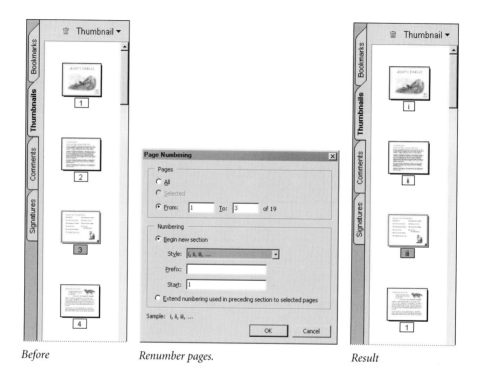

Before   *Renumber pages.*   *Result*

5 Choose Document > Go to Page. Enter **1**, and click OK.

Notice that the number 1 is now assigned to the first page of the body, the Introduction, and matches the page number appearing at the top right of the page.

Editing text and images

You use the touchup text tool to make last-minute corrections to text in a PDF document. You use the touchup object tool to make last-minute corrections to images in a PDF document.

Editing text

The touchup text tool lets you edit text, one line at a time, and change text attributes such as spacing, point size, and color. In order to edit text contents, you must have a licensed copy of the font installed on your system; you can change text attributes without having a licensed copy of the font installed.

You'll use the touchup text tool to change the color of a heading.

1 Click the Bookmarks tab.

2 If needed, click the Introduction bookmark.

3 Select the touchup text tool (𝕋), and click in the heading, "Introduction" to select the heading.

The bounding box encloses the text that can be edited.

4 Drag through the text to highlight it.

5 Choose Tools > Touchup Text > Text Attributes.

6 In the Text Attributes dialog box, click on the Color option at the bottom left. Choose a color for the heading. (We used Green.)

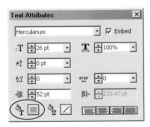

7 Close the dialog box, and click outside the text selection to view the result.

You can experiment with changing other text attributes.

8 Choose File > Save to save the file in the Lesson06 folder.

Editing images

In this part of the lesson, you'll use the touchup object tool to reposition the dog image on the page. The touchup object tool lets you modify the placement of images and layout elements on the page. You can also launch Adobe Photoshop from within Acrobat to edit the composition of a PDF image. If you want to edit the contents of the dog image, for example, you can do so if you have Adobe Photoshop installed, as described in "Exploring on your own" on page 157.

1 Go to page 4 (7 of 19) of the document.

2 Select the touchup object tool (↖), located under the touchup text tool in the toolbar.

3 Click the dog image at the bottom of the page. A rectangular border indicates that the image is selected.

4 Drag the dog to its new location just to the right of the moral.

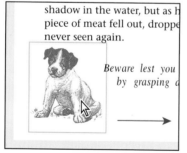 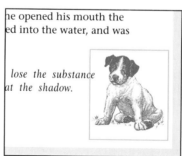

Select dog image, and drag to its new   Result
location.

5 Choose File > Save to save your work.

Editing text

You can perform last-minute corrections to PDF documents using the touchup text tool. You can choose from a variety of properties to apply to selected text, including font size, embedding, color scale, baseline shift, tracking, word spacing, and line alignment.

Editing text with the touchup text tool

While you can use the touchup text tool to edit text, you can only do so one line at a time. As a result, editing large sections of text can be a slow and laborious task. In general, you should reserve use of the touchup text tool for minor text edits in a PDF document. For extensive revisions, you should edit the document in the original document creation program and then regenerate the PDF file. You may choose to regenerate only the corrected pages and insert these corrected PDF pages into the document that needs to be corrected.

Copying tables and formatted text (Windows)

The table/formatted text select tool allows you to select tables and text in a PDF document and retain the original formatting when the material is copied (or imported) into other applications. You can specify vertical or horizontal format, the type of text flow, and whether you want ANSI Text (simple text), OEM Text, Unicode Text, or Rich Text Format (RTF).

–From the Acrobat 5.0 online Help.

Using links and bookmarks to play actions

In most cases, you use links and bookmarks to jump to different views of a document. However, you can also use links and bookmarks to execute commands from the menus and to play movies, sound clips, or perform other actions.

Creating a link that executes a menu item

You'll add a link to the title page that can perform an action.

1 Go to page i (the first page) of the book, and click the Fit in Window button (▣).

2 Select the hand tool and position the hand over the button labeled "Full Screen" at the bottom right corner of the page.

Notice that the button is not currently linked. You'll create a link so that users can click the button to display the book in Full Screen mode.

Full Screen mode maximizes the page display area by hiding the menu bar and toolbar.

3 Select the link tool (🔗), and marquee-drag around the Full Screen button.

4 Under Appearance, for Type, choose Invisible Rectangle; for Highlight, choose Invert. Under Action, for Type, choose Execute Menu Item.

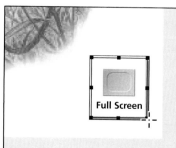

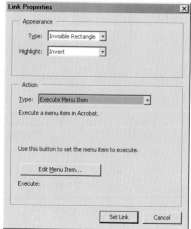

Drag with link tool . . .

. . . and then define link's appearance and action.

5 Click Edit Menu Item. In Windows, in the Menu Item Selection window that appears, choose View > Full Screen, and click OK. In Mac OS, choose View > Full Screen in the Acrobat menu bar, and click OK in the alert box.

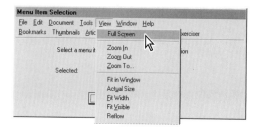

Notice that the command name now appears in the Link Properties dialog box.

6 Click Set Link.

7 Select the hand tool (☜) and test the link that you have created. In Full Screen mode, use Enter or Return to turn pages.

8 Press Esc to exit Full Screen mode.

9 Choose File > Save to save your work.

Creating a bookmark that plays a sound

Now you'll create a bookmark that plays sound. You'll be able to hear the sound if your computer has the proper audio hardware installed.

1 If needed, click the Show/Hide Navigation Pane button (📧) to show the navigation pane.

2 In the navigation pane, click the Bookmarks tab to view the bookmark list.

3 Click The Lion and the Mouse bookmark text to jump to that fable.

You'll create a bookmark that will play the moral of this story aloud.

4 With The Lion and the Mouse bookmark selected, choose New Bookmark from the Bookmark palette menu, and name the new bookmark **Mouse Moral**.

5 Drag the page icon for the Mouse Moral bookmark up and to the right until the insertion bar appears under the "The" in The Lion and the Mouse bookmark.

6 Release the mouse. Click OK to confirm the placement of the bookmark.

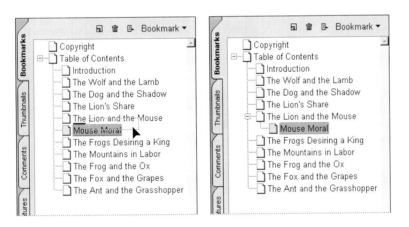

7 Select this new bookmark, and choose Edit > Properties.

8 For Type, choose Sound. Then click Select Sound.

9 Select Mouse.wav (Windows) or Mouse.aif (Mac OS) from the Lesson06 folder, and click Open.

This sound file was created using a sound-editing program and then saved in a file format recognized by Acrobat.

10 Click Set Action.

11 Click in the blank area in the Bookmarks palette to deselect all bookmarks.

12 Click the new bookmark to test it.

You'll hear the moral if you have the proper audio hardware installed on your computer.

For more information on sound system requirements and the types of sound file formats you can use with Acrobat, see "Using actions for special effects" in the Acrobat 5.0 online Help.

13 Choose File > Save to save Afables1.pdf in the Lesson06 folder.

Later in this book, you'll learn how to add more multimedia features to your PDF documents.

Copying text from a PDF file

Now that the book is edited to your satisfaction, you can reuse the text in other applications. For example, you might wanted to prepare a Web page using the same text. In this section, you'll copy all the text of the PDF file in rich text format so you can import it into your authoring application for reuse.

1 Choose File > Save As.

2 For Save as Type (Windows) or Format (Mac OS), choose Rich Text Format (*.rtf).

3 Click Save.

The file is saved as Afables1.rtf in the Lesson06 folder.

Open the file using your text editing or authoring application, such as Microsoft Word. Notice that all the text is copied and that spacing and formatting is retained to simplify reuse of the text. Close the .rtf file and the authoring application when you are finished.

Converting a PDF file to an image format file

In the last section you copied the text of *Aesop's Fables* so that you can repurpose it for your Web page, but you may also want to include sample pages of the book or some of the graphic images. You could extract a PDF page from the file and use that, but it may be easier to include a JPEG version of the page or a TIFF file of an image.

Converting PDF pages to image pages

To be able to show a sample page of *Aesop's Fables,* you'll create a JPEG version of page 1 of the book.

1 Click the Introduction bookmark to go to page 1 of the document.

You should be looking at the page headed, "Introduction."

2 Choose Document > Extract Pages. Make sure that you are extracting only page 1 and that you deselect the Delete Pages after Extracting option.

3 Click OK.

A copy of page 1 of *Aesop's Fables* is created in a separate PDF file. Now you'll convert this one PDF page to JPEG format.

4 Choose File > Save As, and choose JPEG Files for Save as Type (Windows) or Format (Mac OS). Rename the file Aesop.jpg.

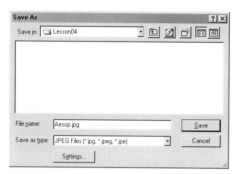

5 Click Settings to select the compression, resolution and quality of your image. (Since we'll be using our JPEG for a Web page, we used JPEG (Quality:Medium), Baseline (Standard), Colorspace to be determined automatically, and a resolution of 72 dpi.) Click OK to accept your settings.

6 Click Save to convert the page to JPEG format.

You can experiment with different Settings values and compare file size and image quality for the Settings you choose.

7 Choose Window > Close All to close all open PDF files. (You don't need to save the PDF version of the page you extracted.)

You can open and view the Aesop.jpeg file if you have Photoshop or an equivalent application. When you are finished, close the .jpeg file and the associated application.

Converting PDF graphic images to image files

If you want to use the art from the *Aesop's Fables* book on your Web page, it would be useful to have the art in an image file format. In this last section, you'll extract all the art into separate PNG files. You can also extract art into TIFF and JPEG file formats.

1 Choose File > Open, and open the file **Afables1.pdf** in the Lesson06 folder.

2 Choose File > Export > Extract Images As > PNG Files.

Note: You set the minimum size of the images that will be extracted in the Extract Images Preferences. (To see the Extract Images Preferences, choose Edit> Preferences > General, and select Extract Images in the left pane.) The default setting is one inch by one inch.

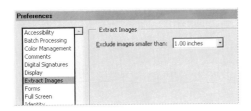

3 Click Settings, and look at the options. We used the default values. Click OK to return to the Extract Images and Save As dialog box.

For information on the Settings options, see Copying images from a PDF file in the Acrobat 5.0 online Help.

4 For Save In, select the Lesson06 folder.

5 Click Save to save the files to the Lesson06 folder.

6 Each piece of art is saved in a separate file. Open one or more of the files using Photoshop or an equivalent application.

7 When you are finished, close all the open image and PDF files.

Exploring on your own

Now that you have finished this lesson on modifying PDF documents, you can explore other document-editing features in Acrobat. In addition to adjusting the position of a PDF image, you can edit its contents by launching Adobe Photoshop from within Acrobat. You can then save the edited image in Photoshop to update and replace the original image in the PDF document. To complete these steps, you must have Photoshop installed and configured correctly on your computer.

1 Select Afables1.pdf in the Lesson06 folder, and click Open.

2 Navigate to page 4 (7 of 19), where the "Dog and the Shadow" fable appears.

3 Select the touchup object tool ( ).

4 Hold down Ctrl (Windows) or Option (Mac OS), and double-click the dog image. Adobe Photoshop launches.

Hold down Ctrl or Option, and double-click image.

Photoshop launches automatically.

5 Make the desired changes in Photoshop, and if needed, flatten the image by choosing Layer > Flatten Image.

Flattening an image merges all visible layers into the background, discards all hidden layers, and fills the remaining transparent areas with white.

6 Choose File > Save.

7 Close the image file and exit or quit Photoshop. Return to Acrobat to view the change to the image.

Review questions

1 How do you change the order of pages in a document?

2 What kinds of text attributes can you change from within Acrobat?

3 How do you select multiple thumbnails?

4 How do you insert an entire PDF file into another PDF file?

5 How do you insert one page or a range of pages from one PDF file into another?

6 What types of actions can you assign to links and bookmarks?

Review answers

1 You change the page order by selecting the thumbnails corresponding to the pages you want to move, and dragging them to their new locations.

2 You can use the touchup text tool to change text formatting—font, size, color, letter spacing, and alignment—or to change the text itself.

3 To select more than one thumbnail, click the first thumbnail. Hold down Shift and click additional thumbnails to add them to the selection.

4 To insert all the pages from a PDF file into another PDF file, choose Document > Insert Pages and select the file you wish to insert.

5 To insert a selection of pages from one PDF file into another, open both files with their thumbnails visible. Select the thumbnails for the pages you wish to insert, and drag the thumbnails to the desired location in the Thumbnails palette of the other document.

6 You can assign these actions to links and bookmarks: Execute Menu Item, Go to View, Import Form Data, JavaScript, Movie, Open File, Read Article, Reset Form, Show-Hide Field, Sound, Submit Form, World Wide Web Link, and None.

Lesson 7

7 Using Acrobat in a Document Review Cycle

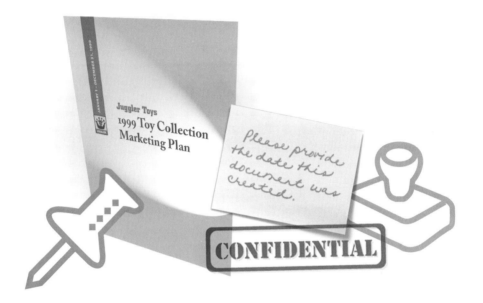

Acrobat can play an effective role in streamlining you document review cycle, where a PDF document is distributed to an audience of reviewers. You can receive comments back in the form of notes, text, sound, stamps, files, graphic markups, and text markups added to the file. You can then collate the comments and compile them in a single file for easier viewing. If you put your review document on a shared server, your colleagues can review and add comments simultaneously from within their Web browsers.

In this lesson, you'll learn how to do the following:

- Use and create comments.

- Export, import, and summarize comments.

- Digitally sign documents.

This lesson will take about 60 minutes to complete.

If needed, remove the previous lesson folder from your hard drive, and copy the Lesson07 folder onto it.

Note: *Windows users need to unlock the lesson files before using them. For information, see "Copying the Classroom in a Book files" on page 3.*

Opening the work file

In this lesson, you'll work with a marketing plan document for the Juggler Toys Company. This document is at an intermediate draft stage, and some of the marketing strategies are still being developed. You'll review existing comments in the document and add a variety of your own comments. You'll digitally sign the document to show the status of the document when you handed it on.

1 Start Acrobat.

2 Choose File > Open. Select Mktplan.pdf in the Lessons/Lesson07 folder, and click Open. Then choose File > Save As, rename the file **Mktplan1.pdf**, and save it in the Lesson07 folder.

Working with comments

Acrobat's comment feature lets you attach comments to an existing document. These comments can be in the form of notes, text, sound files, stamps, application files, graphic markups, and text markups. Multiple reviewers can comment on and incorporate their comments into the same review version. And if you put your document on a shared server, your colleagues can simultaneously review and add comments from within their Web browsers. (For sharing comments online, Acrobat 5.0 supports standard protocols such as Web Distributed Authoring and Versioning (WebDAV) on Windows and Mac OS and Open DataBase Connectivity (ODBC) and Microsoft Office Server Extensions on Windows.)

About comments

There are three types of comment and markup tools available on the toolbar—comment, graphic markup, and text markup. Each has a hidden tool menu.

• The comment tools—note tool, free text tool, sound attachment tool, stamp tool, and file attachment tool—allow you to attach comments to a PDF document in a variety of formats. Each tool provides a unique method for conveying comment information.

• The graphic markup tools—pencil tool, square tool, circle tool, and line tool—allow you to visually mark an area of a PDF document with a graphic symbol and associate a note with the markup for additional comments.

• Text markup tools—highlight tool, strikeout tool, and underline tool—allow you to visually mark up text on a PDF document page and associate a text note with the markup for further comments.

--From the Acrobat 5.0 online Help.

Reviewing comments

1 Choose Window > Comments to display the Comments palette.

A list of comments associated with the open document appears. By default, the list is sorted by page. You can also sort the list by type, author, and date. You'll resort the list by author.

2 Click the Comments palette menu at the top of the Comments palette, and choose Sort by Author.

3 Expand the comments for each author by clicking the plus sign (Windows) or triangle (Mac OS) next to the author name.

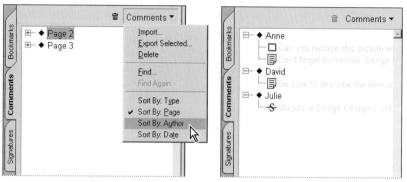

Sort annotations by author.   Result

4 Double-click the yellow note listed under Anne to jump to the page that contains that comment and automatically open the note.

Single-clicking a comment in the Comments palette takes you to the page that contains the comment and highlights the comment. Double-clicking a comment takes you to the page and opens any note associated with the comment.

5 Click the Fit in Window button (▣) to view the entire page. Notice the different colored comments that appear on the page. The blue note is highlighted and open, indicating it is the comment that you selected from the Comments palette.

6 Double-click the yellow note on the page to read it also.

The note's label is different from the previous note. Comments can be set to different colors to indicate that they were created by different reviewers.

Note: In Windows, the note icon in the Comments palette is always yellow, regardless of the color of the note in the document pane.

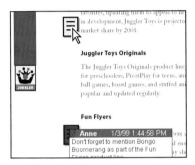 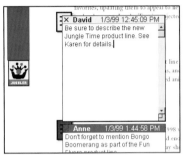

Double-click yellow note to open it.   *Result*

7 Click the close box at the top of each of the note windows when you have finished reading the notes.

Comments in the form of stamps, graphic markups, and text markups can also have notes associated with them. As with notes, double-clicking the comment opens the associated note window.

8 Select the zoom-in tool (🔍) from the toolbar, and marquee-zoom around the Pastime Playthings section at the bottom of the page.

9 Select the hand tool (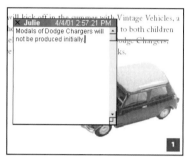), and double-click the green line that strikes out the phrase Dodge Chargers. A note associated with the text markup appears. The note contains a typographical error that you'll correct later in this lesson. Close the note when you have finished reading it.

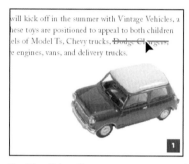 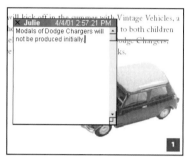

Double-click strikeout text comment.   *Result*

Except for text markups, comments can be easily moved around on a page.

10 Click the Fit in Window button. Then drag the blue note to the right margin.

11 Double-click the blue note to read it. The note window is no longer aligned with the associated comment.

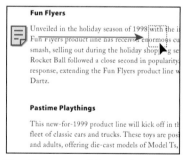 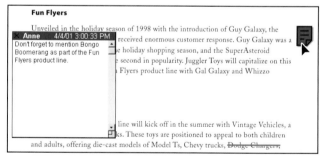

Drag blue note to right margin.   *Note window is no longer aligned with note.*

You can easily reset the location of the note window.

12 Position the pointer over the blue note. Hold down the right mouse button (Windows) or Control-click (Mac OS). Choose Reset Note Window Location from the context menu.

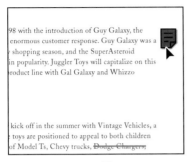

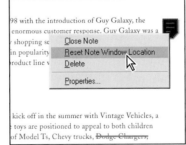

Position pointer over blue note.

Choose Reset Note Window Location from context menu.

The note window realigns with the associated comment.

13 Click the note window to select it, and close the note when you have finished viewing it.

You'll add a variety of your own comments to this document, but first you'll customize your comment style by setting preferences.

Setting comment preferences

1 Choose Edit > Preferences > General. Click Comments in the left pane.

You use the Comments Preferences to determine whether the user login name is used as the author identifier, whether text boxes open automatically when you use the comment and markup tools, how transparent the text boxes are, whether comments are numbered to show the order in which they were added, and whether text boxes and their contents will print when the file is printed. You can experiment with these options to find the mix that best suits your work style.

In this section, you'll specify a new font for displaying the note text. However, keep in mind that this font preference applies only to your system. Users viewing your comments on other systems may see a different font, depending on their own preference settings.

2 Choose a font. (We used Arial®.) For Font Size, choose 12.

3 Select the Automatically Open Note Pop-up option. Click OK.

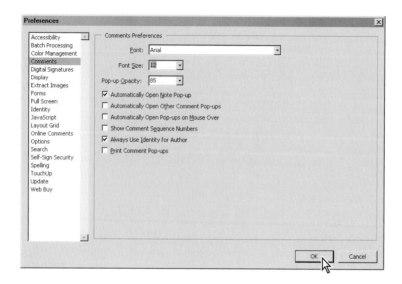

Adding a note

You use the note tool in Acrobat to create your own notes using the preferences that you have just specified. Although you can view notes and other comments in a PDF file using Acrobat Reader, you can only create or edit comments using Acrobat.

1 Click the First Page button (◄) to go to page i (1 of 5).

2 Select the note tool (▤) in the toolbar, and click in the blank space beneath the title on the page.

An empty note window appears.

3 Type the note text as desired. (We used the following: "Please provide the date this document was created.") Then close the note.

4 Position the pointer over the note, hold down the right mouse button (Windows) or Control-click (Mac OS), and choose Properties from the context menu.

5 Select the Comment icon to represent your type of note. Scroll through the Appearance box if needed.

6 Click the Color button to select a color for the note. (In Windows, click the More Colors button to experiment with the various ways of selecting a color for the comments.)

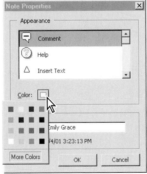

You can change the author name using the Note Properties dialog box. However, any name change that you make in this dialog box applies only to the current comment. If you want the name change to apply to all subsequent comments and all types of comments, you must also deselect the Always Use Identity for Author option in the Comments Preferences dialog box.

7 Click OK.

8 Select the hand tool (🖑), and double-click the note that you have just created to view the message. Close the note when you have finished viewing it.

Adding a stamp

Acrobat's stamp tool lets you apply a stamp to a document in much the same way you would use a rubber stamp on a paper document. In addition to using stamps from the Acrobat stamp library, you can create your own custom stamps, as described in "Exploring on your own" on page 193.

1 Expand the note tool button by holding down the mouse button on the note tool (📄) to display the set of hidden tools. Select the stamp tool (📚).

Select stamp tool.   Click in page to add stamp.

2 Click in the blank space at the top of the page. By default, the Approved stamp appears. You'll change the stamp using the Stamp Properties dialog box.

3 Click on the stamp to select it, and then choose Edit > Properties.

4 For Category, choose Standard. Select Confidential from the list in the left pane of the dialog box. A preview of the stamp that you have selected appears in the right pane of the dialog box.

Notice the Pop-up Color button above the stamp preview. You use this button to specify the color of the note associated with the stamp. You cannot change the color of the stamp itself.

5 Click the Pop-up Color button to select a color for the note associated with the stamp. Then click OK to close the Stamp Properties dialog box.

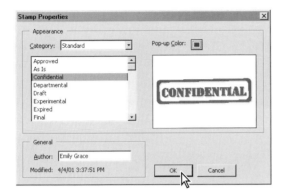

You'll add a note associated with the stamp.

6 Move the pointer over the stamp until it changes to an arrow. Then double-click to create a note window.

7 Type the note text as desired. (We used the following: "Be sure to let reviewers know this document is for internal use only.") Then close the note.

Double-click stamp to open a note window.

Type note text as desired.

8 Select the hand tool (☝), and double-click the stamp to view the message. Close the note when you have finished viewing it.

Adding a file attachment

You use the file attachment tool in Acrobat to embed a file at a specified location in a document, so the reader can open it for viewing. You can attach any type of file as a file attachment. To open an attached file, however, the reader must have an application that can recognize the attachment.

1 Go to page 3 (4 of 5) of the market plan.

As a reviewer of the document, you would like to see information added to the Worldwide Marketing Overview section, and the information you would like added is in a word-processing document called Update.doc. You'll attach the Update.doc file to the marketing plan.

2 Select the file attachment tool (📌).

3 Click in the blank space to the left of the Worldwide Marketing Overview heading.

4 In the dialog box, select Update.doc, located in the Lesson07 folder, and click Select. Be sure the Type of File (Windows) or Show (Mac OS) option is set to All Files.

5 In the File Attachment Properties dialog box, select the Attachment icon to represent this type of file attachment.

6 Click the Color button to select a color for the icon. If needed, click OK to return to the File Attachment Properties dialog box.

7 For Description, type the following: **Worldwide marketing update**. Then click OK.

A pushpin appears on the page.

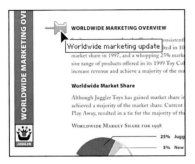

8 Select the hand tool (ξ^m), and position the pointer over the pushpin.

The description of the file appears below the pushpin.

If you have the appropriate application installed on your system, you can open the file that you have just attached.

9 If you have the appropriate application installed, double-click the pushpin to open the file. Click OK or Open to confirm that you want to open the file. When you have finished viewing the file, exit or quit the associated application.

Marking up a document with graphic markup tools

Acrobat's graphic markup tools let you emphasize a specific area of a document, such as a graphic or table. The pencil tool creates a free-form line, the square tool creates a rectangular boundary, the circle tool creates an elliptical boundary, and the line tool creates a straight line between two specified points. You can add a note associated with a graphic markup to comment on the area of the page being emphasized. Graphic markups are saved as comments and appear in the Comments palette.

You'll add a rectangle to the marketing plan, and then add a note associated with the rectangle.

1 Click the Next Page button (▶) to go to page 4.

2 Click the zoom-in tool (⊕), and marquee-zoom around the Production Schedules for the "Super Six" section at the bottom of the page.

3 Hold down the mouse button on the pencil tool ($\mathcal{O}$) to display the set of hidden tools, and drag to select the square tool (□).

4 Drag a rectangle around the table on the page.

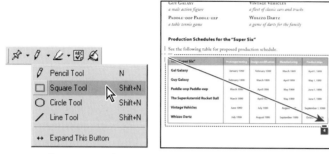

Drag to select square tool.   *Drag to create a rectangle around table.*

5 Select the rectangle, and choose Edit > Properties.

6 Choose a line width for the rectangle from the Thickness menu. Click the Border Color button to select a color for the rectangle. Then click OK.

7 To associate a note with the rectangle, move the pointer inside the rectangle until it changes to an arrow, and double-click to create a note window. (If needed, delete content from the newly opened note.) Type the note text as desired. (We used the following: "Can you use a time line here instead of a table?") Then close the note.

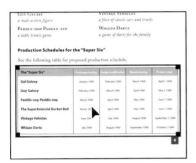

Double-click inside rectangle to open   *Type note text as desired.*
a note window.

8 Select the hand tool (), and double-click the border of the rectangle to view the message. (Be sure to double-click the border of the rectangle, not inside the rectangle.) Close the note when you have finished viewing it.

Marking up a document with text markup tools

You use the text markup tools in Acrobat to emphasize specific text in a document, such as a heading or entire paragraph. You can choose from the highlight tool, the strikeout tool, and the underline tool. You can add a note associated with a text markup to comment on the text being emphasized. Text markups are saved as comments and appear in the Comments palette.

You'll highlight text in the marketing plan, and then add a note associated with the highlighted text.

1 Select the highlight tool ( ) in the toolbar.

2 Drag the I-beam to highlight the word "schedule" in the last sentence on the page.

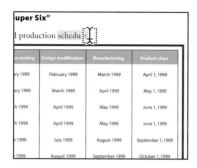

Drag to highlight "schedule."

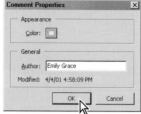

Change properties in Comment Properties dialog box.

3 Select the highlight markup, and choose Edit > Properties.

4 Click the Color button to select a color for the highlighted text. Then click OK. To associate a note with the highlighted text, move the pointer over the highlighted text until it changes to an arrow, and double-click to create a note window. Type the note text as desired. If needed, delete content from the newly opened note. (We used the following: "Make this word plural. Remember to check grammar before the final draft.") Then close the note.

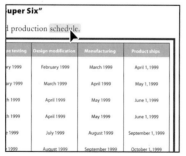

Double-click highlighted text to open note window.

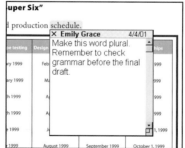

Type note text as desired.

5 Select the hand tool (✋), and double-click the highlighted text to view the message. Close the note when you have finished viewing it.

Deleting a comment

You can easily delete unwanted comments from a document.

1 Click the Fit in Window button (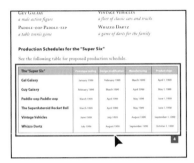).

2 Using the hand tool, click the border of the rectangle on page 4 to select it, and press Delete.

Click border of rectangle to select it, and press Delete.

3 Choose File > Save to save the Mktplan1.pdf file.

Exporting comments

The marketing plan includes comments from several different reviewers. However, another reviewer has placed his comments in a separate copy of the marketing plan. You'll export this reviewer's comments from his copy of the marketing plan and place them in a Forms Data Format (FDF) file. Because the file contains only the comments, it is smaller in size than the original file and therefore more economical to distribute, especially by e-mail. You'll then combine the comments in the FDF file with the existing comments in the marketing plan.

1 Choose File > Open. Select Review.pdf, located inside the Lesson07 folder, and click Open.

2 Choose File > Export > Comments.

3 Name the file **Comments.fdf**, and save it in the Lesson07 folder.

4 Choose File > Close to close the Review.pdf file.

Now you'll import the comments from the Comments.fdf file into the Mktplan1.pdf file, so that you have all the comments in a single document. First take a moment to compare the size of the Comments.fdf file and the Review.pdf file in the Lesson07 folder. (If you need help comparing the size of files, see "Using Default Compression Settings" in Lesson 4.)

Importing comments

1 In the Mktplan1.pdf window, choose File > Import > Comments.

2 Select Comments.fdf, located in the Lesson07 folder, and click Select.

The Comments palette now lists comments from Andrew, as well as those from other reviewers.

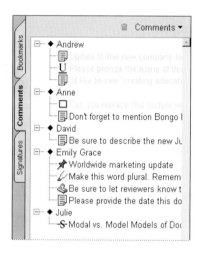

3 Page through the marketing plan and notice the new red comments that have been imported. The imported comments appear in the correct locations on the pages.

4 Choose File > Save to save the Mktplan1.pdf file.

In addition to importing comments from an FDF document, you can import comments directly from one PDF document to another.

Sharing comments on a server

In addition to sharing comments by importing them into your document, you can now share them by keeping them on a server, where they can be quickly accessed by others. Comments shared over a server are secure, meaning they cannot be changed by anyone other than their original author.

Working online versus offline. *You can only read and add comments on a server from a Web browser. This ensures that the file comments on the server are always up-to-date.*

Uploading, downloading, and viewing comments *When you have annotated the file, you can upload your notes so they are available to all the users on the server. You can also view any other comments that have been made to the file by other users. Uploading and downloading comments simultaneously uploads your comments and downloads other comments made to the file. All of these actions must be performed from a Web browser.*

Working offline and sharing comments on a server

Although you can only upload and download comments from a browser, you do have the option of working offline within Acrobat. This is helpful if you will be unable to access the server while creating your comments. You can make your comments to the PDF file in Acrobat, then upload them onto the server from a browser window. Acrobat provides a simple method of going back online, so you do not have to save and reopen your annotated files.

---From the Acrobat 5.0 online Help.

Summarizing comments

At times you may want to display just the text of the notes so that you don't have to open each one individually to read it. You'll summarize the comments in the marketing plan, compiling the text of all the notes into a new PDF document.

1 Choose Tools > Comments > Summarize.

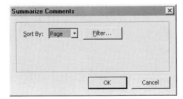

The Summarize Comments dialog box lets you choose whether to sort the summary of comments by page, author, date, or type, as well as apply filters that allow you to choose whether to summarize only comments modified within a given time period, only comments added by one or selected authors, or the type of comments. Any changes you make in this dialog box are reflected in the Comments palette.

For this lesson, you'll use the default settings—sort by page, summarize all comments for all authors. (If you wish, click the Filter button in the Summarize Comments dialog box to review the default filter settings. Click Cancel to return to the Summarize Comments dialog box without making any changes.)

2 Click OK in the Summarize Comments dialog box.

A new PDF file named Summary of Comments on Revised market plan.p65.pdf is created. This document lists each comment that appears in the marketing plan, including the note label, the date and time the comment was added to the file, and the full text of the note.

3 Choose File > Save As, rename the file **Summary.pdf**, and save it in the Lesson07 folder.

4 Close the Summary.pdf file when you have finished viewing it.

Now you'll append the comments summary to the marketing plan.

5 In the Mktplan1.pdf window, choose Document > Insert Pages.

6 Select Summary.pdf, located in the Lesson07 folder, and click Select.

7 For Location, choose After. For Page, select the last page. Click OK to insert the comments summary into the review version of the marketing plan.

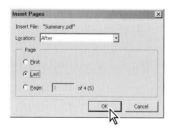

8 Click the Actual Size button (□) to return the page to a 100% view.

9 Go to page 5 of the document to view the first page of the summary of the comments.

The comments are numbered in the comments summary. These numbers show the order in which the comments were created on each page. You can set preferences in Acrobat to display these numbers with the comments in the document. Then you can easily locate comments while reviewing the comments summary.

10 Choose Edit > Preferences > General. Click Comments in the left pane.

11 Select Show Comment Sequence Numbers, and click OK.

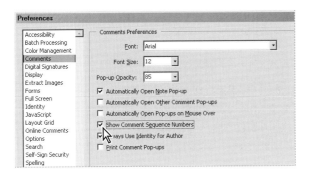

12 Click the First Page button (⏮) to go to page i. Page through the marketing plan and notice the numbers that appear on the comments. These numbers correspond to the numbers listed in the comments summary.

13 Choose File > Save, and save Mktplan1.pdf in the Lesson07 folder.

Spell checking comments

When you looked at the summary of the comments marketing plan document, you may have noticed that note 3 on page 1 contains a typographical error—author Julie typed "Modals" instead of "Models."

You'll use the spell checking feature to quickly spell check all the comments added to the marketing plan document.

1 Choose Tools > Spelling > Check Form Fields and Comments.

2 Click Start.

Any unrecognized text string is displayed in the Not In Dictionary text box. The string "Modals of Dodge Chargers will not be produced initially." is displayed. "Models" is the suggested correction.

3 Click Change to accept the correction.

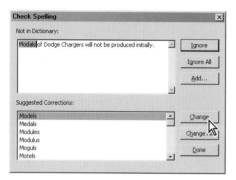

4 Click Done to close the spell checking operation.

5 Choose File > Save, and save the corrected file in the Lesson07 folder.

Printing comments

When you print a PDF file that contains comments, you can print the file so that the comment icons print, you can print the comments with the associated notes open so that the text of the associated notes can be read, or you can hide all the comment icons and associated notes.

• To print only the comment icons, use the default settings in the Comments Preferences dialog box and the Print dialog box. The Print Comment Pop-ups option is not selected in the Comments Preferences dialog box; the Comment option is selected in the Print dialog box.

• To print comments and associated pop-up notes, select the Print Comment Pop-ups option in the Comments Preferences dialog box, and check that the Comments option in the Print dialog box is selected. The associated pop-up notes must be open in the PDF file to be printed.

• To hide all the comments icons and associated pop-up notes so that only the contents of the uncommented PDF file print, deselect the Comments option in the Print dialog box.

Note: In Mac OS, you must choose Acrobat 5.0 from the pop-up menu to display the correct Print dialog box.

Choose Window > Close All to close all open files when you have finished looking at the print options.

Digitally signing documents

In the last section, you saw how easy it is to add comments in a document review cycle. At some point however, you need to "freeze" the document and not allow any more changes. An easy way to do this is to digitally sign the document. Although digitally signing a document doesn't prevent people from changing the document (depending on the security you apply to the document), it does allow you to track any changes made after the signature is added and roll back to the signed version if necessary.

After all the comments were consolidated on the marketing plan, the president of Juggler Toys reviewed, approved, and digitally signed the document. You'll look at the signed document, make a few minor changes to it, and see how easy it is to track the changes made after the president's approval.

1 Choose File > Open. Select DigSig.pdf, located inside the Lesson07 folder, and click Open.

Notice the digital signature at the top right of the first page. Zoom in on the signature to read the details. You set this information in your digital signature profile.

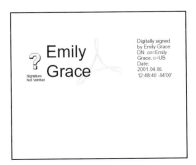

💡 *With Acrobat 5.0, you can sign documents in a browser window using the same tools as you would to sign in an Acrobat window.*

2 Click the Signatures tab to bring the Signatures palette to the front. Click the plus sign (Windows) or triangle (Mac OS) to expand the signature. The Signatures palette gives additional information about the signature.

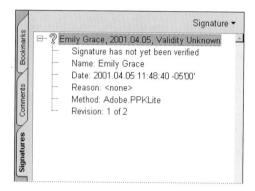

3 With the hand tool (✋) selected, double-click on the digital signature on the document. Notice that the signature is not validated.

Creating a user profile

Before you can validate a signature, you need to log in. For this you need to create a user profile. You'll set up a user profile as the Marketing Manager of Juggler Toys.

1 Click Log In in the Validation Status alert.

2 Click New User Profile in the Log In dialog box.

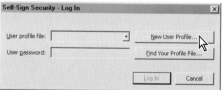

3 In the Name text box, enter **Marketing Manager**. In the Choose a Password and Confirm Password text boxes, enter **123456** as the password.

4 Click OK.

5 Click Save to save your profile file. Click OK to close the alert box.

You use the User Settings command in this dialog box if you want to customize your signature profile and set additional security options.

Verifying a digital signature

Anytime you sign a document using Acrobat Self-Sign, your signature is verified automatically. To verify someone else's signature, however, you must import their user certificate. (User certificates are generated automatically whenever a user creates a signature profile.)

Now that you have a user profile and you're logged in, you can verify the signature on the document.

1 Click Verify Identity.

In real life, you would phone or e-mail the president of Juggler Toys and ask that he send you his certificate information or give you access to his user certificate so that you can check his information against the information in the Verify Identity dialog box. For this lesson, you'll assume the certificate information is correct.

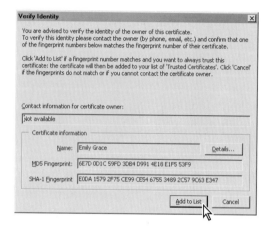

2 Click Add to List.

3 Click OK to close the alert box, and click Close to close the validation status box.

You have validated the signature.

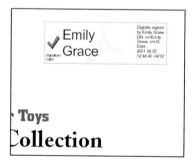

Adding a digital signature

Now you'll make a few minor changes to the document. First you'll remove the reference to the Dodge Charger as one of the reviewers requested, and then you'll add a note authorizing the change.

1 Click the Fit in Window button (▣), and go to page 1 (2 of 5).

2 Select the zoom-in tool (🔍) from the toolbar, and marquee-zoom around the Pastime Playthings section at the bottom of the page.

3 Select the hand tool (✋) and select the green line that strikes out the words *Dodge Chargers*. Press Delete.

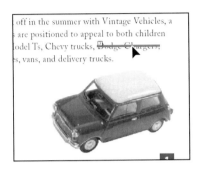

The comment is deleted. Now you'll remove the text that was struck out.

4 Select the touchup text tool (𝕋) from the toolbar, and click in the line of text that contains the text to be edited. A bounding box encloses the text that you can edit. Drag to highlight the text **Dodge Chargers,** (you need to include the comma in the highlighting). Press Delete.

5 Select the hand tool and click anywhere in the document pane to see the results.

A caution immediately appears in the Signatures palette, indicating that the document has been changed.

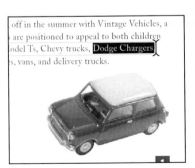
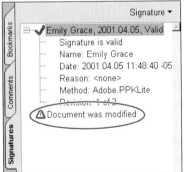

Now you'll re-sign the document. You already set up your user profile as the Marketing Manager of Juggler Toys and logged in to verify the president's signature, so you're ready to sign the document.

6 Select the digital signature tool (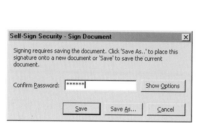), and in the same area where you deleted the phrase "Dodge Chargers," drag to draw a rectangular signature box.

7 In the Sign Document dialog box, enter your password, **123456**.

8 Click Save As, and rename the file DigSig1.pdf to sign and save the document. Click OK to close the alert box.

Again, notice that all the changes you make are reflected in the Signatures palette.

Comparing signed versions of a document

Using the Compare Two Versions Within a Signed Document command, the president of Juggler Toys can quickly see what changes were made to the marketing plan after he signed it.

1 Choose Tools > Compare > Two Versions Within a Signed Document.

2 For Document, choose DigSig1.pdf from the pop-up menu.

Make sure the two documents you want to compare are listed in the Compare and To text fields. You can determine how detailed the comparison process is using the options in this dialog box. You'll do a text only comparison.

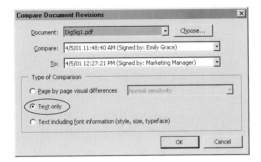

3 Click OK.

Acrobat displays a summary page of the changes between the two document versions. Scroll down or use the next page command to see the differences highlighted.

4 Choose Window > Close All to close all the open files.

Working with digital signatures

The digital signatures feature in Acrobat offers much more than the ability to "sign" a document to indicate that you have read and approved it.

- *You can digitally sign a document to ensure that any changes you make to the document are preserved. If any changes are made to the document after you sign it, you can "roll back" to recover the version that you signed.*

- *You can verify another person's digital signature to verify that their signature is authentic. The verification process uses a user certificate which the signer makes available to you.*

- *You can review all the signatures on a document in the Signatures palette, you can retrieve any signed version of a document, and you can use the Compare Two Versions Within a Signed Document command to compare different versions of a signed document.*

- *You can create different identities (digital signatures) for yourself if you handle documents in more than one capacity.*

- *You can create a signature that uses or includes a graphic such as your company logo.*

About digital signatures

A digital signature, like any other signature, identifies a person or entity signing a document. In Acrobat, a digital signature can appear on a page in many different forms— a handwritten name, a logo or other graphic, or some text explaining the purpose of the signing. The particular appearance of the signature is determined by the signature handler.

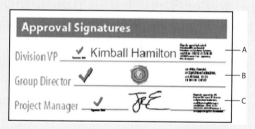

A. Text signature B. Graphic signature C. Handwritten name signature

--From the Acrobat 5.0 online Help.

Exploring on your own

Now that you have learned how to add a stamp to a document, try adding custom stamps to the Acrobat stamp library and using them as comments. Each illustration or graphic for a stamp must be on a separate page in a PDF file. Each stamp can be in a separate PDF file, or several stamps may be contained in one PDF file. We've provided a PDF file with two images that you can use for practice, or you can use your own artwork or photo images saved as PDF files.

1 Choose File > Open. Select Stamps.pdf, located inside the Lesson07 folder, and click Open.

You'll prepare the Stamps.pdf file to be added to the Acrobat stamp library.

The Acrobat stamp library consists of several PDF files, which contain one or more stamps. Each PDF file has a category name, which appears in the Category menu in the Stamp Properties dialog box. Acrobat uses the document title of a PDF file as the category name. You'll specify a document title for the Stamps.pdf file using the Document Summary dialog box.

2 Choose File > Document Properties > Summary.

3 Type **JugglerToys** in the Title text box, and click OK.

To be recognized by Acrobat, each stamp in a stamp file must be named. The name of each stamp should be in the following format:

<CategoryName><StampName>=<StampLabel>

The CategoryName is the name of the stamp category in English, the StampName is the name of the stamp in English, and the StampLabel is the name of the stamp in your native language. Acrobat uses the StampLabel as the name of the stamp listed in the Stamp Properties dialog box. This naming convention ensures that stamps can be easily identified when distributed to users of other languages.

You'll name each stamp in the Stamps.pdf file using Acrobat's Page Templates feature.

4 If needed, go to page 1. Choose Tools > Forms > Page Templates.

5 Type **JugglerToysLibrary=Library** in the Name text box, and click Add. Click Yes to confirm that you are creating a new template using the current page. Then click Close (Windows) or Done (Mac OS) to close the Document Templates dialog box.

6 Click the Next Page button (▶) to go to page 2.

7 Choose Tools > Forms > Page Templates. Type **JugglerToysInternal=Internal** in the Name text box, and click Add. Click Yes. Then click Close (Windows) or Done (Mac OS).

To be part of the Acrobat stamp library, all stamp files must be saved in the Stamps subfolder of the Annotations folder within the Plug-ins folder for Adobe Acrobat 5.0. You'll save the Stamps.pdf file in this location.

8 Choose File > Save As, and save the Stamps.pdf file in the Stamps subfolder of the Annotations folder within the Plug-ins folder for Adobe Acrobat.

9 Choose File > Close to close the Stamps.pdf file.

Now that you have added custom stamps to the Acrobat stamp library, you can use them as comments. You'll apply the custom stamps to the marketing plan.

10 Choose File > Open. Select Mktplan1.pdf, located inside the Lesson07 folder, and click Open.

11 If needed, hold down the mouse button on the note tool (⊟) to display the set of hidden tools, and drag to select the stamp tool (♨). Click in the lower left corner of the page.

The Confidential stamp appears. You'll change the stamp using the Stamp Properties dialog box.

12 Select the stamp, and choose Edit > Properties.

13 For Category, choose JugglerToys. Select Library from the list in the left pane of the dialog box. Then click OK.

Click to add a stamp.   *Change stamp using Stamp Properties dialog box.*

The first page of the Stamps.pdf file appears in the marketing plan as a custom stamp.

Note: *If you don't see JugglerToys in the Category pop-up menu, verify that you saved the stamp.pdf file in the correct location.*

If needed, you can easily adjust the size and position of the stamp. To resize the stamp, drag one of the corner handles. To move the stamp, position the stamp tool inside the stamp and drag.

Drag corner handle to resize stamp.   *Drag stamp to move it.*

14 Select the hand tool (👆?), and click in the blank space in the document to deselect the stamp.

15 Apply the Internal stamp from the JugglerToys category to the marketing plan. When you have finished, close the Mktplan1.pdf file. You do not need to save your changes.

Review questions

1 How do you change the author name of the current comment? How do you change the author name for all subsequent comments?

2 What font is used in a note window when viewed on your computer? On someone else's computer?

3 How do you add a stamp to a document? How do you change the stamp?

4 What type of file can you attach to a document as a file attachment?

5 Name three ways you can mark up text in a document?

6 How do you create a file that contains just the text of the notes added to a PDF document?

7 How can you tell if a digitally signed document has been altered since it was signed?

Review answers

1 To change the author name of the current comment, select the comment, choose Edit > Properties, and enter the required name in the Author text box. To change the author name for all subsequent comments, choose Edit > Preferences > General. Click Comments in the left pane, and deselect Always Use Identity for Author.

2 On your computer, the note window uses the font that you have specified in the Comments Preferences dialog box. On someone else's computer, the note window uses the font that he or she has specified.

3 To add a stamp, select the stamp tool, and click inside an existing PDF document. To change the stamp, select the stamp to be changed in the PDF document, choose Edit > Properties, and select a new stamp from the Stamp Properties dialog box.

4 You can attach any file type as a file attachment. However, to open the file, the reader must have an application that can recognize the attachment.

5 Using Acrobat's text markup tools, you can highlight, strikeout, and underline text.

6 Choose Tools > Comments > Summarize.

7 Look in the Signatures palette. A caution will be displayed if a document has been altered after it was signed.

Lesson 8

8 Creating Forms

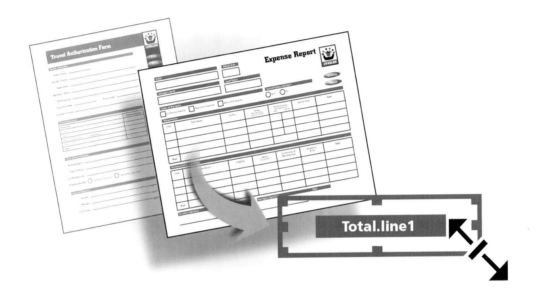

Acrobat lets you create form fields that can be filled out by a user in Acrobat or Acrobat Reader. If all the proper software and hardware components are in place, form data can be submitted over the World Wide Web and collected in a database as with HTML forms.

In this lesson, you'll learn how to do the following:

- Fill out a PDF form and spell check the entries.
- Export information from one form and import it into another form.
- Add form fields, format those fields, and copy them.
- Use the forms layout grid.
- Validate form fields to restrict entries to specific values or characters.
- Perform mathematical calculations on two or more numeric form fields.

This lesson will take about 60 minutes to complete.

If needed, remove the previous lesson folder from your hard drive, and copy the Lesson08 folder onto it.

Note: *Windows users need to unlock the lesson files before using them. For information, see "Copying the Classroom in a Book files" on page 3.*

Working with forms online

With Adobe Acrobat, it's easy to convert your existing paper and electronic forms to Adobe PDF, and then use Acrobat to create PDF form fields, including signature fields. Using an existing form lets you maintain your organization's corporate identity and branding, and saves you from having to re-create the form design itself.

Many forms require the same information—name, address, phone number, and so on. Wouldn't it be nice if you could enter that data once and use it again and again with the various forms that you have to fill out? Acrobat's ability to import and export form data makes it possible for you to populate different forms with the same set of data.

In this part of the lesson, you'll fill out a Travel Authorization form with personal information, export the data, and then import the data into an Expense Report form.

Filling out a form

1 Start Acrobat.

2 Choose File > Open. Select Travel.pdf in the Lessons/Lesson08 folder, and click Open. Then choose File > Save As, rename the file **Travel1.pdf**, and save it in the Lesson08 folder.

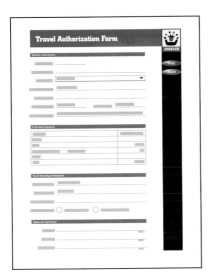

This electronic form was designed using a page-layout application and then converted to PDF. Form fields have been created so that you can fill out the form from within Acrobat. For the purposes of this lesson, some form fields have already been filled out for you.

3 If needed, select the hand tool (✋).

You use the hand tool to enter information in existing form fields; you use the form tool to create new or edit existing form fields.

4 Move the pointer to the right of the Today's Date line. When the pointer changes to an I-beam, click to set an insertion point. Enter the current date in numeric month/day/year format; for example, 3/01/2001. (Be sure to enter the year as four digits to match the field's format and to avoid generating an error message.) Press Tab.

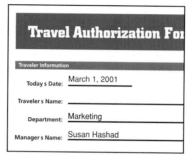

Your date entry automatically updates to a longer date format. Acrobat lets you specify format options, such as currency formats and numbers of decimal places, for data entered in a form field.

5 Enter your name in the Traveler's Name field, and press Tab.

Pressing Tab lets you advance in order through a series of fields. You can set the Tab order of fields when you create a form.

6 Press the triangle to the far right of the Department field to display the *combo box* of department names. Select Engineering from the list.

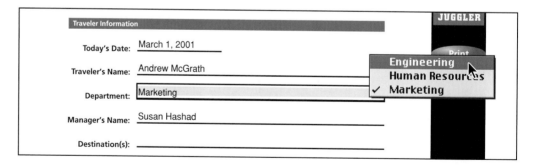

A combo box presents a choice of items in a pop-up menu. You can select only one item from a combo box.

7 Press Tab until you arrive at the Destination(s) field, and enter **Orlando, FL**. Then press Tab until you arrive at the Airfare field of the Estimated Expenses section.

8 Enter **250** for the Airfare field, and press Tab twice.

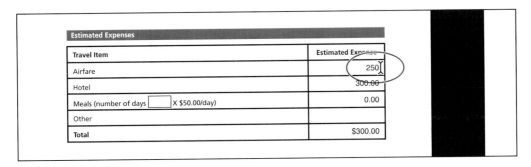

The airfare price automatically updates to a U.S. dollar currency format with two decimal places. Notice also that the Total field automatically recalculates the sum of total expenses.

This section of the form includes a preformatted mathematical calculation in the Meals field, which multiplies the number of travel days by $50.00 (the budget allotted for meals per day). You'll enter a number of days to see the calculation. Later in this lesson, you'll learn to set up predefined and custom calculations for numeric fields.

9 In the Meals field, enter **6** for the number of days and press Tab twice.

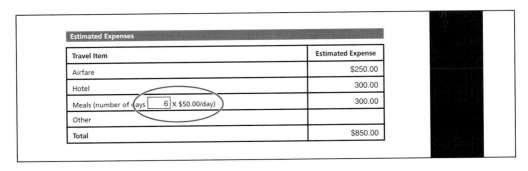

The amount for Meals in the Estimated Expense column changes to $300.00 (6 x $50.00). The calculation is performed automatically when you enter a new value in the number of days field.

10 Press Tab until you arrive at the Confirmation No. field, and try entering **56T123**.

You cannot enter alphabetic characters. This field has been formatted to accept only numeric entries. Delete the current contents of the field, and reenter a confirmation number of **567123**.

11 For Payment Method, click one of the radio buttons to make a payment choice. You can select only one radio button in a set.

The Travel Authorization form was designed to be filled out electronically and then printed for final signature approvals and submission. For the purposes of this lesson, you'll save the form in its current state without printing it.

12 Choose File > Save to save Travel1.pdf in the Lesson08 folder.

Spell checking form fields

By default, Acrobat underlines words that are misspelled as you fill in the form fields. You can also check the spelling in any form fields that you complete unless the creator of the form selected the Do Not Spell Check option in the Options tab of the Field Properties dialog box. You'll check the spelling of your form field entries just to be safe.

1 Choose Tools > Spelling > Check Form Fields and Comments.

2 Click Start to begin spell checking.

Unrecognized words appear in the Not in Dictionary window.

3 Click Ignore to leave the word as is. Click Change next to the Suggested Corrections area to accept the suggested correction that is highlighted.

4 Click Done to close the spell checking operation.

Exporting form data

Now that you have filled out the Travel Authorization form, you'll export the data to a file that contains only the data you entered.

1 Choose File > Export > Form Data. Name the file **Info.fdf,** and save it in the Lesson08 folder (.fdf stands for Forms Data Format, the file format for exported form data).

2 Choose File > Close to close the Travel1.pdf file. You don't need to save the file because the data you entered has already been saved in the exported Info.fdf file.

Importing data

Now you'll open another form, and import the Info.fdf file to populate the common fields with the travel data you just entered.

You can import a form data file repeatedly to fill in multiple forms as long as those forms have the same field names as the original form from which you exported your data. A worldwide standard for naming seems unlikely, but it is certainly possible to create a standard within an organization. You can consistently name fields that ask for the same information with the same name. For example, an address field can always be named *Address,* and a home phone field can always be named *Home Phone* (keep in mind that form field names are case sensitive).

1 Choose File > Open. Select ExpFinal.pdf in the Lesson08 folder, and click Open.

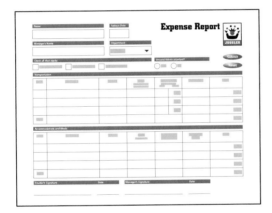

2 Select the form tool (⊞) to display the form fields that have been created in the document. Form fields appear as boxes with highlighted field names.

3 Select the hand tool, and choose File > Import > Form Data. Select Info.fdf in the Lesson08 folder, and click Select.

Name	Today's Date	**Expense Rep**
Andrew McGrath		

Manager's Name	Department
Susan Hashad	Engineering ▼

Check all that apply: | | | | **Unused tickets attached?**
☐ Conference Expense   ☐ Relocation Expense   ☐ Recruiting Expense   ○ Yes   ○ No

The values you entered in the Travel Authorization form for the Traveler's Name, Manager's Name, Department, and Airfare form fields are automatically imported into the corresponding fields in the Expense Report form. (Estimated Airfare from the Travel Authorization form is placed in the first Airfare field in the Transportation section of the Expense Report.)

This Expense Report form contains a number of other premade, formatted fields.

4 Experiment with filling out the Expense Report form. Later in the lesson you'll learn how to create the various types of form fields that appear in the Expense Report.

5 Choose File > Close to close the form without saving it.

Adding form fields

In this part of the lesson, you'll work with an earlier, partially created version of the Expense Report form. You'll create text fields, check boxes, a combo box, and radio buttons. You'll also learn how to validate entries in the fields and calculate the sum of numeric entries in two fields.

You create form fields by using the form tool to draw the area and location of each form field.

Adding and formatting text fields

A *text field* lets users enter alphabetic or numeric values. You can specify formatting for data entered into text fields. For example, you can specify how many decimal places to display for numbers or percentages, or you can specify the month, day, and year format for dates.

1 Choose File > Open. Select Expense.pdf in the Lesson08 folder, and click Open. Then choose File > Save As, rename the file **Expense1.pdf**, and save it in the Lesson08 folder.

2 Select the zoom-in tool (🔍), and marquee-zoom to magnify the Transportation section of the form.

3 Select the form tool (📋) in the toolbar. As you can see from the field names and borders that appear, some form fields have already been added for you.

4 Drag to draw a box inside the first cell under Date in the Transportation section. The field box should sit inside the solid black lines so that any text the user enters remains within the boundaries.

If you have difficulty fitting a box inside the cell, choose View and make sure that the Snap to Grid command is deselected.

Transportation						
Date	Description	Airfare	Fares (Taxi, Bus, Ferry, Parking, & Tolls)	Personal Auto (enter Miles only) Miles Expense		Rental Auto
		Airfare.line1		Miles.line Personal		RentalAuto.line1
Total						

The Field Properties dialog box appears. This dialog box lets you specify form field options such as appearance, format, and mathematical calculations.

ℹ For a complete description of all the available form field options, see "Setting form field options" in the Acrobat 5.0 online Help.

5 For Name, enter **Date.line1**, and for Type, choose Text.

6 Click the Appearance tab. Deselect Border Color and Background Color. Make sure that Text Color is set to black, and choose a sans serif font and a type size. (We used 10-point Helvetica.)

Because the boundaries of the Date field are defined by the form design, you don't need to outline the field with color.

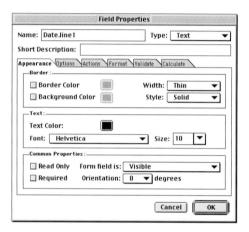

7 Click the Format tab. For Category, select Date. For Date Options, select 1/3/81. Leave the default settings selected for other options, and click OK to add the Date text field to the form.

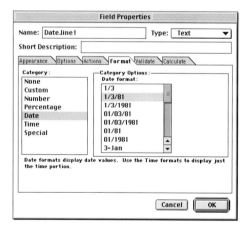

Now you'll create another text field for the Description column.

8 Drag to make a box inside the first cell under Description in the Transportation section.

9 For Name, enter **Description.line1**, and for Type, choose Text. Accept the defaults for other options, and click OK.

Transportation						
Date	Description	Airfare	Fares (Taxi, Bus, Ferry, Parking, & Tolls)	Personal Auto (enter Miles only) Miles Expense		Rental Auto
Date.li	Description.line1	Airfare.line1		Miles.line	Personal	RentalAuto.line1
Total						

10 Click the Actual Size button (⬚).

11 Select the hand tool (✋), and experiment with entering values in the fields you just created, pressing Enter or Return after each value. Notice that the Date value automatically updates to the specified date format.

Duplicating a series of form fields

You've made one form field for the Date column and one form field for the Description column. To fill the second and third rows in these columns you could make new form fields for each cell in the table. In this section, though, you'll learn how to duplicate and automatically rename form fields.

1 First delete any entries you made in the form fields.

Always duplicate empty fields if possible because the duplication process also duplicates any entries in the fields.

2 Select the forms tool (🗒).

3 Shift-drag (Windows) or Command-drag (Mac OS) to create a red rectangle around the three contiguous form fields—Date.line1 form field, the Description.line1 form field, and the Airfare.line1 form field.

Transportation						
Date	Description	Airfare	Fares (Taxi, Bus, Ferry, Parking, & Tolls)	Personal Auto (enter Miles only) Miles / Expense		Rental Auto
Date.li	Description.line1	Airfare.line1		Miles.line	Personal	RentalAuto.line1
Total						

4 With the pointer over one of the bottom selection handles, Ctrl-drag (Windows) or Command-drag (Mac OS) the rectangle to fill the Date, Description, and Airfare columns.

Transportation						
Date	Description	Airfare	Fares (Taxi, Bus, Ferry, Parking, & Tolls)	Personal Auto (enter Miles only) Miles / Expense		Rental Auto
Date.li	Description.line1	Airfare.line1		Miles.line	Personal	RentalAuto.line1
Total						

As you drag to the bottom of the column, two new rows of form fields are created.

5 Click inside the selection to finish creating the columns of form fields.

The form fields are named sequentially, starting from the name you gave to the initial field.

Transportation					
Date	Description	Airfare	Fares (Taxi, Bus, Ferry, Parking, & Tolls)	Personal Auto (enter Miles only) *Miles* *Expense*	Rental Auto
Date.li	Description.line1.0	Airfare.line1.0		Miles.line Personal	RentalAuto.line1
Date.li	Description.line1.1	Airfare.line1.1			
Date.li	Description.line1.2	Airfare.line1.2			
Date.li	Description.line1.3	Airfare.line1.3			

Using form fields to create tables

You can create a table very easily by first creating a row or column of table cells made up of form fields. You then Shift-drag (Windows) or Command-drag (Mac OS) to select the row or column of form fields and Ctrl-drag (Windows) or Command-drag (Mac OS) vertically or horizontally to create the required number of rows or columns. The form fields are numbered automatically, each having a unique number. The original row or column of form fields need not be of the same type. In the finished table, you can edit the properties of individual fields, and even change the field type, as required.

Validating form fields

You use validation to restrict entries in text or combo box fields to specific values or characters. For example, you can restrict a numeric entry to a certain range. Use validation properties to ensure that users enter appropriate data in form fields.

1 With the form tool (⌨) selected, drag to make a box inside the first cell under Fares in the Transportation section.

2 For Name, enter **Fares.line1**, and for Type, choose Text.

3 Click the Options tab and select Right for Alignment. All text you enter will align with the right border of the field.

4 Click the Format tab. For Category, select Number. For Decimal Places, choose 2.

You'll designate the Fares field to accept only values between 1 and 1000.

5 Click the Validate tab. Select Value Must Be Greater Than or Equal To, and enter **1**. Then enter **1000** for the value of And Less Than or Equal To. Leave the default settings selected for other options, and click OK.

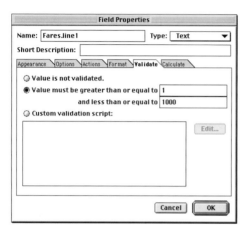

6 Click the Actual Size button (▢). Select the hand tool, and click in the Fares field.

7 Enter **1500**, and press Enter or Return to test the validation for the field.

An alert box appears indicating that the value must be between 1 and 1000.

8 Enter **85** in the Fares field, and press Enter or Return.

The value is accepted and appears in the Fares field formatted as a dollar amount.

9 Choose File > Save to save the Expense1.pdf file.

Using the layout grid

To aid form field creation, you'll display the layout grid. The layout grid makes it easier for you to align, size, and place form fields precisely.

First you'll set the Layout Grid Preferences.

1 Choose Edit > Preferences > General. Select Layout Grid in the left pane.

2 Select values from the Width and Height Between Lines pop-up menus. (We used one inch.) If you want to change the units of measure, you do so using the Page Units option in the Display Preferences.

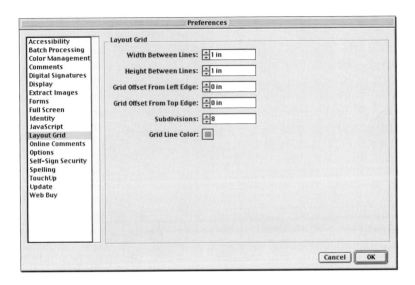

3 Select a value for the Subdivisions option—this is the number of segments between the major layout grid lines (width and height lines). (We used 8.)

4 Click OK.

5 Use the zoom-in tool (🔍) to magnify the Transportation section of the form. Also, click the magnification popup menu, and set the magnification to 125%. (The correct number of subdivisions may not appear if the magnification is set too low.)

Now you'll see how the designer of the form used the layout grid to simplify the alignment of form fields.

6 Choose View > Grid.

7 Select the form tool (📝).

Although the grid is displayed on-screen, it will not print with the rest of the PDF form.

Notice that many of the cell boundaries in the form—the check boxes, for example—follow the lines of the grid. By aligning cell boundaries and form field boundaries with the grid, you can ensure consistent size and even spacing between the fields.

Note: If you used grid values other than those recommended, the form field boundaries may not coincide with the grid lines.

8 Choose View > Snap to Grid.

9 Click the Fares.line1 field to select it.

You can use the form tool to edit the location, size, and properties of a field at any time. You'll resize the Fares.line1 field so that it fills the area of the cell.

10 Position the pointer over a corner of the field to display the double-headed arrow. Then drag to resize the form field. Notice that the field boundary automatically snaps to grid lines.

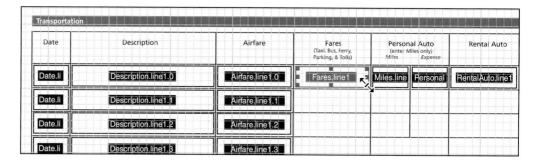

11 If needed, drag the remaining corners of the field to align its boundaries with the cell boundaries.

If desired, you can select and resize the Description.line1 and Date.line1 fields. (You can see that it is useful to resize the fields before duplicating them.)

Adding check boxes

Check boxes allow a user to make multiple selections from a group of items. Adding check boxes to this form will let users select the purpose of their travel (Conference, Relocation, or Recruiting Expense).

1 Click the Fit Width button (🔲). Then select the zoom-in tool (🔍), and marquee-zoom around the area under the phrase "Check all that apply."

Notice that the square boxes in this section follow the lines of the grid for precise sizing and alignment. For this section though, you'll hide the grid to remove the display of distracting grid lines from the form.

2 Choose View > Grid. This command toggles between displaying and hiding the grid lines.

Although you have hidden the display of the grid, the snap-to-grid behavior is still active.

3 Select the form tool (📝), and drag to make a box inside the square just to the left of Conference Expense. Notice that the field automatically snaps to the edges of the square.

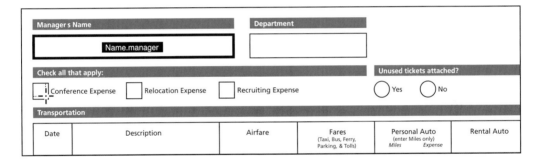

4 For Name, enter **Conference**, and for Type, choose Check Box.

5 Click the Options tab. For Check Style, choose Check (the default style). For Export Value, enter **Yes**.

An export value is the information used by a Common Gateway Interface (CGI) application on a Web server to identify the selected field.

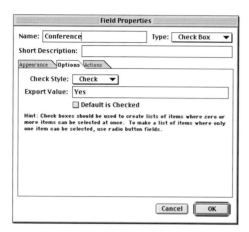

6 Click the Appearance tab. Deselect Border Color and Background Color, and click OK to add the check box to the form.

Earlier in this lesson, you duplicated form fields to create new rows. Now you'll learn how to copy a form field to a new location. Later in the lesson, when you create radio buttons, you'll use a yet another way of copying form fields.

7 If needed, click to select the Conference form field that you just created (selected fields appear highlighted in red), and choose Edit > Copy.

8 Choose Edit > Paste to paste a duplicate of the Conference field in the center of the document window.

You can move a form field and edit its properties at any time with the form tool.

9 Position the pointer inside the duplicate field, and drag it inside the square next to Relocation Expenses. Notice that it snaps to the grid lines.

10 Double-click inside the duplicate field to open the Field Properties dialog box.

Because you copied this field, it has the same name value as the Conference field. You'll rename the field because each check box field must have a distinct name value to work properly.

11 For Name, enter **Relocation**. Accept the current formatting and appearance options, and click OK.

12 Using the same process, duplicate the newly created Relocation field in the square next to Recruiting Expense. In the Field Properties dialog box, rename the field **Recruiting**.

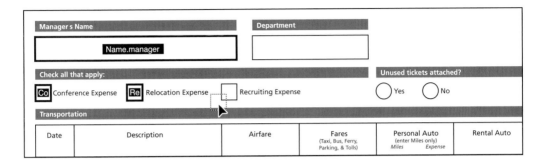

13 Click the Actual Size button (⬚). Select the hand tool, and click inside the newly created check box fields. Notice that you can select more than one check box.

Adding a combo box

A *combo box* contains a list of items that appear in a pop-up menu. You'll create a combo box for the Department section of the form.

1 Use the zoom-in tool (🔍) to magnify the top left portion of the form.

2 Select the form tool (📋), and drag to draw a box inside the cell under Department.

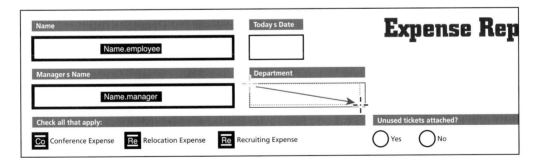

3 For Name, enter **Department**, and for Type, choose Combo Box.

4 Click the Options tab.

Now you'll enter the names of the items you wish to appear in the combo box.

5 For Item, enter **Engineering**, and click Add.

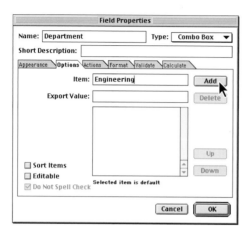

Engineering is added to the combo box list at the bottom of the dialog box, and the Item field is cleared for you to enter additional items.

6 For Item, enter **Marketing**, and click Add.

7 For Item, enter **Human Resources**, and click Add.

Note: *Be sure to click Add after typing each item name to add it to the combo box list. Do not press the Enter or Return key; if you do, you'll exit the dialog box.*

All three items now appear in the combo box list, in the order in which you added them.

8 Select the Sort Items option to rearrange the listed items in alphabetical order.

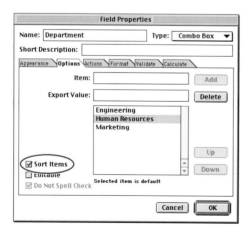

9 Select Marketing to make it the default choice.

10 Click the Appearance tab. Deselect Border Color. Select Background Color, and then click the color box next to it to choose a color:

• In Windows, click More Colors, and then click Define Custom Colors. Enter **255** for Red, **255** for Green, and **204** for Blue. Click Add to Custom Colors, and then click OK.

• In Mac OS, scroll up to select the CMYK Picker. Enter **0%** for Cyan, **0%** for Magenta, **20%** for Yellow, and **0%** for Black. Then click OK.

11 In the Field Properties dialog box, for Type choose a sans serif font and a type size. (We used 10-point Helvetica.) Then click OK.

12 Click the Actual Size button (⬚). Select the hand tool, position the pointer over the triangle in the new field, and click to view the pop-up menu of items.

Adding radio buttons

Unlike check boxes, which let you make multiple selections from a group of items, radio buttons let you select only one item.

When creating radio buttons, keep in mind that the fields must share the same name but have different export values. For example, for the field "Unused tickets attached?" you can have two values: "Yes" or "No." Now you'll set up that radio button.

1 Use the zoom-in tool (🔍) to magnify the top right portion of the form.

2 Select the form tool (🗒), and drag a box that surrounds the circle just to the left of the word "Yes" at the top right of the form.

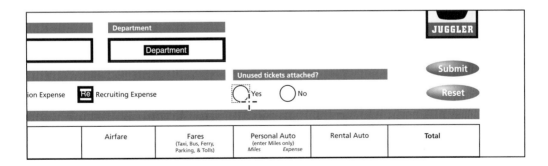

3 For Name, enter **Unused Tickets**, and for Type, choose Radio Button.

4 Click the Options tab. For Radio Style, choose Circle. For Export Value, enter **Yes**.

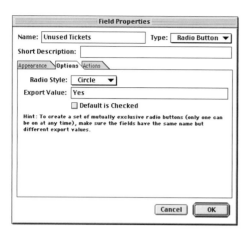

5 Click the Appearance tab. Deselect Border Color and Background Color. For Width, choose Thin, and for Style, choose Solid. Click OK.

Instead of using the form tool to create the other radio button, you'll save time by simply copying the field you just created. When you duplicate a form field, you must remember to edit the appropriate field properties for the new field.

6 Move the pointer inside the Yes field you just created and hold down Ctrl (Windows) or Option (Mac OS). Begin dragging the field to the circle next to No (a hollow arrow appears in Windows and a plus sign in Mac OS, indicating that you are making a copy). As you start dragging, hold down Shift to constrain the motion of the duplicate field along the same horizontal or vertical line as the original field.

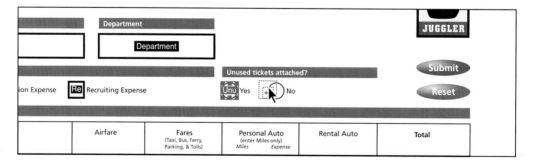

7 Double-click the field next to No to open the Field Properties dialog box. Click the Options tab, enter **No** as the export value, and click OK.

8 Click the Actual Size button ( ). Select the hand tool, and click inside the newly created radio button fields. You can only select one item at a time.

Because you have set the fields to snap to the grid, the radio buttons should line up evenly with the preexisting black circles on the form.

9 Choose File > Save to save the Expense1.pdf file.

Adding a signature field

You'll now create a signature field that will allow the user to sign the form digitally.

Note: A digital signature field is not included in data imported or exported as an FDF file. For a digital signature to be available, the entire PDF file must be made available.

1 Select the form tool ( ), and drag a box that fills the area under the Traveler's Signature label and above the signature line. You may need to scroll down the page to see the signature line.

2 For Name, enter **Traveler's Signature**, and for Type, choose Signature.

3 Deselect Border Color and Background Color.

4 Click the Signed tab, and select Mark as Read Only. Select All Fields from the pop-up menu.

This locks the fields so that no field values can be changed after the document is signed.

5 Click OK to finish adding the signature box.

6 Select the hand tool, and click under the Traveler's Signature label. A Log In dialog box appears, prompting you to log in as a first step in signing the document.

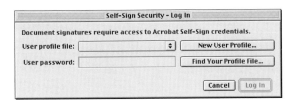

7 Click Cancel to exit the Log In dialog box, and click OK in the alert box.

8 Choose File > Save to save the file.

For information on using digital signatures, see Lesson 7, "Using Acrobat in a Document Review Cycle."

💡 *You can duplicate a signature field (using the Duplicate command in the context menu) and copy it to the same location on more than one page. This is convenient for instances when the user signs the document once, but the signature needs to appear on all pages. Because duplicating the field on each page in this manner automatically adds the signature on each page when the first page is signed, you might want to add a note under the signature field warning the signer of this action.*

Calculating with form fields

You can perform mathematical calculations on two or more existing numeric field entries and display the results. You can apply operations predefined in Acrobat, or you can create custom operations using the JavaScript programming language.

In the first part of this section, you'll create a Total field that adds values from the Airfare, Fares, Personal Auto, and Rental Auto fields in the Transportation section of the form. Then you'll set a custom calculation for the Personal Auto field.

Specifying a predefined calculation

Acrobat lets you assign common mathematical operations to numeric fields—including addition, multiplication, averaging, and finding maximum and minimum values.

1 Use the zoom-in tool (🔍) to magnify the Transportation section of the form.

2 Select the form tool (▦), and drag to draw a box inside the first cell under Total at the right of the Transportation section.

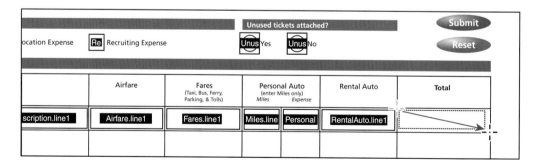

3 Enter **Total.line1** for the name, and for Type, choose Text.

A field must be formatted as a number in order to perform calculations for the field. Now you'll format the Total field as a number.

4 Click the Format tab. For Category, select Number. For Decimal Places, choose 2. For Currency Symbol, choose Dollar.

5 Click the Calculate tab, and select Value Is the <operation> of the Following Fields.

6 Choose sum (+) from the pop-up menu, and click Pick.

7 In the Select a Field dialog box, select Airfare.line1 in the scroll list and click Add (Windows) or Pick (Mac OS).

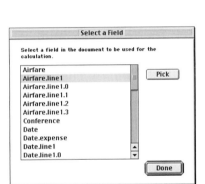
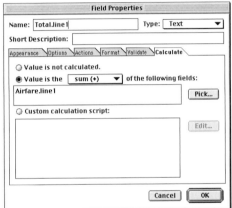

8 Repeat step 7 three times, adding Fares.line1, PersonalAuto.line1, and RentalAuto.line1 to the calculation list.

Values used for calculation must be formatted as numbers in the same way that you formatted the Total field. The Fares.line1, PersonalAuto.line1, and RentalAuto.line1 fields have been preformatted as numbers.

9 Click Close (Windows) or Done (Mac OS).

The Airfare.line1, Fares.line1, PersonalAuto.line1, and RentalAuto.line1 fields appear in the message box next to the Pick button. If you made a mistake in adding fields, you can select the value in the message box and delete it, or you can click Pick to add more fields.

10 Click OK to close the Field Properties dialog box.

11 Select the hand tool ($\mathcal{t}$). The Total field should now contain the value $85.00 (from the 85.00 in the Fares field). Because the other numeric fields are still empty, they do not affect the value in the Total field.

12 Now enter **250** in the first cell under Airfare, and press Tab, Enter, or Return to update the Total field.

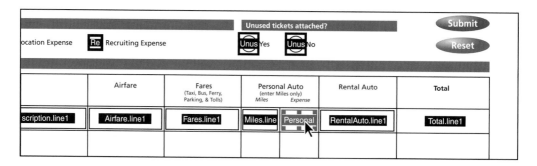

	Airfare	Fares (Taxi, Bus, Ferry, Parking, & Tolls)	Personal Auto (enter Miles only) Miles Expense	Rental Auto	Total
	250.00	85.00			$335.00

Specifying a custom calculation

Now you'll specify a custom JavaScript calculation for the Personal Auto column to calculate the personal transportation expense (number of miles driven multiplied by the expense per mile).

The Miles and Expense fields have been preformatted as numbers. You'll open the Field Properties dialog box for the Expense field and apply the custom calculation option to the field.

1 Select the form tool ($\boxed{\vdots}$), and double-click the PersonalAuto.line1 field under Personal Auto.

	Airfare	Fares (Taxi, Bus, Ferry, Parking, & Tolls)	Personal Auto (enter Miles only) Miles Expense	Rental Auto	Total
scription.line1	Airfare.line1	Fares.line1	Miles.line Personal	RentalAuto.line1	Total.line1

2 Click the Calculate tab. Select Custom Calculation Script, and then click Edit.

To create a custom calculation, you write instructions in JavaScript to tell Adobe Acrobat what operations to perform. You'll enter JavaScript code to multiply the number of miles driven by 32 cents (the allowable expense per mile for personal auto usage).

3 Enter the JavaScript code exactly as it appears below, including a line break after the first semicolon:

**var a = this.getField("Miles.line1");
event.value = a.value * .32;**

For more information on writing in JavaScript, refer to JavaScript documentation.

4 Click OK. Then click OK again.

Now you'll enter values to test the calculating operations.

5 Click the Actual Size button (□). Select the hand tool, and click in the first Miles cell under Personal Auto.

6 Enter **100** and press Enter or Return.

	Airfare	Fares (Taxi, Bus, Ferry, Parking, & Tolls)	Personal Auto (enter Miles only) Miles	Expense	Rental Auto	Total
	250.00	85.00	100	32.00		$335.00

The mileage value appears in the Miles column, and the value 32.00 (100 times .32) appears as the Personal Auto expense.

However, notice that the Total field still displays $335.00, the total excluding the Personal Auto expense. In the next section, you'll fix the calculation order so that the Total field takes the Personal Auto expense into account.

Setting the calculation order

The Total field displays the wrong value because Acrobat is performing the two assigned calculations in the incorrect order. In other words, Acrobat is calculating first the Total, and then the Personal Auto expense. You'll reverse this calculation order so that the Total field displays the correct value.

By default, the calculation order follows the tab order of the fields. For more information on tab order, see "Exploring on your own" on page 235.

1 Choose Tools > Forms > Set Field Calculation Order.

2 Select PersonalAuto.line1, and click Up to move the field to the top of the Calculated Fields list. Then click OK.

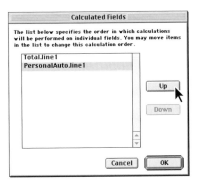

3 In the form, delete 100 from the Miles field under Personal Auto. Then enter **200** for Miles, and press Enter or Return.

The Total field now shows the correct sum, taking into account the Personal Auto calculation.

4 Choose File > Save to save the Expense1.pdf file.

Creating a Reset Form field

You can specify a Reset Form action to clear the data that has already been entered in a form. You might reset a form to clear a mistake, or to clear the form for another user to fill in.

You'll add the Reset Form action as a button field that clears the form when clicked by the user. For this part of the lesson, you'll turn off the snap-to-grid behavior. To learn more about creating buttons for PDF documents, see Lesson 10, "Designing Online Documents."

1 Choose View > Snap to Grid to turn off the snap-to-grid behavior.

2 Select the form tool (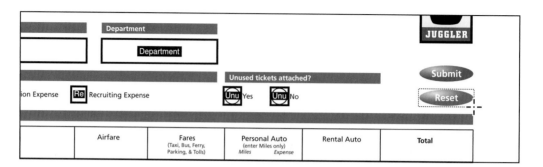), and drag a box around the Reset graphic at the top right of the form.

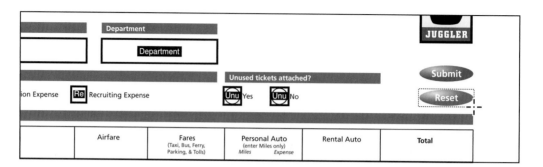

3 For Name, enter **Reset**, and for Type, choose Button.

4 Click the Appearance tab. Deselect Border Color and Background Color, and for Style, choose Solid.

5 Click the Options tab. For Highlight, choose None, and for Layout, choose Text Only.

6 Click the Actions tab. Select Mouse Up to create an action that occurs when the mouse button is released while the pointer is on the Reset button. Then click Add.

The Add an Action dialog box appears, letting you specify the action that will occur after the button is clicked.

7 For Type, choose Reset Form. Click Select Fields.

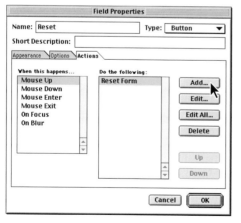
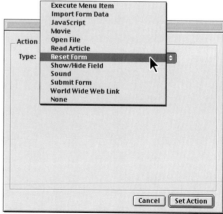

8 In the Field Selection dialog box, select All Fields, and click OK. Click Set Action, and then click OK to add the Reset button to the form.

9 Select the hand tool ($\langle^{\text{th}}\rangle$), and click the Reset button to test it.

The fields in the form are cleared.

10 Choose File > Close to close the file. Click Yes (Windows) or Save (Mac OS) to save your changes.

Submitting forms over the Web

PDF forms can be used for submitting and collecting information over the Web. For this process to work, you must have a Common Gateway Interface (CGI) application on the Web server to collect and route the data to a database. The field names in the forms must also match those set in the CGI application. Any existing CGI application that collects data from forms (in HTML or FDF format) can be used to collect data from PDF forms.

Keep in mind that CGI scripts must be built outside of Acrobat and require some knowledge of computer programming. CGI applications are usually set up by a Web server administrator. For information on creating and managing a form database, see the FDF (Forms Data Format) Toolkit. If you do not have the FDF Toolkit, contact the Adobe Developer Association, or check the Adobe Web site at www.adobe.com.

On the Web or on a network server, you can publish Adobe PDF forms with fields that change dynamically, depending on the data that's input. If an employe filling out a health-insurance form indicates that he or she has children, for example, the form generates new fields on the fly for gathering information about dependents.

For more information, see "Using templates to generate forms dynamically" in the Acrobat 5.0 online Help.

Filling out form fields

Now you can experiment with filling out the fields that you have just created and resetting the form. (Because you haven't set up a CGI application on a Web server, you won't be able to submit the form data.) When you are finished experimenting with the form, choose File > Close to close the file without Adobe saving it.

Using the Fields palette

If you need to modify an existing form that contains form fields, the Fields palette provides a useful overview of all the form fields in a document. It also offers an easy way to lock fields to protect them against accidental changes while you are developing a form. In this section, you'll use the Fields palette to change the properties of a series of related fields.

1 Choose File > Open, and open the Expfinal.pdf file in the Lesson08 folder.

2 Choose Window > Fields.

The Fields palette appears in the document pane as a floating window. To make it easier to work in the form, you'll dock the Fields palette in the navigation pane.

3 If needed, click the Show/Hide Navigation Pane button (▦) to open the navigation pane.

4 Drag the tab of the floating Fields palette into the navigation pane.

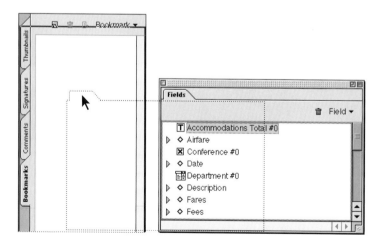

5 Close the floating palette that contains the Tags palette.

6 Click the Fields tab to bring the palette to the front.

Notice that each type of form field has a particular icon. In Windows, you can select the hand tool, and click on a form field in the Expense1.pdf document. As you click on the form field, the corresponding form field in the Fields palette is highlighted.

As with other palettes, the form field markers can be expanded and collapsed. Form fields with related names are grouped under a marker.

7 Select the forms tool ( ), and double-click a marker in the Fields palette to highlight the corresponding field in the form.

This allows you to quickly navigate to fields when you are editing a form, for example.

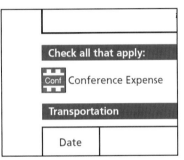

Now you'll use the Fields palette to change the name of the Total field in the Transportation section of the form.

8 Use the zoom-in tool ( ) to magnify the Transportation section of the form.

9 Expand the Total form field marker in the navigation pane to show the entire list of related markers.

You'll change the name of these form fields.

10 Select the Total form field marker, and right-click (Windows) or Control-click (Mac OS). In the context menu, select Rename Field.

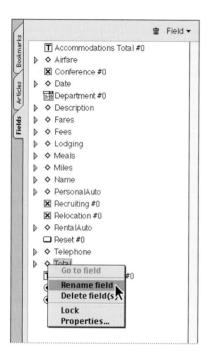

11 Enter the new field name in the form field marker text box. (We renamed the field Expenses.)

Notice that you can also lock form fields using this context menu.

12 Click in a blank area of the navigation pane.

In Windows, the form field marker automatically moves. (Markers are listed in alphabetical order.) In Mac OS, renamed fields are placed at the bottom of the palette. The name of the form field marker is changed, and the names of the subordinate fields are changed correspondingly, as are the names of the form fields on the form itself.

You can change the names of any form fields in the same way.

13 Select the hand tool.

14 Close the file without saving it.

In this lesson, you have learned how to create, maintain, and use PDF forms. Now you can use your new skills to get your existing and future forms online. Work with your Web administrator to collect the data from those forms and keep your databases up to date.

Exploring on your own

You can determine the order in which a user tabs through form fields on a single page. The default tab order is the order in which the form fields were created. You can set the tab order of the Expense Report form so that users tab through fields from left to right, and top to bottom.

1 Choose File > Open, and open the Expensel.pdf file in the Lesson08 folder.

2 Select the form tool ( ).

3 Choose Tools > Forms > Fields > Set Tab Order.

The form fields display numbers indicating the current tab order.

4 To reorder the tabs, click the form fields in the order that they should be numbered. Start with the Name field, and proceed by rows from left to right.

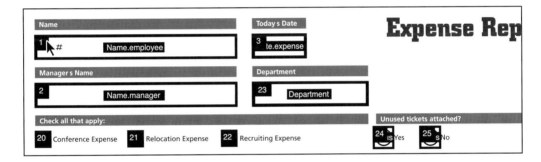

5 Click outside a form field, or select another tool to exit Set Tab Order.

6 Close the file without saving it when you are finished.

Review questions

1 What is the difference between a check box and a radio button?

2 When will a user be able to submit a form over the Web?

3 Which fields will populate in a form if you use the Import > Form Data command?

4 What is a combo box?

5 How do you copy a form field by dragging?

6 How do you restrict entries in text or combo box fields?

7 How do you perform mathematical calculations on two or more numeric fields?

Review answers

1 You can select multiple check boxes, whereas you can select only one radio button in a series.

2 Users can submit a form over the Web after a CGI (Common Gateway Interface) application is set up on a Web server to handle the form data.

3 When you import data from a form data file, the fields that share names in common with the imported data fields will be populated. The signature data for a signature field is not imported.

4 A combo box consists of a pop-up list of items from which users can choose only one item.

5 To copy a form field, select the form tool and make sure that all form fields are deselected. Hold down Ctrl (Windows) or Option (Mac OS) and drag the desired field to create and move a copy of the field.

6 To restrict entries in text or combo box fields and ensure that users enter appropriate data in the form fields, you use validation properties.

7 You perform calculations within text or combo box fields by either applying predefined operations, or by creating custom operations using the JavaScript programming language.

Lesson 9

9 Creating Adobe PDF from Web Pages

Acrobat lets you create editable and searchable PDF files by converting Web pages to Adobe PDF files. You can use the resulting PDF files for a variety of archival, presentation, and distribution needs.

In this lesson, you'll learn how to do the following:

- Convert a Web page to Adobe PDF using Web Capture.

- Download and convert Weblinks from a PDF version of a Web page.

- Build a PDF file of favorite Web pages.

- Update or refresh your PDF version of a Web site.

This lesson will take about 35 minutes to complete.

Create a Lesson09 folder on your desktop, in which to save your converted Web pages.

Note: *Windows users need to unlock the lesson files before using them. For information, see "Copying the Classroom in a Book files" on page 3.*

Converting Web pages to Adobe PDF

You can use Acrobat to download or "capture" pages from the World Wide Web and convert them to Adobe PDF. You can define a page layout, set display options for fonts and other visual elements, and create bookmarks for Web pages that you convert to PDF.

Because captured Web pages are in Adobe PDF, you can easily save, distribute, and print them for shared or future use and review. Acrobat gives you the power to convert remote, minimally formatted files into local, fully formatted PDF documents that you can access at any time.

Web Capture is especially useful for people who make presentations that include Web pages and those who travel a lot. If you need to include a Web site in a presentation, for example, you can convert the Web site to a PDF file so that you have no concern about Web access during your presentation. If you have downloaded all the linked pages, links will behave in the same way as though you were on the actual Web site. Similarly, if you travel extensively, you can create one PDF file containing all of your most visited Web sites. Whenever you have convenient Web access, you can refresh all pages on the site in one simple action. Regardless of the quality or cost of the Web access in your remote location, you can browse your updated PDF versions of the Web sites at your leisure.

Configuring your Internet or proxy settings

Before you use Web Capture, you must configure your Internet or proxy settings for access to the World Wide Web.

1 Start Acrobat.

2 Choose Edit > Preferences > Internet Settings.

3 Do one of the following:

• In Windows, click the Connections tab in the Internet Properties dialog box, and provide the necessary information for your setup. Your system administrator or ISP will give you the information you need.

• In Mac OS, select Use an HTTP Proxy Server, and then enter your proxy URL (if necessary) and port number in the text boxes.

In Windows, if you do not configure your Internet settings using the Internet Settings preferences, Internet Explorer must be installed and the Internet Properties dialog box configured to allow access to the World Wide Web. (In an enterprise environment, you are likely to have to configure your proxy server.) Once Internet Explorer has been installed and configured, you may use any browser as your default browser. If your version of Internet Explorer does not have an Internet Properties dialog box, you must upgrade to a current version of Internet Explorer (available from the Microsoft Web site).

4 Click OK to exit the dialog box.

Setting options for converting Web pages

You set options for capturing Web pages before you download the pages. Here, you'll set options for the structure and appearance of your captured pages.

1 Choose File > Open Web Page.

2 Click Conversion Settings.

3 In the Conversion Settings dialog box, click the General tab.

4 Under Content-Type Specific Settings, select HTML and click Settings.

Note: *If you have difficulty in Mac OS, choose Help > Adobe Online and check for recent upgrades. Alternatively, reinstall Acrobat 5.0 using the custom installation (rather than the standard installation), and install both Acrobat 5.0 and the Asian language fonts. You will be prompted to restart your computer when the installation is complete.*

5 Click the Layout tab and look at the options available.

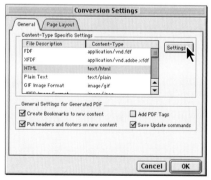
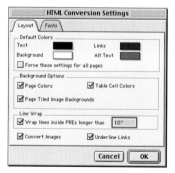

Conversion Settings dialog box   *Layout options for HTML conversion*

You can select colors for text, page backgrounds, links, and Alt text (the text that replaces an image on a Web page when the image is unavailable). You can also select background display options. For this lesson, you'll leave these options unchanged and proceed to selecting font options.

6 Click the Fonts tab.

7 Under Font for Body Text, do one of the following:

• In Windows, click Choose Font. In the Choose Font dialog box, choose a sans serif font from the Font list. (We chose Helvetica.) Choose 12 from the Size list, and then click OK.

• In Mac OS, choose a font and font size from the pop-up menus. (We chose Helvetica, 12 point.)

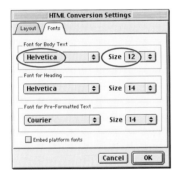

8 Under Font for Headings, do one of the following:

• In Windows, click Choose Font. In the Choose Font dialog box, choose a thick sans serif font from the Font list. (We chose Arial Black.) Choose 14 from the Size list, and then click OK.

• In Mac OS, choose a font and font size from the pop-up menus. (We chose Arial Black, 14 point.)

9 Click OK to accept the HTML conversion settings.

10 On the General tab, under General Settings for Generated PDF, select the following options:

• Create Bookmarks to New Content to create a tagged bookmark for each downloaded Web page, using the page's HTML title tag as the bookmark name. Tagged bookmarks help you organize and navigate your captured pages.

- Add PDF Tags to store a structure in the PDF file that corresponds to the HTML structure of the original Web pages.

- Put Headers and Footers on New Pages (Windows) or Put Headers and Footers on New Content (Mac OS) to place a header with the Web page's title and a footer with the page's URL, page number in the downloaded set, and the date and time of download.

- Save Refresh Commands (Windows) or Save Update Commands (Mac OS) to save a list of all URLs in the PDF file for the purpose of refreshing pages.

11 Click the Page Layout tab.

In Windows, a sample page with the current settings applied appears in the dialog box. You can choose from standard page sizes in the Page Size pop-up menu, or you can define a custom page size. You can also define margins and choose page orientation.

12 Under Margins, enter **0.5** for Left and Right, Top and Bottom.

13 Click OK to accept the settings and return to the Open Web Page dialog box.

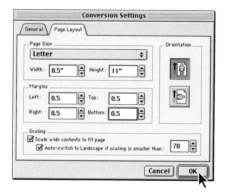

After you have some experience converting Web pages to Adobe PDF, you can experiment with the conversion settings to customize the look and feel of your converted Web pages.

Downloading Web pages in Acrobat

You can download Web pages by specifying a URL in Acrobat, by opening a Weblink in a PDF document you already have open, and by dragging and dropping a Weblink or HTML file to an Acrobat window or Acrobat icon. The Web pages are converted to PDF and open in the Acrobat work area.

Note the following when downloading Web pages in Acrobat:

• Acrobat can download HTML pages, JPEG and GIF graphics (including the last frame of animated GIFs), text files, and image maps.

• HTML pages can include tables, links, frames, background colors, text colors, and forms. Cascading stylesheets are supported. HTML links are turned into Weblinks, and HTML forms are turned into PDF forms.

Note: Acrobat downloads the default/index.html frame only once. Other pages may not open in a frame.

• JavaScript is partially supported at this time; Java applets in HTML pages are not supported.

• To convert Japanese Web pages to PDF on a Roman (Western) system in Windows, you must have chosen to install the Asian language support files at initial installation. (Also, it is preferable to select a Japanese encoding from the HTML conversion settings.) The conversion of Web pages to PDF is not supported for other Asian languages.

About pages on Web sites

Keep in mind that a Web site can have more than one level of pages. The opening page is the top level of the site, and any links on that page go to other pages at a second level. Links on second-level pages go to pages at a third level, and so on. In addition, links may go to external sites (for example, a link at a Web site on tourism may connect to a Web site for a travel agency). Most Web sites can be represented as a tree diagram that becomes broader as you move down the levels.

Important: You need to be aware of the number and complexity of pages you may encounter when downloading more than one level of a Web site at a time. It is possible to select a complex site that will take a very long time to download. Use the Get Entire Site option with great caution. In addition, downloading pages over a modem connection will usually take much longer than downloading them over a high-speed connection.

—From the Acrobat 5.0 online Help.

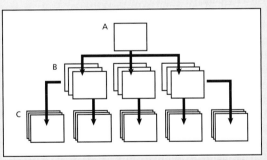

Web site tree diagram. A First level, B. Second level, C. Third level

Creating an Adobe PDF file from a Web page

Now you'll enter a URL in the Open Web Page dialog box and capture some Web pages.

Note: *If you are working from within a company network, you may encounter a firewall that limits your access to external Web pages from Acrobat. For instructions on configuring your system to bypass a company firewall, consult your network administrator.*

1 If the Open Web Page dialog box is not open, choose File > Open Web Page.

2 For URL, enter the address of the Web site you'd like to capture. (We used the NASA Mars Global Surveyor site at http://www.jpl.nasa.gov/mgs/overvu/overview.html.)

You control the number of captured pages by specifying the levels of site hierarchy you wish to capture, starting from your entered URL. For example, the top level consists of the page corresponding to the specified URL; the second level consists of pages linked from the top-level page, and so on.

3 Select Levels, and enter **2** to retrieve two levels of pages in the Web site.

4 Select Only Get Pages Under Same Path to capture only pages that are subordinate to the URL you entered.

5 Select Stay On Same Server to download only pages on the same server as the URL you entered.

6 Click Download. The Download Status dialog box displays the status of the download in progress. When downloading and conversion are complete, the captured Web site appears in the Acrobat document window, with bookmarks in the Bookmarks palette. Tagged bookmark icons differ from the icons for regular bookmarks.

If any linked material is not downloadable you will get an error message. Click OK to close any alert box related to missing material.

Specifying URL to be downloaded   *Error messages indicating missing files*

Note: *In Windows, if you're downloading more than one level of pages, the Download Status dialog box moves to the background after the first level is downloaded. The globe in the Open Web Page button in the toolbar continues spinning to show that pages are being downloaded. Choose Tools > Web Capture > Bring Status Dialogs to Foreground to see the dialog box again. (In Mac OS, the Download Status dialog box stays in the foreground.)*

The captured Web site is navigable and editable just like any other PDF document. Acrobat formats the pages to reflect your page-layout conversion settings, as well as the look of the original Web site. Some of the longer Web pages may be spread across multiple PDF pages to preserve the integrity of the page content.

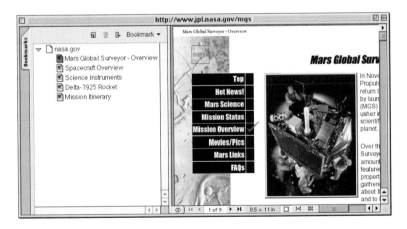

Now you'll use the Bookmarks palette to navigate to another captured page.

7 Select the hand tool (), and click a bookmark in the Bookmarks palette.

The page corresponding to the bookmark appears in the document pane.

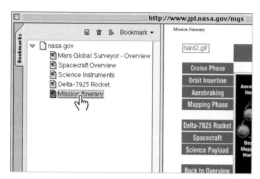
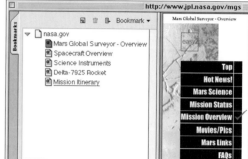

Clicking a tagged bookmark . . .   *. . . links to the corresponding page.*

Downloading and converting links in a converted Web page

When you click a Weblink in the Adobe PDF version of the Web page that links to an unconverted page, Acrobat downloads and converts that page to Adobe PDF. In order to convert linked pages to Adobe PDF, you must set Web Capture preferences to open Weblinks in Acrobat (the default setting) rather than in your default browser.

1 Choose Edit > Preferences > Web Capture.

2 For Open Weblinks, choose In Acrobat. Then click OK.

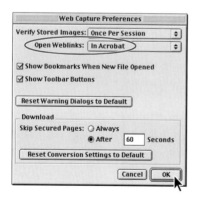

3 Navigate through the captured Web site until you find a Weblink to an unconverted page (we used the link to the Mars Science page), and click the link. (The pointer changes to a pointing finger with a plus sign when positioned over a Weblink.)

Note: If the Specify Weblink Behavior dialog box appears, make sure that Open Weblink in Acrobat is selected, and click OK.

The Download Status dialog box again displays the status of the download. When download and conversion are complete, the linked page appears in the Acrobat window. A bookmark for the page is added to the Bookmarks list.

4 Choose File > Save As, rename the file **Web1.pdf**, and save it in the Lesson09 folder.

Deleting converted Web pages

Because you downloaded and converted two levels of the Web site in the previous section, you have more converted Web pages than you really want to keep. You'll delete an unwanted page.

1 In the Bookmarks palette, click the bookmark Delta-7925 Rocket to view the related page.

This is the page you'll delete.

2 Right-click (Windows) or Control-click (Mac OS) the bookmark, and choose Delete Page(s) from the context menu. Click OK in the alert box.

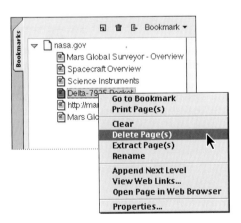

Note: If you click Delete (Windows) or Clear (Mac OS) in this context menu, you delete the bookmark only.

Updating converted Web pages

Because you selected the Save Refresh Commands option when you first converted the Web pages to Adobe PDF, you can refresh or update all pages from one or multiple sites from one Acrobat dialog box.

You can refresh Web pages in a PDF document to retrieve the most up-to-date version from the Web site. Whenever you use the Refresh command, you download the entire Web site or link again and build a new PDF file. Any pages where components have changed—for example, text, Weblinks, embedded filenames, and formatting—are listed as bookmarks in the Bookmarks pane under the New and Changed Pages bookmark. Any new pages that have been added to the site are also downloaded.

Note: The Refresh command may not update converted Web pages that contain forms data. In this case, you will get an error message identifying the pages.

1 With an internet connection open, choose Tools > Web Capture > Refresh Pages.

2 Select Create Bookmarks for New and Changed Pages.

You specify whether Acrobat looks only for text changes or all changes, including text, images, Weblinks, embedded files, etc. (We used Compare All Page Components to Detect Changed Pages.)

3 Click Edit Refresh Commands List.

This window displays the URLs of all the Web sites that have been converted to Adobe PDF in this file. You can deselect any URLs for pages that you don't want to refresh.

Select the URLs for pages you want to refresh.

4 Click OK to accept the default selection, and click Refresh to update your converted PDF pages.

5 Choose File > Save. Notice that this is a new file. If you want to keep the Web1.pdf file for archival purposes, save this file under a different name.

Earlier in the lesson, you deleted a page from the PDF file of the converted Web site. Notice that the page you deleted in the earlier version is present in the refreshed file. Any reorganization or deletion of pages in the PDF file is lost when you refresh.

Building an Adobe PDF file of favorite Web pages

Earlier in the lesson you created a PDF file containing Web pages on the Mars Global Surveyor and its mission. In addition to surfing this site, suppose you also like to check the Adobe home page.

In this section, you'll start to build an Adobe PDF file of your favorite Web pages by appending the Adobe home page to the Mars Global Surveyor file that you have already created.

1 With the Web1.pdf file open, choose Tools > Web Capture > Append Web Page.

2 In the Append Web Page dialog box, enter the URL for your favorite Web site. (We used www.adobe.com.)

3 For Levels, select 1. Select the Only Get Pages Under Same Path option and the Stay On Same Server option.

4 Click Download.

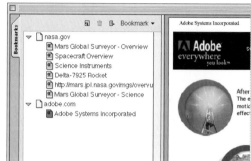

Acrobat appends a PDF version of the Adobe home page to the Mars Global Surveyor pages. You can download any linked pages on this site as described in "Downloading and converting links in a converted Web page" on page 248.

You can repeat this process to build up a file of your favorite Web sites that you can keep on your system, share with friends, and refresh at your convenience.

Exploring on your own (Windows)

Earlier in the lesson you created a PDF file that contains several converted Web pages related to the Mars Global Surveyor and its mission. You can easily and quickly add unrelated pages to this file by dragging and dropping links into the PDF file.

To start building your customized PDF file of Web pages, you'll add a page from the Adobe Web site.

1 If needed, open the Web1.pdf in the Lesson09 folder.

2 In your browser, go to the Adobe home page (www.adobe.com). Resize the browser window so that the Acrobat window is visible beneath.

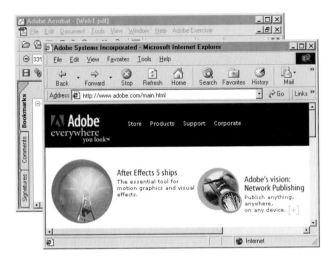

3 Browse the Adobe home page to find a link. (We used the Free e-mail newsletters link under Adobe announces.)

4 Drag the link from the Adobe home page onto the Acrobat window. Release the mouse button when the cursor icon changes to a link icon.

The Web page represented by the link is converted to PDF and appended to the end of your Mars Global Surveyor file.

5 Close the browser window.

6 Choose File > Save to save the file if you wish.

Review questions

1 How do you control the number of Web pages captured by Acrobat?

2 How do you convert destinations of Weblinks to PDF automatically?

3 How do you update your PDF file to show the latest version of the captured Web site?

Review answers

1 You can control the number of captured Web pages by specifying the following options:

• The Levels option lets you specify how many levels in the site hierarchy you want to capture.

• The Only Get Pages Under Same Path option lets you download only pages that are subordinate to the specified URL.

• The Stay On Same Server option lets you download only pages that are stored on the same server as the specified URL.

2 To convert the destination of a Weblink to PDF, first choose Edit > Preferences > Web Capture, and choose In Acrobat for the Open Weblinks option. Then click the Weblink in the PDF file to convert the link's destination to PDF.

3 With an internet connection open, choose Tools > Web Capture > Refresh Pages to build a new PDF file using the same URLs and links. Select the Create Bookmarks for New and Changed Pages option if you want Acrobat to create bookmarks for pages that have been modified or added to the Web site since you last converted the Web site and its links. You also specify whether Acrobat looks only for text changes or for all changes. (You must have selected the Save Refresh Commands (Windows) or Save Update Commands (Mac OS) option in the Conversion Settings dialog box to save a list of all URLs in the PDF file for the purpose of refreshing pages.)

Lesson 10

10 | Designing Online Documents

You can greatly improve the usability of online documents by using a page size customized for on-screen viewing, adding buttons and links to help your users navigate through the documents, setting an uncluttered opening view, and chunking the content for easy readability.

In this lesson, you'll review successful online designs and learn how to do the following:

- Choose a page size for an online document.

- Add buttons and links to help the user navigate through the document.

- Add a link to a Web site.

- Change the formatting and color of text in a document.

- Set an opening view that gives the user an uncluttered screen.

This lesson will take about 45 minutes to complete.

If needed, remove the previous lesson folder from your hard drive, and copy the Lesson10 folder onto it.

Note: *Windows users need to unlock the lesson files before using them. For information, see "Copying the Classroom in a Book files" on page 3.*

About this lesson

Ideally, online documents should be designed to fit the screen or area of the screen on which they are to be displayed, information should be chunked into screen-sized pages, and pages should have consistent and well-placed navigation aids to help the user work through the documents. In this lesson, you'll review the online version of the Adobe Illustrator user guide from Lesson 5 and an award-winning online product overview created to introduce members of the medical profession to new technology. Then you'll work on an online version of a prototype Acrobat user guide, using the tools and techniques you've learned in earlier lessons to convert a simple document into a sophisticated online presentation. You'll also review some of the guidelines for preparing eBooks for the new generation of eBook reading devices.

Looking at design elements in online documents

When you are deciding on your document layout, you should consider how the document will be used. Will it be used in conjunction with other software or on-screen displays, as is the Adobe Illustrator user guide? Or will it be a standalone document like the online product overview, *Continuous Renal Replacement Therapy: Putting It All Together*. Will your document be viewed on a traditional computer monitor or on the newer eBook reading devices? Are your users sophisticated computer users or are they likely to be new to computer systems? These factors and more affect your design decisions.

Looking at the online Adobe Illustrator user guide

In Lesson 5, "Putting Documents Online," you looked at an online version of the Illustrator user guide. This user guide uses a tall and narrow page size to allow the user to view the user guide next to an open Adobe Illustrator application window. This format was chosen to let users conveniently look up reference information without closing their illustration window. Take a few minutes to review the features that made this online document easier to use than its electronic print-on-demand equivalent.

1 Start Acrobat.

2 Choose File > Open, select Online.pdf in the Lessons/Lesson10 folder, and click Open.

The first page has a high-level list of topics, each of which is linked to the appropriate page in the document.

3 With the hand tool selected (✋), click on the List of topics link to see a breakdown of the list of topics.

If you use an authoring program such as Adobe FrameMaker or Microsoft Word, you can create a hyperlinked table of contents automatically when you create your PDF document. (See your authoring program user guide for further information.) If your authoring software doesn't create hyperlinks automatically, you can manually link your table of contents using the Acrobat links tool, as described in "Creating a welcome page" on page 268.

4 Click Viewing and Setting Up Documents, and then click Using Rulers in the list of subtopics. If needed, click the Fit in Window button (▣) to view the entire page.

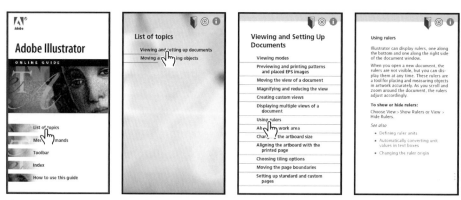

The tall, narrow page size complements the Illustrator work area.

Pages in the online guide are designed so that each topic has its own page. Hot links appear as red text. Again, if your authoring program doesn't allow you to set up cross references automatically, you can add them using the Acrobat link tool. Later in this lesson you'll create links, and you'll change the color of link text using the touchup text tool.

Take a few moments to explore the links and buttons used in this document and to see how topics are "chunked" to fit on a page. You'll see that both the writing and the design are tailored to enhance on-screen usability. The graphics on the buttons are explained in the How To Use This Guide section, and buttons are placed consistently on each page. Users are never more than a click away from the index, the main contents list on the first page of the user guide, or the related topics (parent topics) list.

Note: *For space reasons, not all the files for the online guide are included in the Lessons folder. As a result, some links may not work.*

This Illustrator user guide opens with all the Acrobat screen controls visible, and the How to Use This Guide section instructs users to use the Acrobat Next Page/Previous Page buttons for paging through the document.

5 When you are finished, close the file without saving it.

Looking at an online product overview

Now you'll look at a product overview that was prepared using Adobe FrameMaker and Adobe Acrobat and distributed as a series of linked PDF files on a CD-ROM. This award-winning product overview was created by Larry Prado for Gambro® Inc.

You'll see that this document has all the features that make an online document easy to use and navigate. It has an introductory page that gives users a clear starting point. It has a high-level table of contents, and each of the links on the high-level table of contents (main menu) takes the user to a more detailed table of contents (section menu) for each of the major subject areas (sections). Finally, well-designed buttons are placed consistently throughout the document to help the user navigate through the information. Headings and graphics are also placed consistently on pages to orient the user, especially if a link takes them to another section.

Note: This example of an online document was created using FrameMaker 5.5 and Acrobat 4.0. The design principles are equally applicable to later versions of these software programs, however. Cross references were created in FrameMaker as automatically generated hypertext links, which convert directly to PDF links. The blue, underlined text, indicating a link, was created using FrameMaker character tag included in the cross reference format.

1 Choose File > Open, select Start here.pdf in the Medical folder in the Lessons/Lesson10 folder, and click Open.

Notice that the Acrobat toolbars are hidden.

2 Move the pointer over the page. You'll see that the only link on the first page, the welcome page, is a Start button.

3 Click Start.

The main menu has nine topics plus an index. Notice that Acrobat has opened a new file, mainmenu.pdf. Each section of the product review is contained in a separate file to ensure that links open quickly.

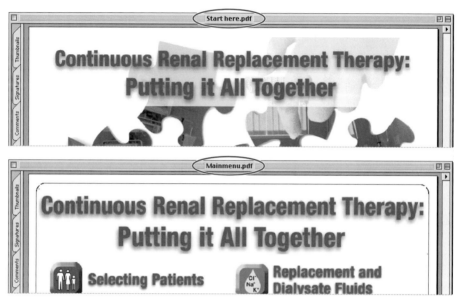

Sections are in separate PDF files so that links open quickly.

4 Move the pointer across the page. As the cursor moves over the section icons, it changes to a pointing finger indicating that all the icons are linked to the relevant sections.

Because of space limitations on the Acrobat 5.0 Classroom in a Book CD, only the Membranes section is included in the Lesson10/Medical folder. If you had the entire product overview CD you would see the following file structure:

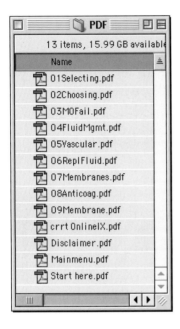

5 Click the Membranes icon to see a high-level list of topics (section menu) in the membrane section.

The first heading on each Section Menu page links to a detailed table of contents for that section. A user who isn't sure that a particular topic on the Section Menu page is going to have the correct information can check the detailed table of contents first. Like the topics on the Section Menu page, the detailed table of contents is also linked to the relevant sections.

6 Click the next page button at the lower right of the screen to advance through the section.

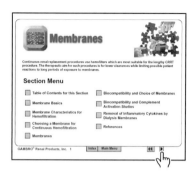 

As you page through the document, notice the following:

• The membrane icon and the Membranes heading are repeated on every page in the section. This repetition of an icon or a heading is a good navigation aid, especially if links in a file are likely to take your user to another file. It is always recommended that you give your user visual clues about where they are in a document, especially in complex help systems or multi-chapter documents.

• The number of buttons changes as you move through the document. On each page, you have just the number of buttons you need—no more and no less. For example, the first page does not have a Previous Page button and the last page does not have a Next Page button.

• The Main Menu button appears on every page in the document except the first page (welcome page) and the Main Menu page. The user is never more than one click away from the Main Menu.

• The Section Menu button appears on every page in the section except the first page of the section, the Section Menu. Again, the user is never more than one click away from the Section Menu.

• An Index Menu button appears on every page except the Main Menu page and the opening page.

7 Click on the Index button to go to the index for the entire document.

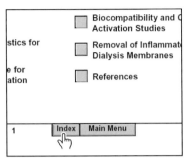 

In addition to the next page, previous page, and previous view navigation buttons at the bottom of the page, at the top of each page in the index are links to each letter of the alphabet for fast navigation through the index.

8 Click the C button. You should be looking at page 3 of the index.

9 Click the membrane considerations entry, the last entry on this page. You should now be looking at page 9 of the Membranes section.

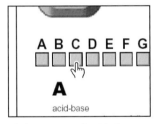 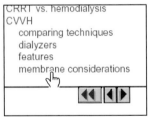 

Click C to go to the C index entries.

Click an index entry to go to that topic.

Result

You'll see that another button, the More button, has been added. The More button indicates that additional related material is on the next page.

Take a few minutes to navigate using only the navigation devices on the document pages. Notice how easy it is to retrace your steps, to move between the index and the related text, and to access the main and section menus.

Note: *For space reasons, not all the files for the product overview are included in the Lessons folder; as a result, some links may not work.*

Setting an opening view

Now you'll look at the Open Options in the Document Properties dialog box. These options determine the opening view for your files.

1 Click the Main Menu button to return to the main menu.

2 Choose File > Document Properties > Open Options to examine the settings for the opening view.

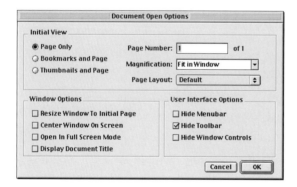

The Initial View is set to Page only. No bookmarks are included—navigation is done using the buttons on the screen, the various tables of contents, or the index. The Magnification is set to Fit in Window to give the user as large a viewing area as possible. The toolbar is hidden to minimize on-screen distractions, but the menu bar and window controls are available for those users who are knowledgeable enough to take advantage of the capabilities of Acrobat.

3 Click Cancel to close the dialog box without making any changes.

Now you'll look at how the icons on this page were linked to the section files.

4 Press the F8 key to show the Acrobat toolbar.

5 Select the link tool (🖑). All links on the page show as black rectangles. Click the icon next to the Selecting Patients text to select the link.

6 Choose Edit > Properties to open the Link Properties dialog box.

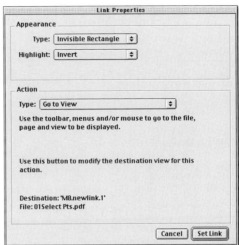

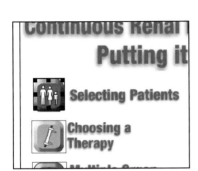

The link action is Go to View; destination and file information is given at the bottom of the dialog box. This information indicates that the links were set using the Adobe FrameMaker hypertext feature. When a FrameMaker or Microsoft Word document is converted to Adobe PDF, links such as these are maintained.

Note: Whenever possible you should set links in your authoring program. Links in Acrobat are useful but they have to be re-created if you need to regenerate the PDF file for any reason.

7 Click Cancel in the Link Properties dialog box to close the dialog box.

8 Select the hand tool ( ).

9 Choose Window > Close All to close all open PDF files.

Creating an online document

Now you'll work on designing a prototype of an online guide for Acrobat, *Acrobat 5.0—A Beginner's Guide*. The files for this portion of the lesson were created in Adobe FrameMaker and then converted to Adobe PDF. Because this is a prototype document designed simply to illustrate a concept, little effort was put into using the features of FrameMaker to generate automatically linked text. Instead, you'll create just enough links using Acrobat to demonstrate how the document will work.

Choosing a page size

Computer monitors generally do not display an 8-1/2 x 11 inch page size in portrait mode well. With this page size, your users would probably be inconvenienced by having to scroll to view material on the lower half of the page. Reducing the page to fit on their screen would make the contents hard or even impossible to read. For these reasons, you should use a landscape page orientation or custom design a page size if your document is to be viewed primarily on-screen.

As with the online product review you looked at in the previous section, you'll use an 8-1/2 x 11 page size with a landscape orientation for this project. You'll use the Acrobat Fit in Window option to ensure that your users always view an entire page rather than a partial page.

Creating a welcome page

We created a title page for *Acrobat 5.0—A Beginner's Guide* for you. This page functions as the welcome page. You'll add two links to this page. You'll add a link to the Adobe Web site, and you'll add a link from this page to the Contents page of the user guide.

You use the link tool to create new links in a document. To specify an activation area for the link, you drag over the desired area with the link tool. Then you set the destination view for the link.

1 Choose File > Open. Select BGTitle.pdf in the BGuide folder in the Lessons/Lesson10 folder, and click Open. Then choose File > Save As, rename the file **BGTitle1.pdf**, and save it in the BGuide folder.

2 Select the link tool ( ) in the toolbar.

The link tool appears as a cross-hair pointer when you move it into the document. When you select the link tool, any existing links in the document appear temporarily as black rectangles.

Place the cross hair above and to the left of the Click Here to Go to the Table of Contents text, and drag to create a marquee that encloses the entire text block.

The Link Properties dialog box appears. This dialog box lets you specify the appearance of the activation area as well as the link action.

3 Under Appearance, choose Invisible Rectangle for Type. For Highlight, choose None.

The following illustration shows the different highlight appearances available in Acrobat.

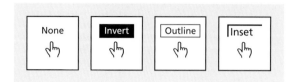

4 Under Action, choose Go to View for Type.

The Go to View option lets you specify a page view as the destination for the link.

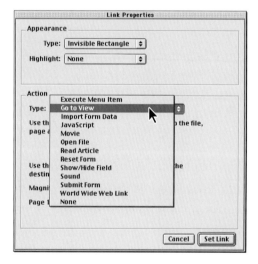

[?] For information on the different types of actions that you can assign to your link, see "About action types" in the Acrobat 5.0 online Help.

5 With the Link Properties dialog box still open, click the Next Page button(▶) to go to page 2, which lists the major topic areas.

6 In the Link Properties dialog box, for Magnification, choose Fit in Window.

Navigate to the link destination. *Set the magnification of the link destination.*

7 Click Set Link. The page view returns to the Title page.

You have now created a link from the Title page to the Contents page.

8 Select the hand tool (), and move the pointer over the Click here to go to the Table of Contents text. The pointing finger indicates the activation area that you have just created.

9 Click the activation area to test your link. You should jump to the Contents page with the same magnification setting.

10 Click the Go to Previous View button (◄) to return to the Title page.

11 Choose File > Save to save the BGTitle1.pdf file.

Later in this lesson, you'll edit an existing link in the Contents. Now though you'll add a link from the title page to the Adobe Web site.

Adding a link to a Web site

On the title page of your document, you'll add a link the Adobe Web site that will take users to the Acrobat home page.

At the bottom of the title page, you'll see text that directs users to check the Adobe Web site for any news or updates to Acrobat 5.0.

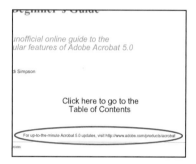

First you'll change the color and style of the text, and then you'll create a link.

Adding color to hyperlinks

Traditionally linked text is colored. If you haven't set the color of any linked text in your authoring program, you can add the color in Acrobat. Because this prototype document uses red as a design color, you'll use the touchup text tool to change the link color from red to blue so users won't get confused.

1 Select the touchup text tool (𝕋) from the toolbar.

2 Click in the text line that contains the URL. A bounding box appears around the text line.

3 Drag through the URL text to select it.

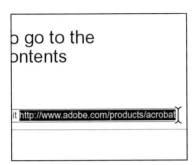

4 Choose Tools > Touchup Text > Text Attributes.

5 Click the text color button, and choose Blue. Click outside the text selection and the Text Attributes dialog box to view the colored text.

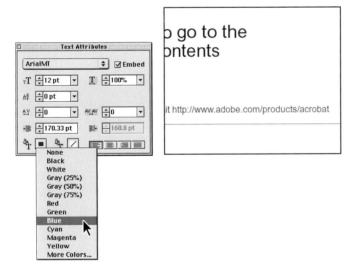

6 Close the Text Attributes dialog box.

7 Choose File > Save, and save BGTitle1.pdf in the BGuide folder.

Underlining links

Now you'll underline the linked text.

1 Select the underline tool (<u>U</u>).

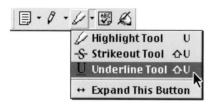

2 Drag to select and underline the URL text.

Now you'll set the color of the underline.

3 With the pointer over the underlined text, right-click (Windows) or Control-click (Mac OS), and choose Properties from the context menu.

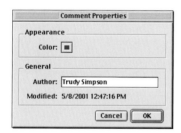

4 In the Comment Properties dialog box, click on the Color box to select the underline color.

5 Choose a blue color, and close the dialog box.

Until you change the comments settings, all subsequent underlining will be done in blue.

6 Choose File > Save, and save BGTitle1.pdf in the BGuide folder.

Creating a link to a Web site

First you'll copy the target URL from the title page.

1 Select the text select tool (T) in the tool bar. Drag to highlight the URL in the text. Then press Ctrl+C (Windows) or Command+C (Mac OS) to copy the text to the Clipboard. Click outside the text to deselect it.

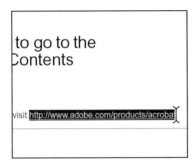

Now you'll assign the action to link to the World Wide Web.

2 Select the link tool (🖉), and drag to create a marquee around the text.

The Link Properties dialog box appears.

3 Under Appearance, choose Invisible Rectangle for Type.

4 For Highlight, choose None.

5 Under Action, choose World Wide Web Link. Click Edit URL for Type.

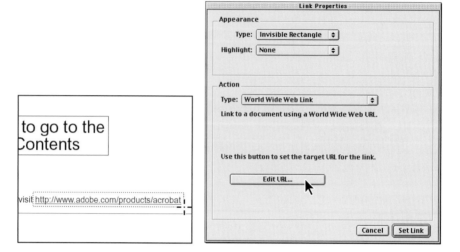

6 Press Ctrl+V (Windows) or Command+V (Mac OS) to paste the URL that you just copied, and click OK.

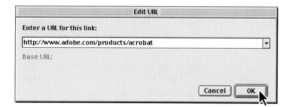

7 Click Set Link.

If you have a Web browser and a connection to the World Wide Web, you can go on to the next step and try out your newly created link.

8 Select the hand tool (), and click on the link. Notice that the hand tool contains a plus sign, indicating that this is a Web link.

Launch your Web browser if prompted to do so.

The link opens the Adobe Systems Web site to the Acrobat home page.

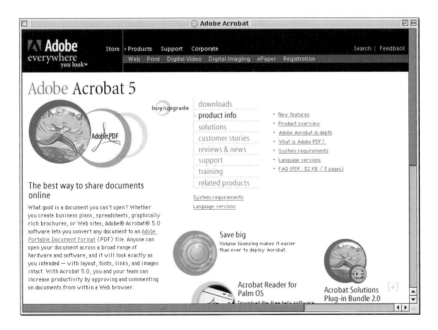

9 Close the browser window when you have finished viewing the Web site, and return to Acrobat.

10 Choose File > Save, and save BGTitle1.pdf in the BGuide folder.

💡 *If you receive a document that contains URLs that are not linked to their respective Web sites, you can quickly make the links active using the Tools > Locate Web Addresses > Create Web Links from URLs in Text command.*

Editing a link type and destination

In this section, you'll edit an existing link on the contents page to correct the link destination. You can edit a link at any time—changing its activation area, appearance, or link action.

1 Using the hand tool, click the Click Here to Go to the Table of Contents text to go to the main table of contents.

2 Click the Signing PDF Files text to follow its link.

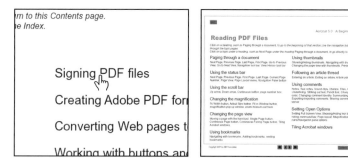

Notice that the link does not take you to the correct section.

***Note:** If new PDF documents do not open in a new window, choose Edit > Preferences > General, and click Options in the left pane. Make sure that the Open Cross-Document Links in Same Window is deselected.*

3 Click the Go to Previous View button (◀) to return to the Contents.

The Go to Previous View button takes you to the previous view, even if it is in a different file.

4 Select the link tool (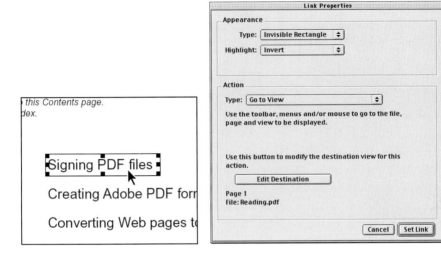), and double-click inside the black rectangle surrounding the Signing PDF Files text to open the Link Properties dialog box.

This dialog box lets you edit the appearance and destination of the selected link.

5 Under Action, for Type, choose Go to View.

6 With the Link Properties dialog box still open, choose File > Open, and select the Signing.pdf file in the Lesson10/BGuide folder, and click Open.

7 Click Edit Destination.

8 For Magnification, choose Fit in Window.

9 Click Set Link.

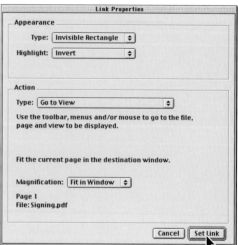

10 Select the hand tool (), and click the Signing PDF Files link to test your revised link. You should now jump to the correct section.

11 Click the Go to Previous View button to return to the Contents.

12 Choose File > Save to save your work.

Now that you've edited the type and destination of a link, you'll change the activation area of a link.

Editing a link activation area

You'll navigate to the section on Reading PDF Files and adjust the activation area of a link on this page.

1 Click the Reading PDF Files link to go to the table of contents for this section.

Notice the topics that are listed under the heading Paging Through a Document.

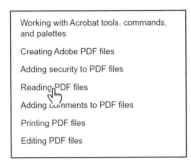

2 Click the Paging Through a Document Link.

All the topics listed under the heading Paging Through a Document are covered on the same page. Rather than create a link for each topic, you'll expand the Next Page link on the contents page to cover all the topics.

3 Click the Go To Previous View button to return to the contents page for Reading PDF Files.

4 Choose File > Save As. Name the file Reading1.pdf and save it in the BGuide folder.

5 Select the link tool ( ), and click once inside the rectangle surrounding the Next Page text.

Handles appear on the edges of the rectangle, indicating that the link is selected.

6 Move the pointer over the bottom right handle so that the double-headed arrow appears. Then drag to stretch the rectangle around the entire text block below the Paging Through a Document heading.

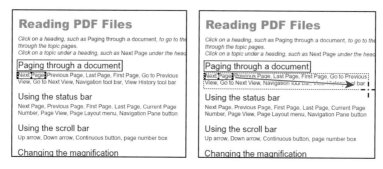

7 Select the hand tool, and move the pointer over the topics. Notice that the activation area includes the entire block of topics.

8 Click the activation area to test your link.

9 Click the Go to Previous View button to return to the contents page for this section.

10 Choose File > Save to save your work.

Adding a destination button

When you set up an online document, you often find that you want to take users to a page other than the first, last, previous, or next page, which are the standard actions available for an Execute Menu Action link. An easy way to do this is to set a page destination using JavaScript.

First, you'll add a button to page 2 in the Reading PDF Files section that links to the first page in the section (the section contents), and then you'll duplicate the button across all the other pages in the section. (Because this is a prototype document, you'll only have to duplicate the button on one content page, page 3.) To set the page action, you'll use JavaScript.

1 Click the Next Page button (▶) to go to page 2 of the Reading1.pdf file.

2 Choose View > Grid.

3 Choose View > Snap to Grid and verify that Snap to Grid is off (Snap to Grid is not checked if it is off).

4 To change the grid spacing, choose Edit > Preferences > General, and choose Layout Grid in the left pane. Select the grid setting that best meet your needs, and click OK. We used 1 inch for the width and height between lines and 4 for the number of divisions.

5 Select the zoom-in tool (🔍) and marquee drag around the navigation buttons at the bottom right of the page.

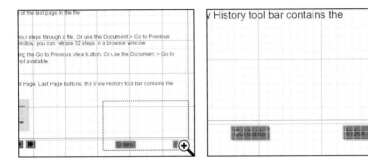

6 Select the form tool (📝) in the toolbar.

7 Between the index and the contents button, drag to draw a rectangle to fill the space.

You should draw the rectangle slightly larger than you want the finished button to appear because Acrobat puts a thin border around buttons.

8 In the Field Properties dialog box, type **Section Contents** in the Name text box, and for Type, choose Button.

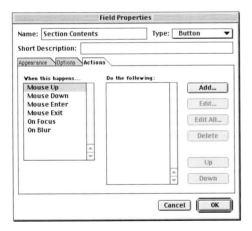

9 Click the Appearance tab in the Field Properties dialog box. Deselect Border Color and Background Color. For Width, choose Thin. For Style, choose Solid. Select Visible for the Form Field Is option.

10 Click the Options tab. For Highlight, choose None, and for Layout, choose Icon only.

11 Click Select Icon, and then click Browse in the Select Appearance dialog box. Locate and select Scontents.pdf in the Lesson10/BGuide/Buttons folder, and click Select.

We created the button image in Adobe Illustrator and converted the Illustrator file to Adobe PDF.

12 Click OK.

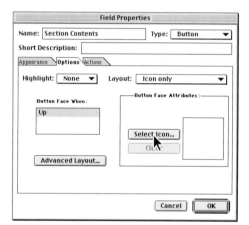

Create button field.

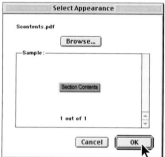

Select a button icon, and click OK.

Now that you've selected the button image, you'll add the JavaScript action that will return users to page 1 of the file.

Using JavaScript to set a button destination

1 Click the Actions tab. Select Mouse Up, and click Add.

2 In the Add an Action dialog box, choose JavaScript for Type. Click Edit to create the JavaScript action.

3 Type in the following code exactly as it appears here:

this.pageNum = 0;

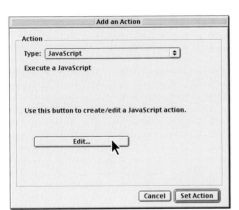

JavaScript considers the first page in a document to have the page number 0. Hence the first page in your document is page 0 in the JavaScript code.

4 Click OK to close the JavaScript Edit dialog box.

5 Click Set Action to return to the Field Properties dialog box.

6 Click OK.

7 Choose View > Grid to hide the grid.

8 Select the hand tool ( ) in the toolbar to view the finished button.

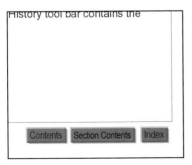

If the button is not sized or positioned correctly, select the forms tool and click once in the button field to select it. The button is selected when handles appear around the edge of the field. Position the pointer over a handle on the corner or edge of the field and drag to resize the it. (You may need to deselect Snap To Grid in the View menu.) To move the field, position the pointer in the field, drag the field to the new location. Release the mouse button when the field is correctly positioned.

9 When the button is correctly sized and positioned, click the Fit in Window button (⬚).

10 With the hand tool selected, test the new button.

11 Click the Go to Previous View button to return to page 2.

Choose File > Save to save the Reading1.pdf file.

You have created a button that will take your users to the first page (the contents page for the Reading PDF Files section) of the document whenever they click on it. Now you'll duplicate this button so it appears on every page except the first page.

Duplicating a button

Now that you have created the Section Contents button, you'll duplicate it so that the users of this document can quickly return to the section contents page from other pages in the section.

1 Select the form tool (▦), and click the Section Contents button to select it.

2 Choose Tools > Forms > Fields > Duplicate.

3 In the Duplicate Field dialog box, select From, and enter from pages **3** to **3**. Click OK. A duplicate button is added to the next page. The button is added in the same location. (If this were a full-length document, you would add the button to all the pages in the section other than the current page and the first page.)

Add button to pages 2 through 3.

Now you'll test the button.

4 Select the hand tool.

5 Click the Next Page button (▶) to go to page 3.

6 Click the Section Contents button.

You automatically return to the Contents page.

7 Choose File > Save to save the Reading1.pdf file.

8 Choose Window > Close All to close all open files.

Duplicating buttons makes it easy to add navigational buttons across multiple pages. Also, Acrobat places the buttons in the same location on all pages. After you have duplicated a button across a series of pages, you can delete the button from any pages on which you don't want it to appear.

You can also cut and paste buttons from one document to another. If you do so, be sure to test that the buttons work in their new location.

Creating an opening view

The opening view of a document should be determined by the design, audience, and purpose of the document. Earlier in this lesson, you looked at the product guide which opened with the Acrobat menu and window controls visible to give knowledgeable users access to Acrobat commands and controls. If you are going to set all the required navigation buttons on the pages of your Beginner's Guide to Acrobat 5.0, you can use the Acrobat Full Screen View to focus the users on the content of the guide rather than on the program running it. However, you might also consider leaving all the Acrobat commands, tools, and window controls visible so the users can relate to them and learn to use them as they search for information.

Throughout this book, you have set various opening views for a number of PDF documents. Take time to look at these opening views again, experiment with different options, and determine which is best for your needs.

Adding an exit or quit button

To distance your online document from the program running it, you can add a button that allows users to quit the file they are reading and close Acrobat from within the document. A Quit button is especially important if you use the Full Screen View.

1 Choose File > Open. Select Signing.pdf in the Lesson10/BGuide folder, and click Open.

2 Select the form tool (🖳) in the toolbar.

3 In the top right of the page, drag to draw a rectangle.

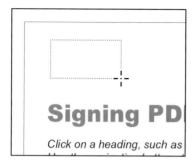

4 In the Field Properties dialog box, type **Quit** in the Name text box, and for Type, choose Button.

5 Click the Appearance tab in the Field Properties dialog box. Deselect Border Color and Background Color. For Width, choose Thin. For Style, choose Solid. Select Visible for the Form Field Is option.

6 Click the Options tab. For Highlight, choose None, and for Layout, choose Icon only.

7 Click Select Icon, and then click Browse in the Select Appearance dialog box. Locate and select Quit.pdf in the Buttons folder in the Lesson10/BGuide folder, and click Select.

8 Click OK.

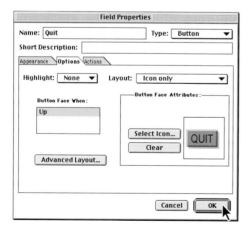

9 Click the Actions tab. Select Mouse Up, and click Add.

10 In the Add an Action dialog box, choose Execute Menu Item for the Type, and click Edit Menu Item.

11 In Windows, choose File > Exit in the Menu Item Selection dialog box. In Mac OS, choose File > Quit from the menu bar. Click OK.

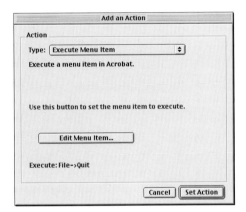

12 Click Set Action, and then click OK.

You now have a button that closes the file and exits Acrobat. You can duplicate this button across all pages in the file, as you did earlier in this lesson, and copy it into other files.

13 Select the hand tool, and click the Quit button.

14 In the alert box, click Yes (Windows) or Save (Mac OS) to save any changes to the open file and exit Acrobat.

Creating eBooks

The growing popularity of eBook reading devices is leading to new guidelines for creating and designing eBooks. Here are some tips if you are designing documents for display on the new generation of eBook readers:

• Use the Distiller eBook job options when creating your Adobe PDF file. (Fonts are embedded as subsets; images are downsampled at 150 dpi; smooth shaded graphics are supported.)

• Prepare a thumbnail of the image of your eBook cover in GIF format. Make the thumbnail image 100 pixels wide and set the resolution at 96 dpi. You can upload this thumbnail of the book cover to the Adobe Content Server for potential buyers to view. (For information on the Adobe Content Server, visit www.adobe.com/products/content-server.)

• Prepare a second thumbnail of an RGB image of your eBook cover in JPEG format. Make the thumbnail image 100 pixels wide, set the resolution at 96 dpi. Attach this thumbnail to the Adobe PDF book file. This is the image that the Acrobat eBook Reader Library will display.

• A 6 x 9 inch page size can be comfortably displayed on a variety of screens and prints well to an 8-1/2 x 11 inch page. A 4 x 3 inch page size is good for screen-focused documents that will not be printed.

• Check out the Adobe WebType™ Collection for typefaces that have been fine-tuned to provide maximum on-screen readability.

• Use larger font sizes than you would for print documents—11 to 13 points are recommended, together with higher leading and tracking.

• Include bookmarks to allow the user to navigate quickly to a specific page or section.

• Renumber pages if necessary so that the page numbers displayed on the document pages match the electronic page numbers.

To see how other people are using third-party tools to customize and enhance Adobe PDF documents, visit www.PDFzone.com.

For more information on designing and creating eBooks, see *How to Create Adobe PDF files for eBooks* and *The Official Adobe Electronic Publishing Guide,* available online at www.amazon.com and www.barnesandnoble.com.

Review questions

1 How do you create a button that needs to appear on multiple pages and that always takes the user to the same page view when clicked?

2 What actions can you assign to a button?

3 Is there a way to display the menu bar or toolbar if they are hidden from view? (Hint: Keyboard shortcuts are listed in the Window menu.)

4 How do you add a graphic to an Acrobat button?

Review answers

1 Create a button field with a JavaScript action that goes to a specified page (this.pageNum = x;). Then duplicate the button field (choose Tools > Forms > Fields > Duplicate) and specify the pages onto which you want to copy the button.

2 You can assign the following actions to a button: Execute Menu Item, Import Form Data, Javascript, Movie, Open File, Read Article, Reset Form, Show/Hide Field, Sound, Submit Form, World Wide Web link, and None.

3 Yes. To show the toolbars, press F8. To show the menu bar, press F9.

4 You must first create the button graphic in a graphics application program and then create a PDF file of the graphic. You use the forms tool to create a button field, and you import the PDF file of the graphic in the Options tab of the Field Properties dialog box.

Lesson 11

11 Enhancing a Multimedia Project

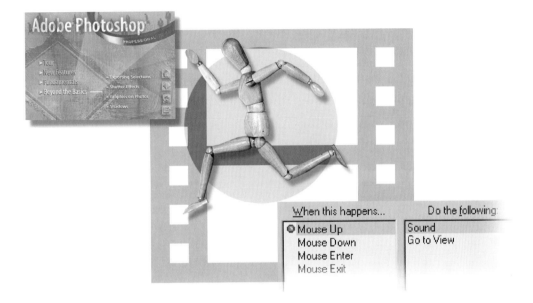

You can enhance your PDF file with buttons, movies, actions, and sounds. Take time to experiment, and have fun.

In this lesson, you'll apply the skills you learned in the previous lessons to create a self-guiding tutorial designed to be used online. You'll do the following:

• Add multiple actions to buttons.

• Combine button and page actions to add sound and graphics.

• Add a movie to a document, and set the movie's appearance and playback properties.

• Edit the playback properties of the movie clip.

This lesson will take about 45 minutes to complete.

If needed, remove the previous lesson folder from your hard drive, and copy the Lesson11 folder onto it.

Note: Windows users need to unlock the lesson files before using them. For information, see "Copying the Classroom in a Book files" on page 3.

Opening the work file

The document that you'll work with in this lesson is part of an actual Adobe Photoshop tutorial shell. It was created to provide users of the Photoshop tutorial with an interface to the instructional movies and step-by-step lessons.

You'll add some of the elements, such as buttons, that existed in the released version of the shell, and also add some other elements just for this lesson.

1 Start Acrobat.

2 Choose File > Open. Select Tutorial.pdf in the Lessons/Lesson11 folder, and click Open. Then choose File > Save As, rename the file **Tutor1.pdf**, and save it in the Lesson11 folder.

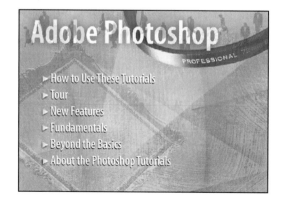

Note: Because there are links to movies in this file, you need to be sure to save this file in the Lesson11 folder to maintain the relative relationship between the PDF file and the movie files. If the relative file relationship is not maintained, you'll receive an error message and the movies will not play when activated by an action or clicked.

3 Take a moment to page through the document using the Next Page button (▶) in the toolbar.

Notice the Home button that appears on every page except the first and last pages. This button has an action assigned to it that always returns the user to the home page, in this case the first page.

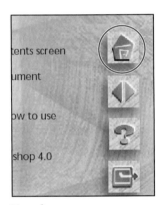

Home button

4 Click the Home button to return to the first page. (If you're on the last page, click the First Page button(◀).)

Adding multiple actions to a button

You can assign more than one action to a button, and also sort the order in which those actions occur after assigning them. You'll add an action that plays a sound as well as returns the user to the home page.

1 Go to page 3 of the tutorial document.

2 Select the form tool (▦), and double-click the Home button.

3 Click the Actions tab in the Field Properties dialog box.

4 Select Mouse Up. Notice that the Execute Menu Item action is already listed in the Do the Following column.

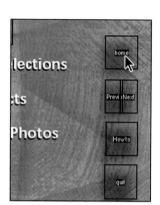

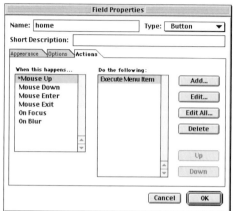

Double-click the button . . .   *. . . to open the Field Properties dialog box.*

Now you'll add a sound file to execute when the user clicks the Home button.

5 Click Add. For Type, choose Sound, and then click the Select Sound button.

6 Locate and select one of the clicking sound files—click1.wav (Windows) or click1.aiff (Mac OS)—in the Lesson11 folder, and click Open. Then click Set Action.

Now two actions are listed in the Do the Following column—Execute Menu Item and Sound. When the button is clicked, the actions will activate in the order listed. But for this tutorial you want the user to hear the sound first, then go to the destination view. So, you'll reorder the actions.

7 Select Sound in the Do the Following column, and click Up. Sound moves up in the list and will now activate before the Execute Menu Item action.

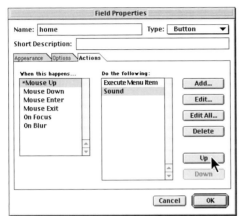

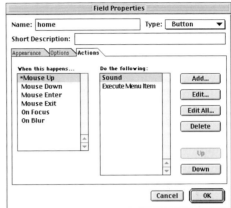

Move Sound up to top of list . . .

. . . to change the order in which the actions are executed.

8 Click OK.

9 Select the hand tool (🖑), and try out the Home button. If you have the correct software and hardware, you will hear the sound as you jump to the first page from page 3 of the tutorial document.

10 Choose File > Save to save the Tutor1.pdf file.

Using actions for special effects

Acrobat allows you to add special effects to PDF documents. You can specify that a particular action will occur when a bookmark, link, or form field is selected, or when a page or form is viewed. For example, you can use links and bookmarks to jump to different locations in a document, but you can also use them to play movies, sound clips, execute commands from a menu, or other actions. Page actions are another way of activating special effects in a PDF document. For example, you can specify a movie or sound clip to play when a page is opened or closed.

Here is a list of the actions available in the Add an Action dialog box:

Execute Menu Item Executes a specified menu command as the action. Click Edit Menu Item, select a menu item, and then click OK.

Import Form Data Brings in form data from another file, and places it in the active form.

JavaScript Runs a specified JavaScript. The Edit button allows you to create or edit a JavaScript action that is activated when the bookmark, link, and so on is selected.

Movie Plays a specified QuickTime or AVI movie. Click Select Movie, and select the movie you want to play when the action is activated. A link to the movie must already be added to the PDF document for you to be able to select it.

Open File Launches and opens a non-PDF file. Click Select File, locate the file, and click Select. If you are distributing a PDF file with a link to a non-PDF file, the reader needs the native application of the non-PDF file to open it successfully.

Read Article Follows an article thread in the active document or in another PDF document. To choose an article from the active document, click Select Article, select an article from the list, and click OK. To choose an article in another PDF document, make the destination file the active document, click Select Article, select an article from the list, and click OK.

Reset Form Clears previously entered data in a form. You can control the fields that are reset with the Select Fields dialog box.

Show/Hide Field Toggles between showing and hiding a field in a PDF document. Click Edit to select a field and whether to show or hide it.

Sound Plays a specified sound file. The sound will be embedded into the PDF document in a cross-platform format that will play in Windows and Mac OS. In Mac OS, you can add QuickTime, System 7 sound files, aiff, Sound Mover (FSSD), and WAV files. In Windows, you can add AIFF and WAV files.

Submit Form Sends the form data to a specified URL.

World Wide Web Link Jumps to a destination on the World Wide Web. You can use http, ftp, and mailto protocols to define your link.

None Specifies no action. This is often used for a bookmark representing a section heading that does not have a specific destination.

---From the Acrobat 5.0 online Help.

Creating special effects with buttons

To add some interesting effects to this tutorial shell, you'll add more buttons. First, you'll see how you can show and hide images and add sound to make buttons come alive.

1 Return to page 3 of the Tutor1.pdf file.

2 Position the pointer over the arrow icon to the left of Shutter Effects. Notice that an image appears, and a sound plays.

3 Move the pointer away from the arrow, and the image disappears. The arrow icon—an Acrobat button—has a Show/Hide Field and Sound actions assigned to it.

Position pointer over arrow to play actions.

Move pointer away to hide image.

In the next section, you'll give the Shadows topic the same combination of multi-media effects.

Creating an image to hide and show

Showing and hiding buttons can be a tricky procedure, but once mastered, it can add interest to any multimedia project. For example, if you don't want to clutter your page with images, but you want to entice your users with previews, you can choose to hide the images until you anticipate a user would actually want to see them.

First, you'll create a button to contain an image of a sun for the Shadows topic.

1 Select the form tool (▤) in the toolbar. Notice the Mouse field that appears on the page. This field contains the image of the white mouse and running figure that appears when the Shutter Effects arrow icon is activated.

2 Drag to draw a rectangle in an open area on the page. The rectangle should be approximately the same size as the Mouse field. After you have formatted this new field, you'll move it on top of the Mouse field so that the image you are adding appears in the same place as the Shutter Effects image when activated.

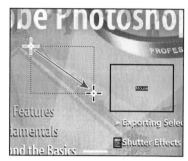

Draw field about same size as Mouse field.

3 In the Field Properties dialog box, type **Sun** in the Name text box. For Type, choose Button.

4 Click the Options tab. For Highlight, choose Push, and for Layout, choose Icon only. For Button Face When, select Up, and then click Select Icon.

5 In the Select Appearance dialog box, click Browse, locate and select Shadow.pdf from the list of files in the Lesson11 folder, and click Select. Then click OK to close the Select Appearance dialog box.

6 Click the Appearance tab in the Field Properties dialog box. Make sure that Border Color and Background Color are not selected. For Style, choose Solid. For Form Field Is, choose Hidden. Click OK.

7 Drag the Sun field on top of the Mouse field.

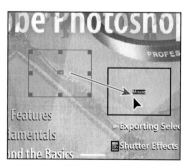

Position Sun field on top of Mouse field.

Adding sound and a Show/Hide Field action

Now you'll add another button field that will show and hide the Sun field, as well as play a sound when you move the pointer over an arrow icon.

1 Using the form tool (📋), drag to draw a rectangle around the arrow icon next to the word "Shadows."

Draw field that covers arrow icon next to
"Shadows."

2 In the Field Properties dialog box, type **Shadows** in the Name text box. For Type, choose Button.

This field will be represented by the image of the arrow on the page, so you don't need to set Button or Appearance options.

3 Click the Actions tab, select Mouse Enter, and click Add.

4 In the Add an Action dialog box, choose Show/Hide Field for Type, and click Edit.

5 Click Show, select Sun in the list, and click OK. Then click Set Action.

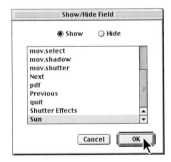

Now you'll add a sound to play.

6 With Mouse Enter still selected in the Field Properties dialog box, click Add.

7 For Type, choose Sound, and click Select Sound. Select Shadow.wav (Windows) or Shadow.aiff (Mac OS) in the Lesson11 folder, and click Open. Then click Set Action.

Now you need to assign an action to hide the Sun image when the pointer is not over the arrow icon.

8 In the Field Properties dialog box, select Mouse Exit and click Add.

9 For Type, choose Show/Hide Field, and click Edit.

10 Click Hide, and then select Sun in the list and click OK. Click Set Action.

11 Click OK to close the Field Properties dialog box.

12 Select the hand tool (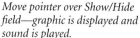) and move the pointer over the arrow icon next to the word Shadows, and then move it away from the arrow to see the effect.

Move pointer over Show/Hide field—graphic is displayed and sound is played.

Move pointer away from Show/Hide field—graphic is hidden.

13 Choose File > Save to save your work.

About movie and sound files

In addition to using movies and sounds with buttons, you can use media clips with your PDF documents in a variety of other ways. The movie tool in Adobe Acrobat lets you add both movies and sounds as playable clips in your document. You can also assign movies and sounds as actions that automatically play when you click a link, bookmark, or open a page.

When you add a media clip to a PDF document using the movie tool, or when you add a movie clip as an action, the clip does not become part of the document—the document simply contains a pointer that references the media file. If you plan to distribute your PDF document, you must be sure to include these sound or movie files along with the document. However, when you add a sound clip as an action, the sound clip does become part of the PDF file; in this case, you do not need to include the original sound file.

Although you can add movie and sound clips to a PDF document, you cannot create or edit the content of these files using Acrobat. You must create your clip using a sound- or video-editing program first, and then save the file in a format that Acrobat can recognize.

For a list of suitable sound and movie formats, see "Integrating media clips into PDFs" in the Acrobat 5.0 online Help.

Adding a movie as a page action

In the previous section, you added a sophisticated button that showed an image and played a sound file when the user moved the cursor over the button. To complete the combination of multimedia effects, you'll add a movie to the Shadows topic page that will play automatically when the page is displayed. You could also add a sound file, just as you did with the button.

1 Click the Shadows link to go to that topic.

First, you'll insert the movie in front of the sun image.

2 Select the movie tool (⊞) in the toolbar, and click *once* in the center of the sun image.

When you click to place a movie, the pixel size of the movie frame determines the activation area for the clip in the document. You can also drag with the movie tool to specify the activation area, but this is not advised because the movie frame must then be stretched or compressed to fit into the specified area. This resizing often results in distortion and poor image quality.

When you're adding a movie using a floating window, however, you can drag freely with the movie tool to set the activation area. The size of a floating window is determined by its Movie Properties setting, not by the activation area you set by dragging.

3 Click Choose to locate and select Shadow2.mov from the list of files in the Lesson11 folder, and click Open.

4 In the Movie Properties dialog box, for Movie Poster, choose Don't Show Poster.

5 Under Player Options, deselect Show Controller. For Mode, choose Play Once Then Stop. Deselect Use Floating Window. Under Border Appearance, for Width, choose Invisible. Click OK.

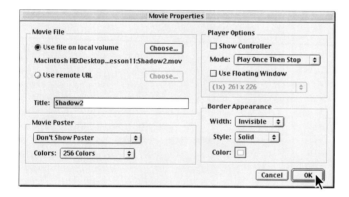

6 Drag the movie field to position it over the sun image. (Be careful not to adjust the size of the field.)

Now you'll set a page action to play the movie when the page is opened.

7 Select the hand tool (🖑), and choose Document > Set Page Action.

8 In the Page Actions dialog box, select Page Open, and click Add.

9 In the Add an Action dialog box, choose Movie for Type, and click Select Movie. For Select Movie, choose Shadow2. For Select Operation, choose Play.

10 Click OK, and then click Set Action.

11 Click OK to close the Page Actions dialog box.

Now you'll try out the page action.

12 Click the Go to Previous View button (◆).

13 Move the pointer over the arrow icon to the left of the word "Shadows" to see the effect you added earlier again.

14 Click the Shadows link. The short movie plays immediately after the page opens.

Movie plays . . .   *. . . when page is opened.*

15 Click the Go to Previous View button to return to page 3.

16 Choose File > Save to save the Tutor1.pdf file.

17 Now click the Shutter Effects link to go to that topic.

Adding a movie with the movie tool

You've added movies with page actions and buttons. Now you'll add a short animation movie to the Shutter Effects page that will play directly inside its activation area in the document. You'll add this movie using the movie tool.

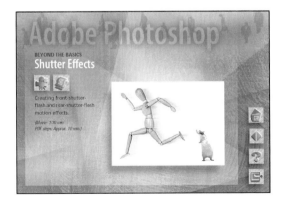

1 If necessary, click the Actual Size button (▯) to return to a 100% view.

Because movies have a set number of pixels and therefore a set size, it's important to keep the magnification at 100% to prevent the added movie clip from being scaled inadvertently.

2 Select the movie tool (⊞) in the toolbar.

3 Click in the center of the graphic to set the location for the movie. Be sure to click, not drag, with the movie tool.

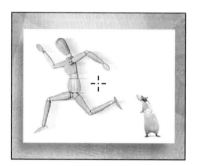

4 For Movie File, select the Use File on Local Volume option, and click Choose. Select Shutter2.mov, located in the Lesson11 folder, and click Open.

The Movie Properties dialog box lets you set the appearance and playback behavior of the movie. You can also specify whether to place a poster (a still image of the first movie frame) in the document.

5 For Title, enter **Shutter.** For Movie Poster, choose Don't Show Poster.

If you're working with a document that has no representative illustration of the movie, choose Put Poster in Document to add a still shot of the first frame to the document page.

6 Under Player Options, select Show Controller. For Mode, choose Repeat Play. Deselect Use Floating Window.

Selecting Show Controller displays the controller bar, which lets the viewer stop, pause, and rewind the movie.

7 Under Border Appearance, choose Invisible for Width. Then click OK.

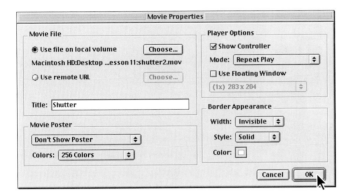

8 Move the pointer over the poster until the arrow (▶) appears, and drag the movie poster to position it inside the illustration area.

You can also resize the poster by dragging the corners of the poster. However, remember that resizing the movie area may result in a distorted image.

9 Select the hand tool (✋), and test the movie you just added. Notice that the pointer changes to a movie frame pointer. Use the buttons and the slider in the controller bar to pause, rewind, and advance through the movie.

You can stop a movie at any time by pressing Esc or clicking outside the movie image.

10 Choose File > Save to save the Tutor1.pdf file.

Editing movie properties

You can change the playback properties of a movie at any time.

1 Select the movie tool (⊟), and double-click within the image to display the Movie Properties dialog box.

2 Under Player Options, deselect Show Controller. For Mode, choose Play Once Then Stop. Then click OK.

3 Select the hand tool, and click in the graphic to see the effect of the modified playback properties.

4 Choose File > Save to save your changes. Then choose File > Close to close the file.

> **Tips for adding movie and sound clips**
>
> *When adding movie and sound clips to PDF documents, consider the following suggestions:*
>
> • *Use a graphic image for the activation area of the link to a movie. You can do this by inserting an image that you capture from the movie. (Capture the image using a movie authoring application.) Once the image is incorporated into the PDF document, draw a rectangle around it to specify the play area for the movie. Then deselect the Display Poster option from the Movie Properties dialog box, and select Use Floating Window.*
>
> • *Use a miniature version of the movie poster to create an icon for the movie. The movie can play in a separate window. You can create the icon by adjusting the movie boundaries to less than full size, and then selecting Display Poster. The Use Floating Window option sets the movie to play in a separate window.*
>
> • *Use a play action other than Play Once Then Stop when a controller bar is used with a clip. Selecting the controller bar stops the clip. Double-clicking inside the movie frame starts it playing again.*
>
> • *Use movie and sound files that are located on your hard disk or on a CD-ROM with your PDF files. This ensures optimum performance. If you link your PDF documents to movie or sound files residing across a network or on the World Wide Web, performance decreases.*
>
> --From the Acrobat 5.0 online Help.

Take some time to experiment with the actions that you can assign to buttons, links, bookmarks, and pages. You may find that actions add a new level of communication possibilities and fun to your PDF documents that you never thought possible.

Exploring on your own

In this lesson, you have added movies and sound to create interesting multimedia effects. Here are a couple of additional projects you can experiment with that will help you create a unique product.

Using the Full Screen View

Many types of presentations may improve when the document takes over the entire screen, and hides the menu bar, toolbar, and other window controls. This is useful for presentations that aren't interactive or that have all the controls and buttons built into the PDF pages.

To learn how to set up a full-screen presentation, you'll use the tutorial shell from this lesson. You'll set it up to work as a full-screen slide show on your computer with pages that turn automatically, as in a stand-alone kiosk display.

1 Choose File > Open to open the Tutor1.pdf file you saved earlier in the Lesson11 folder.

2 Choose File > Document Properties > Open Options.

3 Under Window Options, select Open in Full Screen Mode. For Magnification choose Fit in Window, and for Page Layout, choose Single. Click OK.

The next time the file is opened, the image and a solid background will automatically fill the entire screen.

4 Choose Edit > Preferences > General, and click Full Screen in the left pane.

5 Under Full Screen Navigation, select Advance Every 5 Seconds. Make sure that Escape Key Exits is selected.

Full-screen mode also lets you choose special effects for transitions between pages.

6 For Default Transition, choose Dissolve, and then click OK.

7 Choose File > Save As, and save the file as **Tutor2.pdf** in the Lesson11 folder.

8 Choose File > Close.

9 Choose File > Open and reopen the Tutor2.pdf document.

10 To stop the slide show, press Esc. To stop the slide show and quit Acrobat, click the Quit button on one of the pages, and then click Yes.

Creating button icons

Try creating your own button icons. All button icon files must be saved as PDF files, and each page of a PDF document can be used as an individual button icon.

First, use your favorite drawing or photo-editing application to create an image, or locate an existing image file. Be sure to save the image file in one of the following formats: BMP, JPEG, PCX, PICT (Mac OS only), PNG, or TIFF. Then follow the steps below to import the image, and crop it in Acrobat if necessary.

1 In Acrobat, choose File > Open as Adobe PDF. For File of Type (Windows) or Show (Mac OS), select your image format. Select your image file, and click Open.

The image is converted to PDF and placed in a new document. If you want to use only a portion of the page as the button icon, you need to crop the page. Acrobat's crop tool allows you to adjust page margins by setting specific parameters or by visually setting page boundaries. You cannot undo a crop operation.

2 Select the crop tool (✠) in the tool bar, and drag a rectangle around the button icon on the page.

3 Double-click inside the rectangle to display the Crop Pages dialog box.

4 Use the left, right, top, and bottom increment arrows to adjust the page margins.

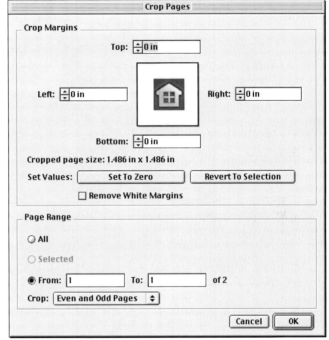

Drag rectangle around button icon.   *Adjust page margins in Crop Pages dialog box.*

5 Click OK to accept the new page margins.

6 Choose File > Save to save the file.

7 If you want, you can add more button icons to your button icon file by importing additional images to the current document, cropping them if necessary, and saving your file.

8 Choose File > Close to close the file.

Now that you have created your own button icons, you can add buttons with these icons to an existing PDF document by following the general instructions in "Adding a destination button" on page 282 in Lesson 10.

Review questions

1 When selected, what does the Hidden option on the Appearance tab of the Field Properties dialog box do?

2 What actions can you assign to a button?

3 To what other types of elements can you assign actions?

4 What happens to the display of a movie when you use the Use Floating Window option in the Movie Properties dialog box?

Review answers

1 The Hidden option on the Appearance tab of the Field Properties dialog box makes the field invisible until another action shows it.

2 You can assign the following actions to a button: Execute Menu Item, Import Form Data, JavaScript, Movie, Open File, Read Article, Reset Form, Show/Hide Field, Sound, Submit Form, World Wide Web Link, and None.

3 Besides buttons, you can assign actions to links, bookmarks, page actions (opening or closing a page), and other types of form fields.

4 The movie plays inside a floating window that appears in front of the document temporarily rather than on the document page.

Lesson 12

12 | Managing Color

Acrobat 5.0 supports the same color engine, the Adobe color engine, as is used in Adobe Photoshop 6.0 and Adobe Illustrator 9.0. Sharing this core color-management technology provides you with a consistent color experience when migrating files between programs. The soft proofing capability of Acrobat lets you save time and money by doing your color proofing on screen. And when you're ready to print a color file from Acrobat, you can specify whether color is managed on the printer or from Acrobat.

In this lesson, you'll do the following:

- Look at how Acrobat handles unmanaged color spaces.

- Set up Acrobat to proof a color image on-screen (soft proofing).

- Preview overprinting.

- Look at host-based and printer-based color printing.

This lesson will take about 30 minutes to complete.

If needed, remove the previous lesson folder from your hard drive, and copy the Lesson12 folder onto it.

Note: *Windows users need to unlock the lesson files before using them. For information, see "Copying the Classroom in a Book files" on page 3.*

In this lesson, you'll learn some basic color management concepts and terminology. You'll learn how Acrobat handles unmanaged color by temporarily assigning ICC profiles based on the settings in the Acrobat Color Preferences dialog box. You'll also learn how to set up your system for on-screen color proofing and previewing overprinting.

Color Management: An Overview

Colors on a monitor are displayed using combinations of red, green, and blue light (called RGB), while printed colors are typically created using a combination of four ink colors—cyan, magenta, yellow, and black (called CMYK). These four inks are called *process colors* because they are the standard inks used in the four-color printing process.

RGB image with red, green, and blue channels

 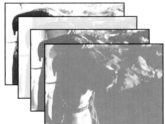

CMYK image with cyan, magenta, yellow, and black channels

Because the RGB and CMYK color models use very different methods to display colors, they each reproduce a different gamut, or range of colors. For example, because RGB uses light to produce color, its gamut includes neon colors, such as those you'd see in a neon sign. In contrast, printing inks excel at reproducing certain colors that can lie outside of the RGB gamut, such as some pastels and pure black.

But not all RGB and CMYK gamuts are alike. Each model of monitor and printer is different, and so each displays a slightly different gamut. For example, one brand of monitor may produce slightly brighter blues than another. The *color space* for a device is defined by the gamut it can reproduce.

RGB model

A large percentage of the visible spectrum can be represented by mixing red, green, and blue (RGB) colored light in various proportions and intensities. Where the colors overlap, they create cyan, magenta, yellow, and white.

Because the RGB colors combine to create white, they are also called additive colors. Adding all colors together creates white—that is, all light is transmitted back to the eye. Additive colors are used for lighting, video, and monitors. Your monitor, for example, creates color by emitting light through red, green, and blue phosphors.

CMYK model

The CMYK model is based on the light-absorbing quality of ink printed on paper. As white light strikes translucent inks, part of the spectrum is absorbed and part is reflected back to your eyes.

In theory, pure cyan (C), magenta (M), and yellow (Y) pigments should combine to absorb all color and produce black. For this reason these colors are called subtractive colors. Because all printing inks contain some impurities, these three inks actually produce a muddy brown and must be combined with black (K) ink to produce a true black. (K is used instead of B to avoid confusion with blue.) Combining these inks to reproduce color is called four-color process printing.

––From Acrobat 5.0 online Help.

Although all color gamuts overlap, they don't match exactly, which is why some colors on your monitor can't be reproduced in print. The colors that can't be reproduced in print are called out-of-gamut colors, because they are outside the spectrum of printable colors. For example, you can create a large percentage of colors in the visible spectrum using programs such as Adobe Photoshop, Adobe Illustrator, and Adobe® InDesign™, but you can reproduce only a subset of those colors on a desktop printer. The printer has a smaller gamut than the application that created the color.

To compensate for these differences and to ensure the closest match between on-screen colors and printed colors, applications use a color management system (CMS). Using a color management engine, the CMS translates colors from the color space of one device into a device-independent color space, such as CIE (Commission Internationale d'Eclairage) LAB. From the device-independent color space, the CMS fits that color information to another device's color space by a process called color mapping, or gamut mapping. The CMS makes any adjustments necessary to represent the color consistently among devices.

A CMS uses three components to map colors across devices:

• A device-independent (or reference) color space.

• ICC profiles that define the color characteristics of particular devices and documents.

• A color management engine that translates colors from one device's color space to another according to a rendering intent, or translation method.

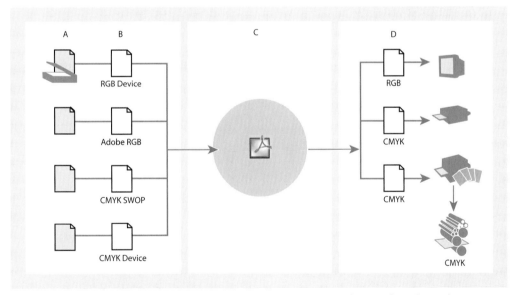

A. *Scanners and software applications create color documents. Users choose document's working colorspace.*
B. *ICC source profiles describe document color spaces.* **C.** *A color management engine uses ICC source profiles to map document colors to a device-independent color space.* **D.** *The color management engine maps document colors from the device-independent color space to output device color spaces using destination profiles.*

About device-independent color space

To successfully compare gamuts and make adjustments, a color management system must use a reference color space—an objective way of defining color. Most CMSs use the CIE LAB color model, which exists independently of any device and is big enough to reproduce any color visible to the human eye. For this reason, CIE LAB is considered *device-independent*.

About ICC profiles

An ICC profile describes the gamut of a device—that is, it describes how a device or standard reproduces color using a cross-platform standard defined by the International Color Consortium (ICC). ICC profiles ensure that images appear correctly in any ICC-compliant applications and on color devices. This is accomplished by embedding the profile information in the source file or assigning the profile in your application.

At a minimum, you must have one *source profile* for the device (scanner or digital camera, for example) or standard (SWOP or Adobe RGB, for example) used to create the color, plus one *destination profile* for the device (monitor or contract proofing, for example) or standard (SWOP or TOYO, for example) that you will use to reproduce the color.

About color management engines

Sometimes called the color matching module (CMM), the color management engine interprets ICC profiles. Acting as a translator, the color management engine converts the out-of-gamut colors from the source device to the range of colors that can be produced by the destination device. The color management engine may be included with the CMS or may be a separate part of the operating system.

Translating to a gamut—particularly a smaller gamut—usually involves a compromise, so multiple translation methods are available. For example, a color translation method that preserves correct relationships among colors in a photograph will usually alter the colors in a logo. Color management engines provide a choice of translation methods, known as *rendering intents*, so that you can apply a method appropriate to the intended use of a color graphic. Examples of common rendering intents include *Perceptual (Images)* for preserving color relationships the way the eye does, *Saturation (Graphics)* for preserving vivid colors at the expense of color accuracy, *Relative* and *Absolute Colorimetric* for preserving color accuracy at the expense of color relationships.

Color management resources

You can find additional information on color management on the Web and in print. Here are a few resources:

• On the Adobe Web site (www.adobe.com), search for **color management** or go directly to http://www.adobe.com/support/techguides/color/.

• On the Apple Web site (www.apple.com), search for **ColorSync**.

• On the LinoColor Web site (www.linocolor.com), open the *Color Manager Manual*.

• On the Agfa Web site (www.agfa.com), search for the publication *The Secrets of Color Management*.

• On the ColorBlind Web site (www.color.com), click Color Resources.

• At your local library or bookstore, look for **GATF Practical Guide to Color Management,** by Richard Adams and Joshua Weisberg (May 1998); ISBN 0883622025.

Do you need color management?

You might not even need color management if your production process is tightly controlled for one medium only. (For example, you or your prepress service provider may prefer to tailor CMYK images and specify color values for a known set of printing conditions.) Whenever you have more variables in your production process though, you can probably benefit from color management.

Color management is recommended if you anticipate reusing color graphics for print and online media, using various kinds of devices within a single medium (such as different printing presses), if you manage multiple workstations, or if you plan to print to different domestic and international presses. If you decide to use color management, consult with your production partners—such as graphic artists and prepress service providers—to ensure that all aspects of your color management workflow integrate seamlessly with theirs.

—From the Acrobat 5.0 online Help.

Managing color in Acrobat

Colors must often be converted when they are displayed to a monitor or sent to a printer. This will always be the case when the color models do not match (for example, when CMYK color is displayed on an RGB monitor). The techniques used for these conversions are based on the use of ICC profiles. For managed colors, this conversion is well understood because managed colors are described using ICC profiles.

A PDF file may also contain unmanaged color spaces, however—that is, color spaces that have no ICC profile attached. In this case, Acrobat temporarily assigns an ICC profile to determine how the images will be converted for display. You control the choice of profiles to use for the conversions of unmanaged colors from the Color Management Preferences dialog box.

In this section, you'll set the Acrobat Color Management preferences for a file that contains an unmanaged color space and view the results using the Acrobat soft proofing feature.

1 Start Acrobat.

2 Choose Edit >Preferences > General, and click Color Management in the left pane.

Take a few minutes to examine the Working Spaces options and the Conversion Options for different values of Settings that you can select from the pop-up menu. Notice that if you change any of the values for the Working Spaces or Conversion Options in the Color Management Preferences dialog box, the value for Settings changes to Custom. The predefined Settings files cannot be edited.

For this lesson, you'll assume that the image is eventually going to be reproduced on a four-color press.

3 From the Settings pop-up menu, choose U.S. Prepress Defaults.

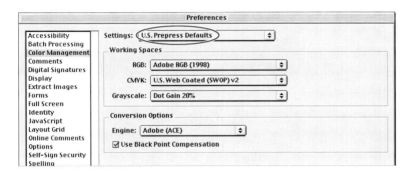

The U.S. Prepress Defaults option manages color for content that will be output under common press conditions in the U.S.

4 Click OK.

Note: These settings apply to any unmanaged color spaces in a PDF file, and they remain in effect until you change them again. Acrobat uses the profiles and color management system information from the color settings file to convert only unmanaged color for display and printing.

Now you'll open a PDF file that doesn't have an embedded ICC profile.

5 Choose File > Open, select SeaDog.pdf in the Lessons/Lesson12 folder, and click Open. Then choose File > Save As, rename the file SeaDog1.pdf, and save it in the Lesson12 folder.

6 Click the Fit in Window button (▣).

In a traditional workflow, you would print a copy of a color document to see how colors look on a specific printer or output device. With soft proofing, Acrobat lets you see on-screen a close representation of what your job will look like when printed. The Acrobat soft proofing capability is similar to (but not as extensive as) that of Photoshop.

Setting up color proofing

Now you'll set up the on-screen proofing parameters for color proofing with Acrobat so you can see an on-screen representation of how the PDF file will look when printed.

Note: *If you plan on using soft proofing extensively, you should characterize or calibrate your monitor for better results using a utility such as Adobe Gamma (or ColorSync) and set up a controlled viewing environment.*

Creating a viewing environment

Your work environment influences how you see color on your monitor and on printed output. For best results, control the colors and light in your work environment by doing the following:

• *View your documents in an environment that provides a consistent light level and color temperature. For example, the color characteristics of sunlight change throughout the day and alter the way colors appear on your screen, so keep shades closed or work in a windowless room. To eliminate the blue-green cast from fluorescent lighting, consider installing D50 (5000 degree Kelvin) lighting. Ideally, view printed documents using a D50 light box.*

• *View your document in a room with neutral-colored walls and ceiling. A room's color can affect the perception of both monitor color and printed color. The best color for a viewing room is polychromatic gray. Also, the color of your clothing reflecting off the glass of your monitor may affect the appearance of colors on-screen.*

• *Match the light intensity in the room or light box to the light intensity of your monitor. View continuous-tone art, printed output, and images on-screen under the same intensity of light.*

• *Remove colorful background patterns on your monitor desktop. Busy or bright patterns surrounding a document interfere with accurate color perception. Set your desktop to display neutral grays only.*
View document proofs in the real world under which your audience will see the final piece. For example, you might want to see how a housewares catalog looks under the incandescent light bulbs used in homes, or view an office furniture catalog under the fluorescent lighting used in offices. However, always make final color judgments under the lighting conditions specified by the legal requirements for contract proofs in your country.

1 Choose View > Proof Colors. Make sure that Proof Colors is checked. The Proof Colors option toggles the proof display on and off.

2 Choose View > Proof Setup > Simulate Paper White.

Original

Simulate White Paper

Selecting Simulate Paper White simulates the color and tone of the printed document. If the paper or medium on the output device is darker, for example, the image on the monitor will appear muted, presenting a more realistic rendition of the actual print image.

Simulate Ink Black simulates the lightness or density of black on the printed piece, which is usually lighter than on a monitor.

The final step is to choose a profile for the printer or output device you plan to print the photograph on.

3 Choose View > Proof Setup > Custom.

4 In the Proof Setup dialog box, choose a press profile to emulate. The default for the current setting is U.S. Web Coated (SWOP) v2.

5 Click OK. The colors in the on-screen image change to more closely represent the output that you'd get from your printer.

Notice that the on-screen color looks muted.

6 Choose View > Proof Colors to turn color proofing off.

Notice that the colors become less muted. Acrobat is no longer simulating the print output.

Proof Colors off.   *Proof Colors on.*

7 Choose View > Proof Colors to turn color proofing on again.

Now you'll select a different output device.

8 Choose View > Proof Setup > Custom. In the Proofing Space menu, choose a different output device, such as a color desktop printer. Click OK.

9 Notice the change in on-screen color again.

Take time to experiment with the Proof Setup settings. If you have a color printer, check the quality of the soft proof of a file against a printed copy. When you are finished, close the file without saving it.

Previewing overprinting

If you create files in graphics programs such as Adobe Illustrator, your final file may well contain one or more spot colors on a CMYK image. When such a file is printed, the spot colors can be overprinted as spot colors or they can be separated into their process color equivalents (CMYK).

Acrobat 5.0 supports overprint preview both in display and printing, with spot colors being converted to process colors for the preview. The overprint preview results obtained via these two paths are essentially the same, although there may be some differences depending on the complexity of the source file. The overprint preview obtained using the Apply Overprint Preview option in the Advanced Print Settings dialog box is generally more accurate than that obtained with the Overprint Preview command in the View menu.

In this section, you'll use Acrobat 5.0 to preview some simple overprinting.

1 In Acrobat, choose File > Open. Select Overprint.pdf in the Lessons/Lesson12 folder, and click Open.

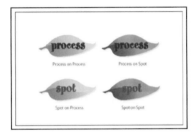

This PDF file was generated from an Illustrator 9.0 file. The two leaves on the left (green) were painted by applying a gradient blend to a process (CMYK) color. The two leaves on the right (brown) were painted by applying a gradient blend to a spot color. In each case, the leaf shadow was painted using a process color. A word was then overlaid on each leaf. In each case, the word *process* was created using process colors and the word *spot* was created using spot colors.

You'll save this file as a PostScript file and then re-create the PDF file first with the Apply Overprint Preview on and then with Apply Overprint Preview off.

Note: If you have a LanguageLevel 3 PostScript printer attached to your system, you can print the original pdf file directly to your printer with the Apply Overprint option selected in the Advanced Print dialog box.

Using the Apply Overprint Preview option

1 Choose File > Save As.

2 In the Save As dialog box, choose PostScript file for Save as Type (Windows) or Format (Mac OS). Click Settings.

First you'll create the PostScript file with the Overprint Preview off.

3 Under File Format Options, select LanguageLevel 3 from the PostScript pop-up menu. Verify that Apply Overprint Preview is not selected. Click OK.

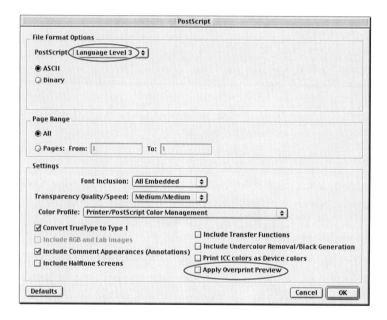

4 Change the filename to OvrPrOFF.ps, and click Save to save the PostScript file to the desktop.

Now you'll create the PostScript file with the Overprint Preview on.

5 Choose File > Save As.

6 In the Save As dialog box, choose PostScript file for Save as Type. Click Settings.

7 For File Format Options, select LanguageLevel 3 for PostScript. Select the Apply Overprint Preview option. Click OK

8 Change the filename to OvrPrON.ps, and click Save to save the PostScript file to the desktop.

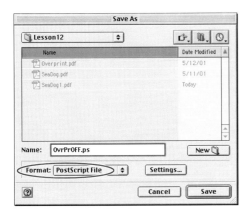

You now have two PostScript files, one printed with Overprint Preview off and one printed with Overprint Preview on.

9 Close the Overprint.pdf file without saving any changes.

Now you'll re-create the PDF file from each of these PostScript files to view the effect of the OverPrint Preview option.

10 Choose Tools > Distiller.

11 In Distiller, choose File > Open, and select the file OvrPrOFF.ps. Click Open, and click Save to save the resulting PDF file to the desktop with the same file name. Repeat this process for the file OvrPrON.ps. The Distiller window opens and you can see the progress of each conversion. (Alternatively you can drag the PostScript files in turn into the Distiller window.)

12 Choose File > Exit or Quit to close Distiller.

13 In Acrobat, choose File > Open, and select OvrPrON.pdf and OvrPrOFF.pdf (Shift-click to select both files.) Click Open to open both files in the Acrobat window.

14 Choose Window > Tile > Horizontally. Scroll if necessary to view the overprint area.

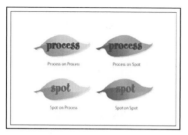
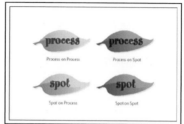

*PDF file created with Overprint
Preview Off.*

*PDF file created with Overprint
Preview On.*

Notice the change in colors when the Overprint Preview option is on. The preview shows the effect of blending the top inks with those below.

15 Choose Window > Close All to close the files without saving them.

Using the OverPrint Preview command

A faster but less precise preview is obtained with the Overprint Preview command.

1 Choose File > Open. Select Overprint.pdf in the Lessons/Lesson12 folder, and click Open.

2 Choose View > OverPrint Preview. Overprint Preview is checked when the preview is on.

Toggle the OverPrint Preview command on and off and observe the difference in the display.

Choose File > Close to close the file without saving it.

Managing color at print time

Printing in Acrobat 5.0 supports a number of options that control color management. Color can be managed either on the printer or on the host (your computer system). Overprinted colors and spot colors are printed using composite colors, and the printing of transparent objects is supported using the same transparency settings as are used in Adobe Illustrator 9.0.

If you work with a color-managed workflow, you should take time to explore the Advanced Print Settings dialog box. Because printing varies with your operating system, this section is divided into a Windows and Mac OS section.

Here's a brief introduction to one component in advanced printing.

In Windows

1 Choose File > Open, select SeaDog.pdf in the Lessons/Lesson12 folder, and click Open. Then choose File > Save As, rename the file SeaDog2.pdf, and save it in the Lesson12 folder.

2 If you have a PostScript printer attached to your system, select it in the Printer Name pop-up menu, or select Acrobat Distiller.

3 Click the Advanced button.

4 To have Acrobat manage color using the color management engine selected in the Acrobat Color Management preferences, choose the appropriate press profile from the Color Profile pop-up menu. (We chose U.S. Web Coated (SWOP) v2.)

Notice that a description of the option appears in the text window at the bottom of the dialog box. You can click in any text box in this dialog box to see a description of the option.

5 Click OK to return to the Print dialog box.

Notice the text at the bottom of the dialog box says that color is managed on the host.

6 Click the Advanced button.

7 To force color management on the printer, choose Printer/PostScript color management in the Color Profile pop-up menu.

8 Click OK to return to the Print dialog box.

Notice that color is now managed on the printer.

9 Click Cancel or OK to close the Print dialog box.

Now you'll look at the options for a non-PostScript printer.

10 Choose File > Print.

11 In the Printer Name pop-up menu, select a non-PostScript printer if you have one.

Notice the text at the bottom of the dialog box says that color is managed on the printer.

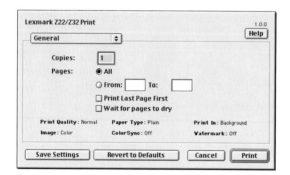

12 Click the Advanced button.

Notice that many of the options, including Color Profile, are grayed out. Some items in the Advanced Print Settings dialog box are available for PostScript printers only.

13 Click Cancel to return to the Print dialog box.

14 Choose File > Close, and close the file without saving it.

For information on the other options in the Advanced Print Settings dialog box, see "Managing color on a printer" in the Acrobat 5.0 online Help.

In Mac OS

1 In the Chooser, select a PostScript printer.

2 In Acrobat, choose File > Open, select SeaDog.pdf in the Lessons/Lesson12 folder, and click Open. Then choose File > Save As, rename the file SeaDog2.pdf, and save it in the Lesson12 folder.

3 Choose File > Print.

4 Select your PostScript printer in the Printer Name pop-up menu or select Create Adobe PDF.

5 Select Acrobat 5.0 in the pop-up menu.

6 Click the Advanced button.

7 To have Acrobat manage color using the color management engine selected in the Acrobat Color Management preferences, choose the appropriate press profile from the Color Profile pop-up menu. (We chose U.S. Web Coated (SWOP) v2.)

8 Color is now managed on the host.

Notice that a description of the option appears in the text window at the bottom of the dialog box. You can click in any text box in this dialog box to see a description of the option.

9 To force color management on the printer, choose Printer/PostScript Color Management in the Color Profile pop-up menu.

10 Click OK to return to the Print dialog box.

Color is now managed on the printer.

11 Click Cancel or OK to close the Print dialog box.

Now you'll look at the options for a non-PostScript printer.

12 In the Chooser, select a non-PostScript printer.

13 In Acrobat, choose File > Print.

14 In the Printer Name pop-up menu, select your non-PostScript printer.

15 Select Acrobat 5.0 in the pop-up menu.

Notice that there is no Advanced button in the print dialog box. The number of options is limited.

16 Click Cancel to return to the Print dialog box.

17 Choose File > Close, and close the file without saving it.

   For information on the other options in the Advanced Print Settings dialog box, see "Managing color on a printer" in the Acrobat 5.0 online Help.

In this lesson you have had a brief introduction to the color management features in Acrobat 5.0 and a quick look at some of the advanced printing features. If you use Acrobat as part of a work flow that includes Photoshop and Illustrator, you should talk to your graphics professionals to ensure that you take full advantage of the shared color management technology.

Review questions

1 What does the color management engine do?

2 What is an ICC profile?

3 How does Acrobat handle unmanaged color?

4 What is the purpose of Simulate Paper White?

Review answers

1 The color management engine translates colors from the color space of one device to another the color space of another device by a process called color mapping.

2 An ICC profile describes how a particular device or standard reproduces color using a cross-platform standard defined by the International Color Consortium (ICC). ICC profiles ensure that images appear correctly in any ICC-compliant applications and on color devices.

3 Acrobat handles unmanaged color by temporarily assigning ICC profiles based on the settings in the Acrobat Color Preferences dialog box. Choose Edit > Preferences, and click Color Management in the left pane to set the Color Management preferences.

4 Selecting Simulate Paper White simulates the color and tone of the printed document. If the paper or medium on the selected output device is darker, for example, the image on the monitor will appear muted, presenting a more realistic rendition of the actual print image.

Lesson 13

13 Distributing Document Collections

Platform independence and small file sizes make Adobe PDF an attractive format in which to distribute your documents on the Web, an intranet, or a CD. You'll put the finishing touches on a collection of documents—including adding a linked Welcome document and indexing the document collection—to finalize them for electronic distribution.

In this lesson, you'll learn how to do the following:

• Examine the issues associated with distributing PDF documents.

• Compare image quality and file size between PDF documents.

• Add links to a *Welcome* document.

• Add document properties information to a PDF document.

• Set an opening view for a collection of documents using the Batch Processing command.

• Index a document collection with Acrobat® Catalog.

• Examine a Web server administrator's checklist.

This lesson will take about 45 minutes to complete.

If needed, remove the previous lesson folder from your hard drive, and copy the Lesson13 folder onto it.

Note: *Windows users need to unlock the lesson files before using them. For information, see "Copying the Classroom in a Book files" on page 3.*

Distributing PDF documents

The ability of PDF to faithfully maintain the formatting of a document while offering smaller file sizes, searchable text, printability, and integration with the most Web browsers, makes it a popular choice for distributing documents on the Web, company intranets, CDs, and via e-mail. Of course you could simply create your PDF documents and send them out to the world without any more effort than printing. With a little extra effort, though, you can make the information in your documents more accessible to your users and thereby make the documents more successful.

Collecting the documents to publish

The first step is to create or collect your PDF documents. In this project, you'll prepare, arrange, stage, and test documents from the Seybold 98 Internet Publishing archives for distribution. You can assume that the contents of the documents you are going to use are complete.

Your documents should be at the point where you would normally print the final copy. If you are going to distribute your documents electronically, however, you must first check a few extra things—image quality, file size, and filenames—to ensure that the documents you distribute have the desired quality, are as efficient as possible, and work across computer platforms.

Checking image quality and file size

Making bitmap images small enough for network distribution or for mass storage on CD volumes generally requires compression—saving images in a way that uses less disk space.

When you create Adobe PDF files using Distiller, the default job options usually provide the optimum balance between compression and quality. In this section, you'll look at two sets of default Distiller job options and the files they produce.

• The eBook job options are recommended for Adobe PDF files that will be read primarily on-screen—on desktop or laptop computers or eBook reading devices, for example. This set of options balances file size against image resolution to produce a relatively small self-contained file.

• The Screen job options are recommended for Adobe PDF files that will be displayed on the World Wide Web or an intranet, or that will be distributed through an e-mail system for on-screen viewing. This set of options uses compression, downsampling, and a relatively low resolution to keep the file as small as possible.

You'll open and view an image that has had no compression applied to it. You'll create two Adobe PDF files from a PostScript version of that image using the eBook and Screen job options of Distiller. And then you'll then compare the image quality and file size of the original file with the compressed files.

1 Start Acrobat.

2 Choose File > Open. Select Image.pdf in the Lessons/Lesson13 folder, and click Open. (If needed, set type of file to open or show to All Files.) Then choose File > Save As, rename the file **Image1.pdf**, and save it in the Lesson13 folder.

3 Click the triangle next to the Magnification pop-up menu in the Viewing toolbar, and choose 400% to zoom in on the image.

Examine the image. No compression was applied to this file when it was converted to Adobe PDF.

Uncompressed Image1.pdf at 100% magnification

At 400% magnification

Choosing a compression setting

Now you'll choose two different compression settings in Distiller and convert the PostScript version of the Image.pdf file to Adobe PDF. You'll use two of the standard Distiller job option settings—eBook and Screen. (For information on customizing the job option settings rather than using the predefined job options, see Lesson 4, "Customizing Adobe PDF Output Quality.")

1 Choose Tools > Distiller.

2 In the Distiller window, choose eBook from the Job Options pop-up menu.

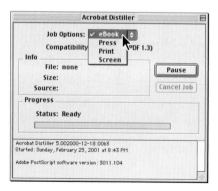

3 In the Distiller window, choose File > Open. Select Image.ps from the Lesson13 folder, and click Open.

4 Name the file **EBkImage.pdf**, and save the file in the Lesson13 folder.

5 Repeat steps 2 through 4, selecting Screen from the Job Options pop-up menu in the Distiller window, and naming the file **ScrImage.pdf**.

6 Reset the Distiller job options to eBook. Exit or quit Distiller.

Distiller always uses the last set of job options defined; it does not automatically revert to the eBook job options.

Comparing the files in Adobe Acrobat

Now you'll compare the image quality and file size of the original file with the two compressed files.

1 In Acrobat, choose File > Open. Select EBkImage.pdf, which you just converted to Adobe PDF and saved in the Lesson13 folder, and click Open.

2 Choose 400% magnification from the Viewing toolbar of the EBkImage.pdf document.

3 Choose File > Open, and select ScrImage.pdf, which you also saved in the Lesson13 folder, and click Open.

4 Choose 400% magnification from the Viewing toolbar of the ScrImage.pdf document.

All three image files should be open and viewed at 400% magnification. If other PDF files are open, close or minimize them.

5 Choose Window > Tile > Vertically to compare the three images. Adjust your viewing area to view the same portion of the image in each file. We viewed the text in the upper right of the monitor screen.

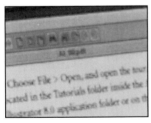
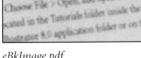

Uncompressed Image1.pdf   eBkImage.pdf   ScrImage.pdf.

As you can see, there is some slight quality degradation in the EBkImage.pdf file, whereas there is a significant degradation in quality in the ScrImage.pdf file. Now open the Lesson13 folder and check the file sizes—Image1.pdf is approximately 730 KB, EBkImage.pdf is approximately 148 KB, and ScrImage.pdf is approximately 52 KB.

Before you close the files, compare the three images at 100% magnification.

When you select the Distiller job options to use when creating Adobe PDF files, you must often balance file size against resolution. The eBook job options clearly create small files with good resolution.

6 If needed, select the hand tool ($\textrm{\tiny{🖑}}$).

7 When you have finished viewing the files, choose Window > Close All.

Checking filenames

When you plan on distributing your files, Adobe recommends that you use filenames consisting of one to eight characters (no spaces) followed by an extension (a period and from one to three characters) of your choice. Use .pdf as the file extension for your PDF documents. Most Web browsers, Web servers, and versions of Microsoft Windows have been configured to associate .pdf files with Adobe Acrobat, Acrobat Reader, or the Web Capture command. If properly configured, these applications will launch the appropriate program when PDF files are encountered.

You can view PDF documents in Web browsers compatible with Netscape Navigator 4.0 (or later) or Internet Explorer 4.0 (or later) on Windows and Internet Explorer 5.0 or later on Mac OS. (Netscape Navigator 6.0 is not compatible with Acrobat's Web browser plug-in and does not support viewing PDF documents in the browser.) The Web browser you use, the Web server, and several other factors determine how your system handles the PDF documents.

For more information on viewing PDF documents in Web browsers, see "Viewing PDF documents on the Web" in the Acrobat 5.0 online Help.

Naming PDF files for cross-platform compatibility

When you name PDF documents and build indexes for cross-platform document collections, the safest approach is to observe MS-DOS® filenaming conventions. Although Acrobat has a sophisticated mapping filter for identifying formats of indexed documents, ambiguities caused when names created for one platform are mapped to usable names on another platform can slow down the searches. There may even be cases where this prevents documents from being located.

Consider the following guidelines when naming PDF files and documents:

• If you are using the Mac OS version of Catalog to build a cross-platform indexed document collection, and if you don't want to change long PDF filenames to MS-DOS filenames, select Make Include/Exclude Folders DOS Compatible in the Catalog Preferences before you build your index. If you check this preference, you must use MS-DOS filenaming conventions for the folder names (8 digits with 3 digit extension); however, you do not have to use these conventions for the names of the files inside the folders.

• If you are using Mac OS with an OS/2® LAN Server, and if you want to be sure that the indexed files are searchable on all PC platforms, either configure LAN Server Macintosh (LSM) to enforce MS-DOS filenaming conventions, or index only FAT volumes. (HPFS volumes may contain unretrievable long filenames.)

• If you are indexing PDF documents with long filenames that will be truncated for Windows use, be consistent in your use of either the Windows or Mac OS version of Catalog to build or update the index.

• If you are creating documents that will be searched only by Macintosh users, do not use deeply nested folders or pathnames longer than 256 characters.

• If you are planning to deliver the document collection and index on an ISO 9660-formatted CD, you should use ISO 9660 filenames. With the Macintosh version of Catalog, check Log Compatibility Warnings in the Logging Preferences to be warned of noncompliant filenames. For more information, see "Naming PDF documents" in the Acrobat 5.0 online Help.

***Important:** Avoid using extended characters, such as accented characters and some non-English characters, in the names of files and folders used for the index or the indexed files. The font used by Catalog does not support character codes 133 through 159.*

Preparing a Welcome document

In many cases, you may want to distribute material in a collection of PDF documents rather than in a single document. When first opening a CD or visiting a Web site, users may have difficulty determining where to start or what's in the document collection. It often helps users if you include a "welcome" PDF page in your collection to point them in the right direction.

On the Web or an intranet, you might want to use an HTML Web page as your Welcome document. The page typically gives an overview of the documents and provides links to specific places in them.

⚲ *On CD volumes, you should also include a ReadMe text file that contains Acrobat Reader installation instructions and any necessary last-minute information about the CD.*

Adding links to a Welcome document

A Welcome document has been provided for you to use with this lesson. The Welcome document includes a table of contents for the Seybold 98 Internet Publishing newsletters. Now you'll open the document and add cross-document links to some of the documents in the Lesson13 folder.

1 In Acrobat, choose File > Open. Select Welcome.pdf in the Lesson13 folder, and click Open. Choose File > Save As, rename the file **Welcome1.pdf**, and save it in the Lesson13 folder.

2 If desired, resize the Welcome1.pdf document.

Now you'll use the link tool to add some cross-document links.

3 Select the link tool (🔗), and drag a link rectangle to enclose "January."

4 For Appearance Type, choose Invisible Rectangle.

5 For Action Type, choose Go to View.

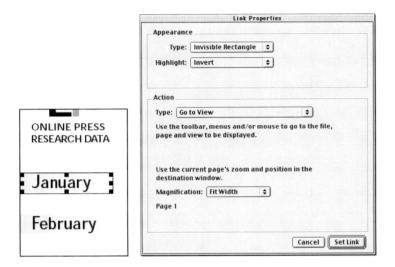

6 With the Link Properties dialog box still open, choose File > Open, select ip0198.pdf in the Seybold folder, located inside the Lesson13 folder, and click Open. The file opens in front of the Welcome1.pdf document.

7 In the Link Properties dialog box, choose a magnification level with which you are comfortable:

• Fixed displays the destination at the magnification level and page position in effect when you create the bookmark or link. Use the zoom-in or zoom-out tool, other buttons on the toolbar, or the scroll bar to adjust the view before accepting this setting.

• Fit View displays the visible portion of the current page as the destination. The magnification level and window size vary with monitor resolution.

• Fit in Window displays the current page in the destination window.

• Fit Width displays the width of the current page in the destination window.

• Fit Height displays the height of the current page in the destination window.

• Fit Visible displays the width of the visible contents of the current page in the destination window.

• Inherit Zoom displays the destination window at the magnification level the readers are using when they click the bookmark or link.

8 Click Set Link. The Welcome1.pdf document appears frontmost on-screen.

9 Using the hand tool (🖑), click the link to test it. Click the Go to Previous View button (◀) to return to the Welcome1.pdf document.

10 Using the link tool (🖗), add a second link by dragging a link rectangle to enclose "April." Then in the Link Properties dialog box do the following:

• For Appearance Type, choose Invisible Rectangle.

• For Action Type, choose Go to View.

• Choose File > Open, select ip0498.pdf in the Seybold Reports folder, located inside the Lesson13 folder, and click Open.

• Accept the same magnification level you chose in step 7.

• Click Set Link.

11 Using the hand tool, click the link to test it. Click the Go to Previous View button to return to the Welcome1.pdf document.

12 Choose File > Save to save the Welcome1.pdf file.

13 Close all of the files except the Welcome1.pdf file. The files must be closed before they can be batch processed, which you'll do later in the lesson.

Adding document properties information to PDF files

The Document Summary dialog box provides users with basic information about a file and another way to index a file in a collection of documents. The Title, Subject, Author, and Keyword fields in the Document Summary dialog box can be completed and edited in Acrobat.

For tips on using the document properties information in document searches, see "Using Document Info fields in a search" on page 377 in Lesson14.

First, take a look at the information loaded in the fields for the Welcome1.pdf document.

1 Choose File > Document Properties > Summary.

By default, the filename Welcome.ai appears in the Title field. Note the Subject, Author, and Keyword fields are empty. The other entries represent file information generated by the PDF creator.

Because many Web search engines use the document properties information fields to search for information and display results in a Search Results list, you should fill in document properties information fields for each document you distribute. Because the filename often is not an adequate description of the document, consider replacing it with the document title. You should fill in the document properties information text boxes for all of your files if you plan to index your document collection with Acrobat Catalog.

In this section, you'll enter document properties information in only the Welcome1.pdf file. In a normal workflow, you would enter document properties information for all files in a document collection.

2 In the Document Summary dialog box, fill in the following text boxes:

• Title. (We entered "Online Press Research Data.")

• Subject. (We entered "Internet Publishing.")

• Author. (For example, enter your name.)

• Keywords. (We entered "Seybold, Internet publishing, Online Press." Be sure to enter a comma and space between each keyword.)

3 Click OK.

4 Save the file and close it.

Now you're ready to set the opening view for each document. In the next section, you'll use a batch processing operation to make sure that all the documents open at the same view and magnification.

Setting an opening view for the document collection

Acrobat allows you to create and execute a series of commands on one document, several documents, or an entire collection of documents in one automated process called batch processing. (In Windows, all the documents must be contained in the same folder.)

First you'll edit a batch processing sequence to set a consistent opening view for the document collection. You could also use this same batch processing sequence to apply security to all your documents.

1 In Acrobat, choose File > Batch Processing > Edit Batch Sequences.

You'll notice that a number of useful batch processing sequences—Opening View, Set Security to No Changes, and Fast Web View, for example—are already defined for you.

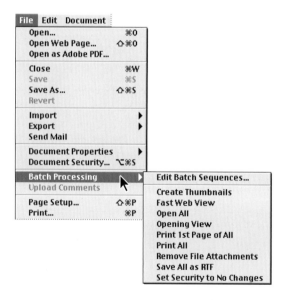

You'll edit the Opening View sequence to customize the opening view for your document collection.

2 In the Batch Sequences dialog box, select Opening View in the right pane, and click Edit Sequence.

Now you'll edit the sequence of commands that will set the opening view for all the documents in our collection.

3 In the Batch Edit Sequence dialog box, click Select Commands.

4 In the right pane of the Edit Sequence dialog box, click the triangle to the left of the Set Open Options command to expand the command. The options listed under the command are all the options you can set using this one batch processing command.

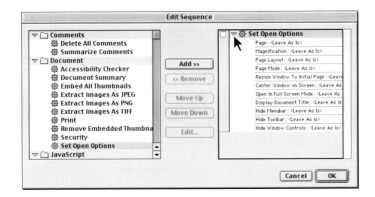

5 Select the Set Open Options command in the *right* pane, and click Edit to change the opening view options for your document collection.

Take a moment to look at all the options you can set in this dialog box. You're going to simply set the documents to open at the first page, with no bookmarks or thumbnails showing, and with a Fit in Window magnification.

6 In the Set Open Options dialog box, select Page Only for Initial View.

7 Under Open Action, deselect Leave As Is, and select Fit in Window from the Magnification pop-up menu. Click OK.

Notice that the values under the Set Open Options command have changed to reflect the new settings.

8 Click OK.

In the Batch Edit Sequence dialog box, you can also define which files the batch processing commands are run on (Run Commands On) and where the processed files are saved (Select Output Location). In both cases we used the default values.

9 Click Output Options.

Notice that the Fast Web View option is selected. The Fast Web View command removes unused objects, consolidates duplicate page backgrounds, and reorders objects in the PDF file format for page-at-a-time downloading. For information on page-at-a-time downloading, see "Optimizing for page-at-a-time downloading" on page 355.

10 Click OK to accept the default values for file naming and the output file format options.

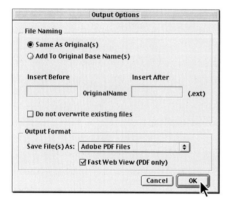

11 Click OK.

12 Make sure the sequence you just defined—Opening View—is highlighted, and click Run Sequence.

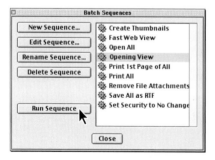

Now you'll select the files for which you want to set the opening view.

13 Click OK, and in the Select Files to Process dialog box, select all the files in the Seybold folder. (Shift-click to select multiple files.)

14 Click Select. The progress box tells you when the batch processing is complete. When processing is complete, click OK.

15 Click Close to close the Batch Sequences dialog box.

16 Open one or two files to check that the opening settings are correct.

17 When you are finished, choose Window > Close All to close all open files.

Now that you have added document properties information and set the opening view for all the documents to be the same, you are ready to stage, optimize, and index your documents.

Organizing the staging area

When you have collected all the PDF documents and the Acrobat Reader installer, set up a staging area (that is, a central location or folder) for the collection on a network file server. Then test the document links, bookmarks, actions, forms, and indexes on the server to make sure everything works the way you planned.

In a normal workflow, you should set up a staging area on a network file server if possible. Also, always keep a copy of the original files in another location. Backup copies can save you from having to re-create files if they are mistakenly deleted or corrupted. For this lesson, you'll use the Lesson13 folder as the staging area.

Organizing the documents in folders lends an intuitive organization and leads readers to the information they need. Before you publish your document collection, consider asking others to use the folder structure in your staging area to make sure your organization is easy to understand.

Optimizing for page-at-a-time downloading

If you're distributing your documents on the Web or via a company intranet, you should use the Fast Web View command to remove unused objects, consolidate duplicate page backgrounds, and reorder objects in the PDF file format for *page-at-a-time downloading*. With page-at-a-time downloading (also called byte-serving), the Web server sends only the requested page of information to the user, not the entire PDF document. This is especially important with large documents, which can take a long time to download from the server.

You can apply the Fast Web View command to all your documents using the predefined Fast Web View command in the Batch Processing submenu. (The Fast Web View option is also selected by default in the Output Options in the Batch Edit Sequence dialog box.)

🔃 For more information on the Fast Web View command, see "Optimizing or creating Fast Web View files" in the Acrobat 5.0 online Help.

The files are almost ready for distribution.

Indexing your document collection

If your document collection will be distributed on a CD, you should index the collection using Acrobat Catalog so that users can search the entire set of documents quickly. If you are distributing your documents over the World Wide Web or a company intranet, you should index them using a Web search engine that supports indexing PDF documents. (An index created by Catalog is not searchable over the World Wide Web or a company intranet.) For a list of Web search engines that support PDF indexing, check the Support Knowledgebase on the Adobe Web site (www.adobe.com).

Now you'll index the documents in the Lesson13 folder.

1 Choose Tools > Catalog.

2 In Mac OS, choose Preferences > General. Make sure that Make Include/Exclude Folders DOS Compatible is deselected, and click OK.

3 Click New Index, and enter a title for the index. (We entered "Online Press.")

The Index Description box provides users with more information about the documents included in the index.

4 Click inside the Index Description box, and enter information about the index you are building. (We entered "Internet publishing newsletters, Seybold 1998.")

5 Under Include These Directories, click Add.

6 Click to select the Lesson13 folder, and then click OK (Windows) or Choose (Mac OS).

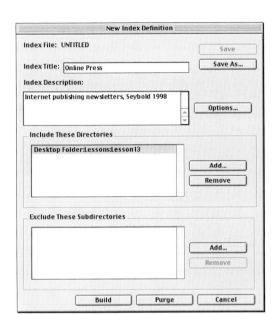

7 Click Build, and name the index **onlinepr.pdx**. Click Save.

8 When the message Index Build Successful appears in the Catalog message window, click Close. You may have to scroll down the message window to see the message.

Automatically loading an index

Before you can search an index, that index must be loaded in the available index list. You can load an index manually, but it is easier for your user if you associate the index with a file so that the index is added automatically to the available index list whenever that file is opened. In this section, you'll associate the Seybold 1998 Newsletters index with the Welcome1.pdf document, so that whenever the Welcome document is opened, the Seybold 1998 Newsletters index will automatically be available for searching.

1 In Acrobat, choose File > Open, select Welcome1.pdf in the Lesson13 folder, and click Open.

2 Click the Search button ( ) in the toolbar, and click Indexes. Notice that the Online Press index is not listed as an available index.

3 Click OK.

4 Close the Acrobat Search dialog box.

5 In Acrobat, choose File > Document Properties > Associated Index.

6 Locate the index:

• In Windows, click Choose.

• In Mac OS, select Choose Index and then click Choose.

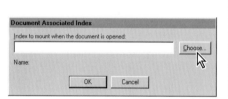

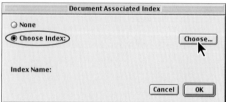

Click Choose, and locate index (Windows).   *Select Choose Index, and click Choose (Mac OS).*

7 Select onlinepr.pdx, located in the Lesson13 folder, and click Open.

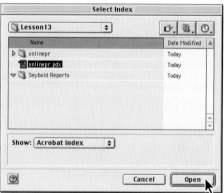

Associating an index with Welcome1.pdf file in Windows (left) and in Mac OS (right)

8 Click OK.

9 Choose File > Save, and save Welcome1.pdf in the Lesson13 folder.

10 Close the file.

Testing an associated index

Now you'll reopen Welcome1.pdf to see the index automatically associated with the file. It's a good idea to check that the associated index works as expected before distributing your documents.

1 Choose File > Open, and reopen the Welcome1.pdf file.

2 Click the Search button ( ) in the toolbar.

3 In the Acrobat Search dialog box, click Indexes.

The Online Press index now appears as an available index in the Index Selection dialog box. If any other indexes are checked, deselect them.

4 Click OK.

5 Enter **multimedia** in the Find Results Containing Text box, and click Search.

The Search Results palette lists the documents containing the term.

6 Select any of the documents in the list, and click View to view the file.

7 When you have finished viewing the file, choose Window > Close All to close all open files.

Once you have completed all cross-document links and indexed your collection, it is important to maintain relative file relationships. (A relative file relationship keeps the same organization of a file in a folder, within the same hierarchy of folders and subfolders.) Moving a file outside of the folder in which a link was created or that Catalog indexed will alter the relative file relationship. This causes linking and searching to produce error messages instead of link destinations and highlighted search terms.

Adding Acrobat Reader installers

Acrobat Reader is available free of charge for distribution with your documents so that users can view your PDF documents. It's important either to include a copy of the Reader installers on your CD or to point Web users to the Reader installers on the Adobe Web site at www.adobe.com.

If you're including the Reader installers on a CD-ROM, include a ReadMe text file at the top level of the CD that describes how to install Reader and provides any last-minute information. If you're posting the Reader installers on a Web site, include the Reader installation instructions with the link to the downloadable software.

If you're distributing documents on the Web, you'll probably want to point users to the Adobe Web site for the downloadable Reader software.

You may make and distribute unlimited copies of Reader, including copies for commercial distribution. For complete information on distributing and giving your users access to Acrobat Reader, visit the Adobe Web site at http://www.adobe.com/products/acrobat/.

A special "Includes Adobe Acrobat" logo is available from Adobe for use when distributing Reader. See the Adobe Web site for details.

Testing your document collection

When you have staged your documents and the Reader installers by organizing them in one location, it's important to test your document links, bookmarks, actions, forms, and indexes to ensure that everything works the way you planned.

In this lesson, you tested your document links and the associated index as you prepared the document collection. You can test documents in other collections that you're preparing by opening the documents and randomly testing any links, bookmarks, actions, and forms, and by using the Search command to test any associated indexes.

Double-checking the checklist

You should double-check content, layout, artwork, and so forth of any document that you intend to distribute. As you have seen with this lesson, electronic documents add a few other items to your checklist. We have created a checklist to help you double-check the basics. Of course, feel free to add to the list to help you complete your own projects.

Checklist:

- Content is complete.

- Electronic enhancements, links and bookmarks, and so forth are complete.

- Document properties information has been added to all files.

- Filenames have one to eight characters plus a .pdf extension, following the DOS naming conventions.

- Files are organized appropriately.

- The Fast Web View option has been applied (if intended for Web distribution).

- Files are indexed (if intended for CD distribution).

- Files have been tested in staging area.

- The file structure is maintained when delivering the document collection to the Web server administrator or CD creator.

This completes the lesson. You have learned how to organize and prepare documents for electronic distribution. For additional practice in building indexes from a series of PDF files, see Lesson 14, "Building a Searchable PDF Library and Catalog."

Review questions

1 Describe three ways you can make a document collection more accessible to users.

2 Why is providing a Welcome document important?

3 Why is it recommended that you name your files with one to eight characters plus a .pdf extension?

4 What does the Fast Web View option do to your PDF files?

5 Are you allowed to include the Acrobat Reader installers on CDs that you publish?

Review answers

1 You can make the information in a document collection more accessible to users in these ways:

• By compressing files to ensure that they're small enough for network distribution or for mass storage on CD volumes.

• By using filenames that work across computer platforms.

• By including a Welcome document with links to the document contents.

• By ensuring that the collection includes document properties information such as title, subject, author, and keywords.

• By organizing the files intuitively.

• By indexing the document collection.

• By including the Acrobat Reader application for viewing the documents.

• By testing any electronic enhancements such as bookmarks, links, and forms, to make sure that they work as expected.

2 Users may have difficulty determining where to start when first opening a CD or visiting a Web site, or determining what's in the document collection. A Welcome document can give users an overview of a document collection and can include links to specific places in the collection.

3 Naming files with one to eight characters (no spaces) plus a .pdf extension enables properly configured applications to launch the appropriate program when they encounter PDF files. Most Web browsers, Web servers, and versions of Microsoft Windows have been configured to associate .pdf files with Adobe Acrobat, Acrobat Reader, or the Web browser plug-in.

4 When you apply the Fast Web View option, Acrobat restructures files to prepare for page-at-a-time downloading (byte-serving) from Web servers. With page-at-a-time downloading, the Web server sends only the requested page of information to the user, not the entire PDF document.

5 Yes, Adobe allows you to distribute the Acrobat Reader installers and application with PDF documents that you publish.

Lesson 14

14 | Building a Searchable PDF Library and Catalog

Converting all of your electronic and paper publications to PDF lets you distribute and search large collections of documents quickly and easily. You can use the Acrobat Catalog feature to create a full-text index of your PDF publications, and then use the Search command in Acrobat or Acrobat Reader to search the entire library almost instantly.

In this lesson, you'll learn how to do the following:

- Build an index using the Acrobat Catalog feature.

- Choose Catalog options.

- Use the Search command to locate information contained in the files indexed by Catalog.

- Set Search options.

- Refine a search.

- Use Document Info fields in searches.

- Search for information using Boolean expressions.

- Search for a phrase.

This lesson will take about 50 minutes to complete.

If needed, remove the previous lesson folder from your hard drive, and copy the Lesson14 folder onto it.

Note: Windows users need to unlock the lesson files before using them. For information, see "Copying the Classroom in a Book files" on page 3.

Building an index

You use the Acrobat Catalog feature to build full-text indexes of PDF document collections. A full-text index is a searchable database of all the text in a document or set of documents. Your documents should be complete in content and electronic features such as links, bookmarks, and form fields before you use Catalog to index them.

To use Catalog and Search on secured documents that do not allow content extraction, you must have selected the Certified Plugins Only option in the Options General preferences. Also, you cannot use Catalog on documents that require a password for opening.

In this lesson, you'll work with chapter files from the book, *Hawaii: The Big Island Revealed*, by Andrew Doughty and Harriett Friedman. You'll create an index of these files and then search that index to find exciting information about what to do on your next trip to Hawaii.

1 From the desktop, open the Hawaii folder in the Lessons/Lesson14 folder. Notice the files contained within this folder. All of the PDF files in this folder will be indexed by Catalog.

Before you index a document collection, you need to organize the documents on the disk drive or network server volume, make sure the filenames comply with cross-platform conventions, break large documents up into smaller files (to enhance search performance), and complete the document information using the Document Properties menu for each document, if appropriate.

⊞ For information on adding document information, see "Adding searchable information and setting the binding" in the Acrobat 5.0 online Help.

2 Open Acrobat.

3 Choose Tools > Catalog.

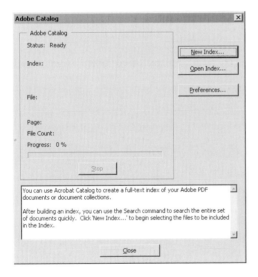

4 In Mac OS, choose Preferences. Make sure that Make Include/Exclude Folders DOS Compatible is deselected, and click OK.

5 Click New Index. For Index Title, enter **Hawaii: The Big Island**.

The Index Description box provides users with more information about the documents included in the index.

6 Click inside the Index Description box, and enter information about the index you are building. (We entered "The Ultimate Guidebook. The most comprehensive, yet easy to use guidebook ever written for the Big Island.")

7 Under Include These Directories, click Add.

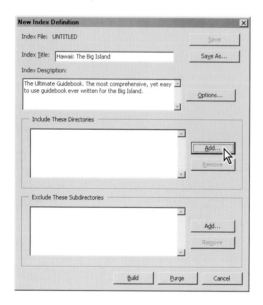

Now you'll select the folder or folders that contain the documents to be indexed.

8 Click to select the Hawaii folder in the Lesson14 folder, and then click OK (Windows) or click Choose (Mac OS).

By default, Catalog indexes subdirectories, but you can exclude subdirectories by using the Exclude These Subdirectories option. You can also add more than one directory to the index. For this lesson you'll index one directory or folder.

9 Click Build. Catalog automatically prompts you to save the index file within the Hawaii folder.

⊞ For information on changing the default location of the index using the Index File Location preferences, see "Setting Acrobat Catalog preferences" in the Acrobat 5.0 online Help.

10 Name the index **Guide.pdx**, and click Save. The file extension PDX identifies a file as an Acrobat index.

Enabling index options, such as Case Sensitive, Sounds Like, and Word Stemming, can enhance how well an index can be searched, as described in "Creating a new index and choosing options" on page 381. (To see the index defaults, choose Tools > Catalog > Preferences > Index Defaults.)

11 Click Close when the Index Build Successful message is displayed in the Adobe Catalog message window.

You may need to scroll down the message box to view the message.

Creating the file structure

Begin the indexing process by creating a folder to contain the documents you want to index, the index definition file (PDX) and its support folder. Adobe Acrobat Catalog generates the PDX file and its support folder in the same folder with the document collection. The index definition file will have the same name as the index folder and a .pdx extension. The support folder has the same name as the PDX file, and contains related folders that are auto-matically generated by Acrobat Catalog. The following guidelines apply:

• *Your documents should be complete in content and electronic features, such as links, bookmarks, and form fields, before you use Acrobat Catalog to index them.*

• *Consider creating a separate PDF file for each chapter or section of a doc-ument. When you separate a document into parts and then search it, search performance is optimized.*

• *The entire index—both the PDX file and the support folder—must be located inside a single folder.*

--From the Acrobat 5.0 online Help.

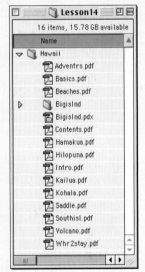

In this section, you'll create an index so that you can practice using the Search command. If you're creating an index for a document collection that you're distributing to other users, you want to be sure that the index is attached automatically as described in "Automatically loading an index" on page 357.

Searching an index

Now you'll use the Search command in Acrobat to perform searches of the PDF documents you just indexed with Catalog. You'll also use the Search command to limit and expand the definition of the term for which you are searching.

Using a full-text index, you can quickly search a collection of PDF documents; in contrast, the Find command works only with a single PDF document and reads every word on every page, a much slower process.

For information on the Find command, see "Finding words in PDF documents" in the Acrobat 5.0 online Help.

1 Begin the search by clicking the Search button ( ) in the toolbar. The Search button is on the File toolbar. If needed, choose Window > Toolbars > File to show the File toolbar.

The Adobe Acrobat Search dialog box appears. First you'll select an index to search.

2 If needed, click Clear to clear the Search Dialog box.

3 Click Indexes to display the Index Selection dialog box.

4 Click Add.

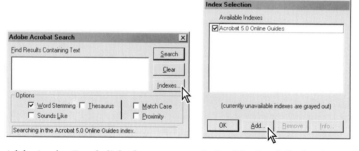

Adobe Acrobat Search dialog box

Index Selection dialog box lists available indexes.

5 Browse to select Guide.pdx, located inside the Hawaii folder, and click Open. The Hawaii: The Big Island index now appears under the list of available indexes.

6 Deselect any other indexes in the list by clicking the boxes next to them to clear the checkmark. Then click OK.

Acrobat searches only the selected index or indexes in the Available Indexes list. Here, you'll search only for entries in the Hawaii index.

To find information contained in the Hawaii index, you enter a word or phrase representing the desired topic.

7 In the Find Results Containing Text box, enter **hiking**.

8 For Options, select Word Stemming, and deselect all other search options.

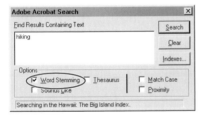

The Word Stemming option tells Search to look also for words that share the same word stem as "hiking," such as "hike" or "hiked."

For more information on each search option, see "Using the Search command" in the Acrobat 5.0 online Help.

9 Click Search.

Looking at the Search Results list

The Search Results dialog box lists the documents that contain the word or words you searched for. The dialog box also displays how many documents were searched and how many were found to contain the words. In this example, 13 documents were searched, with 11 containing variations of the word "hiking."

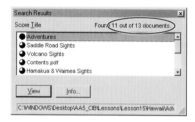

The documents are listed by relative ranking—documents with solid circles have more occurrences of the search words relative to the other documents in the list.

Acrobat Search uses five icons to indicate a document's relevance ranking:

Relevance ranking from highest (solid circle) to lowest (empty circle)

If needed, use the scroll bar or resize the Search Results dialog box to view the entire list. You can open any of the documents in the list and view the highlighted search words.

1 Select the Adventures entry at the top of the list, and click View to display the corresponding document. If needed, click the Fit in Window button ( ) to view the entire document page.

If needed, drag the Search Results list by its title bar to reposition the list so that it doesn't obscure the document.

Notice the highlighted occurrences of the word "hike." Because the Adventures document contains many occurrences of the searched word, it is ranked near the top of the Search Results list. If desired, use the zoom-in tool (🔍) to magnify a section in which "hike" is highlighted.

> **MAUNA ULU CRATER**
> This short hike is n
> frightened or the faint
> Ulu erupted between 1
> When it was all over, it
> maw 400 feet deep and
> (That's a guess—it get
> time.) This crater is acc
> minute hike from Chain
> in Hawai'i Volcanoes N
> man on following page

2 Now scroll to the bottom of the Search Results list, and double-click Kohala Sights to open that document. If needed, click the Fit in Window button to view the highlighted occurrence of "hiking."

The Kohala Sights document is ranked at the bottom of the Search Results list because it has fewer occurrences of the searched word than the other files in the list.

3 Close the Search Results dialog box.

4 Choose File > Close.

Narrowing the search

To make searching more effective, you should narrow your search criteria as much as possible. So far, you have found 11 documents that contain some information about hiking on the island of Hawaii. Now you'll refine your search to list only those documents that contain information about hiking near volcanoes.

1 Click the Search button.

2 In the Find Results Containing Text box, after "hiking," enter the words **and volcanoes**.

3 For Options, deselect Word Stemming to search only for the specific words you entered.

You are about to do a refined search. A refined search tells Search to look only at the documents in your current results list and to apply the new search criteria (instead of searching the index completely from scratch).

4 Hold down Ctrl (Windows) or Option (Mac OS) to change the Search button in the dialog box to Refine, and click Refine.

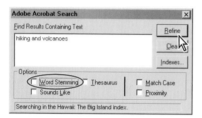
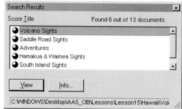

Word Stemming option deselected   *Results of refined search*

Notice that 6 documents out of the 11 in the last Search Results list meet the new search criteria. Using very specific search criteria helps you quickly identify which documents, if any, contain the information for which you are looking.

Also notice that you've eliminated five documents with this search, but that the ranking of the remaining six documents is very close.

5 Close the Search Results dialog box.

Affecting the ranking order

You need to know which, if any, of the six listed documents is the best candidate for information about hiking near volcanoes. You can affect the relative ranking order by using any of the options displayed in the Adobe Acrobat Search dialog box.

1 Click the Search button ( ) in the toolbar.

2 For Options, select Proximity. This option finds documents in which the search words occur within three pages of each other. If the words are more than three pages apart, the search criteria aren't met and the document won't be listed in the Search Results window.

3 Hold down Ctrl (Windows) or Option (Mac OS) to make the Search button change to Refine, and click Refine.

The Search Results list has narrowed the field to three documents with very different relative rankings.

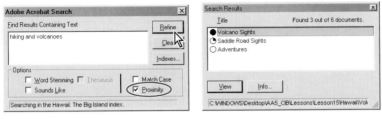

Refining search   *Result*

4 Select Volcano Sights in the list and click View, or double-click Volcano Sights. To view the whole document page, click the Fit in Window button.

Nearby occurrences of "hiking" and "volcano" are highlighted. You can zoom in on the highlighted text to read the information.

5 Choose File > Close to close the document.

6 Close the Search Results dialog box.

Using Document Info fields in a search

In addition to conducting a search based on specific words, you can search a collection of documents using any one of the Document Info fields. In this section, you'll search for documents that have a specific entry in their Subject fields.

First, you'll make sure that the Adobe Acrobat Search dialog box displays Document Info fields.

1 Do one of the following:

• In Windows, choose Edit > Preferences > General, and click Search in the left pane.

• In Mac OS, choose Edit > Preferences > Search.

2 For Include in Query, select Document Information, and click OK.

3 Click the Search button ( ) in the toolbar.

The Adobe Acrobat Search dialog box now displays Document Info fields in which you can enter additional search information. For example, before you create an index for a document, you can enter relevant information in the Title, Subject, Author, and Keywords fields of the Document Summary dialog box for that document's PDF file to make a search more efficient. Users can then search for this specific information.

For information on adding document information, see "Adding searchable information and setting the binding" in the Acrobat 5.0 online Help.

> ### Document MetaData
> *Adobe PDF files created with Acrobat 5.0 contain document metadata in XML format. This document metadata contains (but is not limited to) information that is also in the document properties. Any changes you make in the document properties using the Acrobat Document Summary dialog box are reflected in the document metadata. To view the document metadata, choose File > Document Properties > Document Metadata.*

4 If needed, click Clear to clear the text and Document Info fields in the Adobe Acrobat Search dialog box. Notice that your search options are not cleared.

5 For Subject, enter **beaches**, and click Search. Three documents meet the search criteria.

Entering search criteria

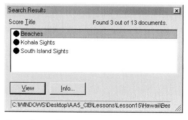
Search results

6 Double-click Beaches to open that document. To view the whole page, click the Fit in Window button (▣).

7 Click the Next Highlight button (▶📄) to open the next document in the Search Results list. (The Next Highlight button is a hidden tool. If needed, click the More Tools button adjacent to the Search button, and drag to select Next Highlight.) You use the Next Highlight and Previous Highlight buttons to browse through a Search Results list.

Note: Alternatively, use the Next Document and Previous Document commands in the Edit > Search menu to browse the search results.

8 Choose File > Close to close the document.

9 Close the Search dialog box.

🔲 For information on using the document creation and modification dates to limit searches, see Searching with Document Info and Date Info in the Acrobat 5.0 online Help.

Searching with Boolean expressions

You can use AND, OR, and NOT operators to build a logical expression (called a *Boolean expression*) that searches for words in a specific relation to each other. For example, earlier in this lesson you used the AND operator to build an expression that searched for occurrences of both "hiking" and "volcanoes" in the same document.

Using the OR operator

Use OR to find documents containing any of two or more search terms. Maybe you aren't sure what you want to do one day on your vacation—you could go diving or you could go to Kailua.

1 Click the Search button (🔍) in the toolbar.

2 Click Clear to clear the text and Document Info fields. Deselect all search options.

3 In the Find Results Containing Text box, enter **diving or Kailua**.

4 Click Search.

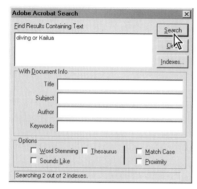

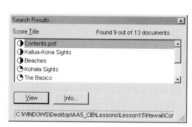

Using OR Boolean expression　　*Results*

The Search Results dialog box lists nine documents that contain information about either diving or Kailua. You can open any of the documents to find information about one subject or the other, but not necessarily both.

5 Close the Search Results dialog box.

Using the AND operator

If you plan it right, you might be able to go diving and see Kailua in one day trip. Use AND to find documents containing two or more search terms.

1 Click the Search button ( ) in the toolbar.

2 Click Clear. In the Find Results Containing Text box, enter **diving and Kailua**.

3 Click Search. Three documents contain information about both diving and Kailua.

4 Double-click Beaches to open that document. Zoom in on the lower right of the displayed pages to learn about a small cove near Kailua that is excellent for scuba diving.

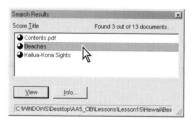

You can also search with the NOT Boolean operator, combine Boolean operators, and search with wildcard characters.

🔢 For more information on searching with Boolean operators, see "Using Boolean operators" in the Acrobat 5.0 online Help.

5 Choose File > Close.

6 Close the Search Results dialog box.

Searching on the Web

An index created by Catalog is not searchable over the Web or a company intranet, but your documents can be indexed by a Web search engine that supports indexing PDF documents. You must first set up the search-engine software that can search PDF files on your Web server. Users can then run a search from your Web page.

Many companies develop search engines that can automatically and continuously update a search index of both PDF and HTML documents on a Web server. For a list of these companies, check the Support Knowledgebase on the Adobe Web site (www.adobe.com).

Choosing Catalog options

You can change the Catalog default options to reduce the size of an index as much as possible, if you plan to post an index (and its associated files) on a network file server, for example, where space is at a premium.

You can change the defaults for most of the options in the Index Defaults group of preferences.

1 Choose Tools > Catalog, and click Preferences to examine at the default options settings.

2 Click OK to close the Catalog Preferences dialog box.

Creating a new index and choosing options

In this section, you'll create another index of the documents contained in the Hawaii folders and choose Catalog options to reduce the size of that index.

1 In the Adobe Catalog dialog box, click New Index.

2 For Index Title, enter **The Island**.

3 Click Options.

The Options dialog box lets you change Acrobat Catalog defaults for a particular index definition. You can exclude specified terms (called *stopwords*) and numbers, and turn off the Case Sensitive, Sounds Like, and Word Stemming features. If the collection contains Adobe PDF files created by version 1.0 of Acrobat PDF Writer or Acrobat Distiller, you can select the Add IDs to Acrobat 1.0 PDF Files option to add unique IDs to the file to assist Search in locating a document.

Use the Words Not to Include in the Index section to enter stopwords—words that you exclude from an index to reduce its file size. Stopwords usually are words that would not be entered as search terms, including articles such as "the" and "a", conjunctions such as "but" and "or", and prepositions such as "for" and "by".

Excluding stopwords from an index makes the index typically 10% to 15% smaller. However, searches won't find phrases (that is, words enclosed in quotation marks) that contain the stopwords. To help users, you should list stopwords in the index description.

4 For Word, enter the following words, pressing Enter or Return (or clicking Add) after each entry: **the, The, and, And, a, A, but, But, or, Or, for, For, by, By.**

Note: *If stopwords include words that are also used in Boolean expressions, such as "and" and "or," the Search feature won't be able to perform logical searches with those Boolean operators.*

You can add up to 500 stopwords to an index. Stopwords can be up to 24 characters long. If you want to stop a word completely, you must enter all capitalization possibilities such as "the" and "The."

5 Select Do Not Include Numbers. This option excludes numbers such as phone numbers, part numbers, and address numbers from an index.

Excluding numbers from an index about Hawaii is appropriate because users of the index will not be looking for specific numbers. Excluding numbers from an index of an auto parts manual, where it is likely people will be searching for numbers, is not appropriate.

6 Select all of the Word Options. These options let you use some of the options in the Search dialog box.

For more information on Word options, see "Setting the search options" in the Acrobat 5.0 online Help.

7 If needed, deselect Optimize for CD-ROM.

Intended for indexes placed on a CD, this option arranges index files for the fastest possible access. This option also allows you to modify document properties information or security settings after you have indexed a document without generating an alert message that warns users that the document has been modified.

8 If needed, deselect Add IDs to Acrobat 1.0 PDF Files, because this collection doesn't contain any 1.0 PDF files. Click OK.

9 In the New Index Definition dialog box, next to the Include These Directories box, click Add. Select the Hawaii folder, located in the Lesson14 folder, and then click OK (Windows) or click Choose (Mac OS).

10 In the Index Description text box, add information on what stopwords were included. (We entered "The following stopwords have been excluded from this index: the, The, and, And, a, A, but, But, or, Or, for, For, by, By.")

11 Click Build. Name the index **Island.pdx,** and save it in the Hawaii folder.

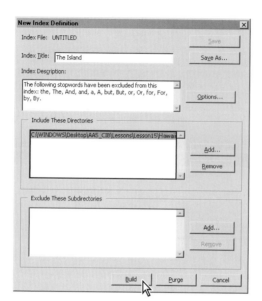

12 Click Close when the Index Build Successful message is displayed.

Comparing index sizes

Indexes consist of an index definition file (PDX) and a folder that contains the supporting data files that are needed to return search results. This folder must travel with the PDX file at all times. An index definition file also contains relative paths between the PDX file and the folders containing the indexed documents. These relative paths must also always be maintained to complete successful searches.

When you set options in Catalog to reduce the size of your index, you are actually reducing the size of the supporting data files and not the index definition file itself. Now you'll compare the sizes of the folders that hold the supporting data files to see how the folder size is reduced.

1 From the desktop, open the Hawaii folder, located in the Lesson14 folder. Among the files, you should see two folders, named Guide and Island.

2 Display the folder size:

• In Windows, right-click the Guide folder and choose Properties.

• In Mac OS, click once to select the Guide folder, and choose File > Get Info > General Information.

3 Write down the folder's size.

4 Repeat steps 2 and 3 for the Island folder.

As you can see, the Island folder is smaller than the Guide folder. If these indexes were larger, you would see an even greater difference in the size of the folders.

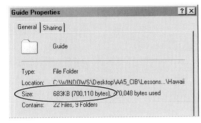
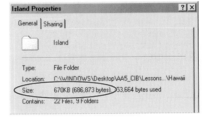

Guide folder size   *Island folder size*

Tips for updating indexes

You must update an index if documents are added to or removed from the collection, or if the hierarchy of the indexed folders has changed.

You should also consider updating an index when documents in the indexed document collection have changed, or when data values are added because a new custom field has been defined.

You can reduce the index update time by following these guidelines:

• Don't support the Sounds Like, Case Sensitive, or Word Stemming search options.

• Use stopwords and exclude numbers.

Searching for a phrase

By using the Search button in Acrobat or Reader, you can search for a phrase that contains two or more words, such as *Marriage license*. But when you search for a phrase containing words that might be confused with Boolean operators such as *and*, *or*, and *not*, or parentheses, you must enclose the phrase in quotation marks.

1 In Acrobat, click the Search button ( ) in the toolbar.

2 Click Indexes.

3 In the Index Selection dialog box, make sure the *Hawaii: The Big Island* index is selected. (If the *Hawaii: The Big Island* index created in this lesson is not in the available indexes list, click Add. Select Guide.pdx, located in the Hawaii folder inside the Lesson14 folder, and click Open.)

Now you'll add the index created in this lesson with stopwords.

4 Click Add. Select Island.pdx, located in the Hawaii folder inside the Lesson14 folder, and click Open. *Hawaii: The Big Island* and *The Island* are listed as available indexes.

5 Deselect *The Island* so that the index remains in the list, but won't be searched. Click OK.

6 In the Find Results Containing Text box, enter **Mauna Loa and Mauna Kea**. Then click Search. (These are the two biggest volcanoes on Hawaii.)

The Search Results dialog box lists eight documents that contain information about the two volcanoes. The search engine returned all documents that contained both Mauna Loa and Mauna Kea to the Search Results list, even if both names weren't in the same sentence. But what if you remember seeing something about the two volcanoes in the same sentence and want to find the phrase "Mauna Loa and Mauna Kea"? If that is the case, you need to add quotation marks.

7 Click the Search button in the toolbar.

8 In the Find Results Containing Text box enter **"Mauna Loa and Mauna Kea"** (with quotation marks) and click Search.

Now the Search Results list returns two documents that contain the phrase "Mauna Loa and Mauna Kea."

9 Double-click Saddle Road Sights to view the information. Close the file when you have finished viewing it.

Seeing the effects of stopwords

As mentioned earlier, excluding certain words from an index results in a smaller index. But searching for phrases that contain stopwords will fail and index users won't be able to find phrases that contain the stopwords.

1 Click the Search button ( ) in the toolbar.

2 In the Adobe Acrobat Search dialog box, click Indexes.

3 Deselect *Hawaii: The Big Island* so that the index remains in the list, but will not be searched.

4 Select *The Island*. Click OK.

5 In the Find Results Containing Text box enter **Mauna Loa and Mauna Kea** (no quotation marks) and click Search. The Search Results dialog box lists eight documents that contain information about these two volcanoes.

6 Click the Search button in the toolbar.

7 Now enter **"Mauna Loa and Mauna Kea"** and click Search.

Remember that you excluded *and* from the index as a stopword. As a result, the current search found no documents that matched your query. The use of stopwords prevents you from locating phrases (as defined by quotation marks) containing words included as stopwords, even though these phrases exist in the document collection.

8 Click OK to close the alert box.

9 Exit or quit Acrobat.

This completes this lesson. You've learned how to build an index using Acrobat Catalog and how to perform various searches. For additional practice in building indexes from a series of PDF files, see Lesson 13, "Distributing Document Collections."

Exploring on your own

If you're including PDF files on a CD, Adobe recommends that you also include an index to help your users access your information with ease and efficiency. You can practice building an index for a CD from PDF files.

For additional practice, you can purge and rebuild an index. Whenever you add or remove documents from an indexed collection or whenever you change document information fields, you must rebuild the index. When you rebuild an index, entries for deleted documents and for the original versions of changed documents remain in the index but are marked as invalid. Eventually this greatly increases the disk space required by the index. Purging and rebuilding an index removes the redundancies that increase the size of the index and slow searches.

You can add some of your own PDF documents to the Hawaii document collection and remove some of the existing documents. Rebuild the index when you're finished, and note the size of your final index. Then purge and rebuild your index, and notice the decrease in the index size.

Purge your index as follows:

1 Open Acrobat.

2 Choose Tools > Catalog.

3 Click Open Index. Browse to select the index you want to update, and click Open.

For example, select Island.pdx in the Hawaii folder, located inside the Lesson14 folder.

4 Click Purge. A message window advises you how long the purge will take.

5 When the purge is complete, click Close.

6 Rebuild (build) the index as described earlier in this lesson.

Review questions

1 How can you distinguish an index file from a PDF file?

2 What does the Search Results dialog box display?

3 How does the Word Stemming option expand your search results?

4 What key do you press to do a refined search?

5 Why should you enter document properties information—Title, Subject, Author, Keywords—in all your PDF documents?

6 Give two examples of Boolean expressions and explain what they do.

7 What are stopwords?

8 How can an index user find out which, if any, stopwords were excluded from an index?

9 When would you not include numbers in an index?

10 When should you purge an index?

11 What is the difference between searching for a phrase with quotation marks and without quotation marks?

Review answers

1 In Acrobat, the file extension PDX identifies a file as an Acrobat index.

2 The Search Results dialog box lists the documents that contain the word or words you searched for and displays how many documents were searched and how many were found to contain the words.

3 The Word Stemming option tells Search to look also for words that share the same word stem. For example, searching for the word "hiking" also finds occurrences of "hike" or "hiked."

4 A refined search is one in which Search looks only at the documents in your current search results list and applies the new search criteria (instead of searching the index completely from scratch). To do a refined search, hold down Ctrl (Windows) or Option (Mac OS) to change the Search button in the dialog box to Refine.

5 To give users more ways to search for information, you should fill in the Title, Subject, Author, and Keywords text boxes in the Document Summary dialog box with the relevant information. Users can search for this specific information and use the title, subject, and keywords as they would index terms to refine their searches.

6 AND, NOT, and OR are Boolean expressions used in searches, as follows:

- AND combines two or more search terms.

- OR searches for any of two or more search terms.

- NOT excludes terms from searches.

7 Stopwords are words that you exclude from an index to minimize the size of the index file or reduce it by 10% to 15%. Stopwords are usually words that would not be entered as search terms; for example, articles such as "the" and "a," conjunctions such as "but" and "or," and prepositions such as "for" and "by."

8 Listing the stopwords in the index description helps users find out what stopwords were excluded from the index.

9 You should exclude numbers from an index that doesn't pertain specifically to numbered information, such as in a guide book or descriptive text. You should include numbers in an index if users would be searching for numbers, for example, for technical specifications, addresses, part numbers, or phone numbers.

10 You should purge and rebuild an index periodically to reclaim disk space and speed up searches.

11 Searching for a phrase enclosed in quotation marks finds the verbatim phrase. Searching for a phrase without quotation marks finds the terms within close proximity in the document.

Index

Production notes

This book was created electronically using Adobe FrameMaker. Art was produced using Adobe Illustrator and Adobe Photoshop. The Minion*and Myriad*families of typefaces are used throughout the book.

Credits

Examples, photographs, and illustrations are intended for instructional use with the Acrobat 5.0 Classroom in a Book only.

Lesson 6

Aesop's Fables retold by Adobe Systems Incorporated from the public domain.

Lesson 9

Use of the Jet Propulsion Laboratory Web site was approved by Caltech/JPL.

Lesson 10

Continuous Renal Replacement Therapy: Putting It All Together, © Gambro® Inc.; used by permission; Cathy DiMuzio and Kevin Highland. Created by Larry Prado with Ginny McDonald and Jim Rambo.

Adobe Acrobat 5.0—A Beginner's Guide, © SBR Associates; used by permission.

Lesson 13

Seybold Internet Publishing archives used by permission.

Photograph: Woman with computer and plant — Lisa Milosevich.

Lesson 14

Hawaii: The Big Island Revealed © Andrew Doughty and Harriet Friedman; used by permission.